R. B.

The History of the House of Orange

William and Mary, King and Queen of England

R. B.

The History of the House of Orange
William and Mary, King and Queen of England

ISBN/EAN: 9783743345980

Manufactured in Europe, USA, Canada, Australia, Japa

Cover: Foto ©ninafisch / pixelio.de

Manufactured and distributed by brebook publishing software (www.brebook.com)

R. B.

The History of the House of Orange

PROTESTANT LANDMARKS.

THE HISTORY

OF THE

HOUSE OF ORANGE:

WILLIAM AND MARY,

KING AND QUEEN OF ENGLAND, SCOTLAND, FRANCE, IRELAND, ETC., ETC.

WITH A SKETCH OF

THE ORANGE INSTITUTION

TO THE PRESENT DAY,

AND

THE REFORMATION;

AND WHAT IT DID FOR SCOTLAND.

TORONTO:
G. M. ROSE & SONS, PUBLISHERS.
1897.

CONTENTS.

	PAGE
PROTESTANT LANDMARKS	7
THE HISTORY OF THE HOUSE OF ORANGE	41
THE HISTORY OF KING WILLIAM AND QUEEN MARY	203
A SKETCH OF THE ORANGE INSTITUTION	271
THE REFORMATION; AND WHAT IT DID FOR SCOTLAND	303

PROTESTANT LANDMARKS.

HOUSE OF ORANGE, ETC.

We need not, at this momentous crisis in the history of our country, offer any apology to the Protestant public for reproducing, for the benefit of the loyal and patriotic Orangemen of Canada, a reliable, condensed, and perfectly trustworthy history of the illustrious Conqueror of the Boyne, William the Third, Prince of Orange. It will be readily understood that such a work as the present cannot fail to prove extremely useful, particularly to the intelligent members of the Orange Institution, large numbers of whom have frequently expressed themselves anxious to obtain a convenient work of historic reference, which should combine, not merely a history of the heroic achievements of "the Glorious, Pious and Immortal Prince of Orange," but one that would also give in convenient form all the more memorable incidents which have marked the progress of the Orange Society since its inception. A detailed work on a subject of such magnitude would be, if not an impossibility, so cumbrous, not to say expensive, as to render its possession next to useless. Besides this, the business of life presses too heavily upon the ordinary run of mankind to allow them time to sit down and digest volume after volume of dry details, which, however interesting in themselves, can possess but little practical influence on the issues at present before the nations of the earth. The great drama is proceeding with ever-varying details. The actors and incidents of the present shall soon have passed into the realms of history, but still the great conflict in all its essential features must remain the same until "the mighty angel" proclaims to the startled nations of the earth—" BABYLON THE GREAT IS FALLEN, IS FALLEN!" " Rejoice over her, thou heaven and ye holy apostles and prophets; for God hath avenged you on her." Under these circumstances, it would be a mere waste of time to dwell upon subordinate issues or seek to elevate into importance men or events which, at best, are but mere "settings" on the historic canvas. Except as a mere matter of curiosity, and that only to a literary antiquarian, it is not important to the Orangemen of the present day to be informed that the Rev. Mr. Boanerges was Grand Chaplain in Ireland in 1844. The fact may be perfectly indisputable, and perhaps even interesting to a few friends who have had the honour of Mr. Boanerges' acquaintance; but such, we submit, is not the class of information that Orangemen should be called upon to pay for. Unfortunately, Orange literature has very largely suffered from the vicious and objectionable habit of giving undue prominence to local and very subordinate characters, to the neglect, or, what is almost worse, the overshadowing of the grand principles for which, as units in a great army, they did noble and gallant service. The imperishable memory of William III. is justly revered by the members of the Orange Institution, not merely on account of those virtues which, in a remarkable degree, he possessed, but especially because the Prince of Orange stands " a head and shoulders " over all his compeers as the exponent, or rather, it should be said, the embodiment of those principles of "Civil and Religious Liberty " the very mention of which sends the blood coursing through loyal hearts with redoubled energy. If the principles that obtained at the time of the Reformation had been left unassailed, and if a perfidious, weak, dishonest and Papistical King had not sought to destroy the glorious heritage of British freedom, there would have been no necessity for the formation of the celebrated "Protestant Association." But the spirit of Popery, then as now, is incompatible with the free exercise of civil rights; and so James II. must needs array himself on the side of the "apostate tyrant " of Rome, in order, if possible, to restore Britain's independent Church as well as Britain's independent nationality to the See of Rome. But the British Church, after asserting herself against the tyrannical usurpations of the " Man of Sin," and after having baptized her liberties in the best and purest blood of her children, was in no humour to listen to the arrogant pretensions of the man who blasphemously proclaims himself the Vicar of Christ. Nay, more; sooner than resume the galling yoke of Rome, British Protestants counted not their lives dear unto them; but with the Bible in one hand and the sword in the other, they taught Rome such a lesson that the very mention of it, even to the present, sends a cold shudder through the whole system of Popery. The man who fails to see a Divine Providence working in all the events of this period must be in a worse than Egyptian darkness; and it is therefore no matter for surprise that when the Orangemen and Protestants of Ireland assemble each July in their thousands to commemorate the victories of the past, that their feelings should find vent, as a favourite channel for expression, in the following words of the Psalmist:—

> "O Lord, our fathers oft have told,
>   In our attentive ears,
> Thy wonders in their days performed,
>   And elder times than theirs;
> For not their courage nor their sword
>   To them possession gave,
> Nor strength that from unequal force
>   Their fainting troops could save:—
>
> "But Thy right hand and powerful arm,
>   Whose succour they implored—
> Thy presence with the chosen race,
>   Who Thy great name adored.
> To Thee the triumph we ascribe,
>   From whom the conquest came;
> In God we will rejoice all day,
>   And ever bless His name."

It would be about as sensible to ignore God in these events of history as it would be to deny His government in the physical universe; and just as our observations of physical phenomena are accurate or the contrary, so we can judge with a greater or less amount of probability of that which is likely to occur at any given period. In this way we are to understand the trite saying, "Coming events cast their shadows before;" and if we would make even an approximate forecast of the future, we must endeavour accurately to gauge the present by the past. Events that appear to us disconnected, and not moving on the same line, are only so relatively; in other words, they appear so to us, because our finite minds are incapable of comprehending the links in the mighty chain of God's providence. The conflict between truth and error is ever in progress; the combatants take sides, fight for a moment, and then disappear in the great vortex of the past. Not so the issues themselves—these are ever the same, and must remain so. Sometimes the battle rages along the whole line; then again the distant cannonading is heard, and we know that some outpost is fighting, it may be to the death; presently the trumpet sounds the advance, and a regular pitched battle ensues. Gradually, the sounds of conflict cease, and then over-sanguine people tell us that we have reached that blessed time when "war shall be no more;" but this pleasing assurance is no sooner made than it is belied, because the conflict has only slumbered, to burst forth with tenfold fury at some other point. Thus the ceaseless strife goes on. Yesterday it was at the north, to-day at the south, and to-morrow it may rage under the burning suns of Asia or Africa. This continent has been comparatively free from those mighty conflicts which have shaken older communities to the very centre. But it may be permitted us to ask how long is this state of things going to last? What reasons have we to hope for immunity from the conflict? None. In all probability the contest on the American continent will be a bloodless one. We trust that it may be; but we have no guarantee that it will be so; because if the Church of Rome ever comes to imagine that she can, on this continent, gain the mastery over Bible truth and Protestant liberty by physical force, that moment she will have recourse to it. Contemplate, if you can, the horrible cruelties of that infernal system of torture which Rome, in the profound goodness of her soul, calls "the Holy Inquisition." An interesting sketch of Rome's patent method of making converts accompanies this volume. It is enough to make our blood curdle to think of what Rome would do if she only had the power; but, fortunately for the sanctity of our homes and altars, she has not that power, and with the blessing of God she never shall have it so long as the Protestants of Canada and the United States are true to the memory of the indomitable heroes who crushed her power on many a well-contested field. At the same time, we need not disguise from ourselves the fact—admitted by all who have given the subject any consideration—that we are approaching, if indeed we have not actually reached, one of the most critical periods that has ever occurred in the history of this country. The attitude of the Romish Priesthood at the present day is nothing short of a challenge to us to forget her bloody persecutions; her blighting misrule; her arrogant impiety; her man-made deities; her contempt of God's holy word; her Jesuitical abrogation of the pure precepts of Christ—to forget that Rome watered the plains of Europe with the blood of the saints ; to forget that she kindled the fires of Smithfield ; to forget that she has crushed the very life out of Spain by her Inquisitions; in fact, to forget that Rome can be anything but Rome, " drunken with the blood of the saints and with the blood of the martyrs of Jesus." Rome, with intolerable audacity, asks the Protestants of Canada and elsewhere to aid her in a work which has for its ulterior object their own extinction ; or, what is equivalent, their subjugation to the Monk of the Vatican—to cast to the winds the priceless heritage of our British freedom, and bow as slaves beneath the ecclesiastical despotism of a Latin priest. What claim has Rome upon the Protestants of the Dominion, that they should surrender at her bidding ; or that which amounts to the same thing, to the bidding of Bishops who carry out the programme of the Syllabus in this country ? We apprehend, however, that but one answer will be given to those who seek to advance the cause of the Papacy at the expense of civil liberty.

The Orangemen of Canada, as the avowed conservators of the principles of civil and religious liberty, are imperatively called upon to declare, in clear and unambiguous language, that they can have no affinities, political or otherwise, with the Ultramontane party in this or any other country. We have been told that such a combination is not alone possible, but that it has been actually consummated. We shall presently vindicate the members of the Orange Institution from this and some other equally foul aspersions that have been cast upon them. The point, however, that we wish to direct attention to is this : namely, that those who make such charges do so apparently on the supposition that the Orangemen as a body are ignorant of the history of the Institution to which they belong; because it is not possible to suppose that any Orangeman, no matter how humble, knowing the history of the past, would for a moment lend himself to countenance a political alliance with Ultramontanism. Those who talk and write about such an alliance are wilfully or ignorantly misrepresenting some of the most prominent landmarks of the Institution. And here we take occasion to say that the history unfolded in the following pages is pregnant with the most valuable instruction; but to no one more valuable than to the honest and conscientious members of the Loyal

Orange Institution. It will be seen that James II. was a most devoted slave of the Pope, and that the great object of his life was to destroy the Protestantism of the English nation, and re-establish the Romish faith. Why, it may be asked, did James imperil the best interests of the kingdom by acting in the way he did? The answer is not difficult to discover. James was what would now be termed "an Ultramontane;" that is to say, a man whose patriotism is extinct, and whose better feelings have been sacrificed at the nod of a foreign priest. James fawned on the Pope, and the Pope blessed James in return. Does not the Pope claim to be the Vicar of Christ, and to have all power committed to him? He does. Then surely, as Heaven's first favourite, James had just grounds for expecting an unusual share of human prosperity; and, indeed, it is on record that when he was informed of the disaster which befell the combined fleets under Admiral Herbert and Vice-Admiral Everson, that he held up his hands in pious exultation and said, "At length, then, the wind has declared itself a Papist;" and on the same occasion James told Barillon, the French Ambassador, very confidentially, that nothing else was possible, "because," said he, "you know that for these three days I have caused the holy mass to go in procession." It is almost impossible to contemplate such gross superstition without a shudder, illustrating as it emphatically does the truth of that Scripture which affirms: "And for this cause God shall send them strong delusion, that they should believe a lie." But it was not the first time that Rome put a lie into the mouth of a King, nor has it been the last. What followed? Why, to use the language of an Irish Grand Chaplain, the Rev. John Flanagan, one of Ireland's most gifted and eloquent divines, "James II. had his crown ignominiously kicked into the Boyne," and he became a pauper, depending upon the bounties of France. Ever since then, the Pope's blessing or alliance has been to the nation that sought it of the most disastrous character. Most people are aware that during the present generation Isabella of Spain was, of all European sovereigns, the most blessed by the Pope; yet so intolerable was her Popery, even in Popish Spain, that she, too, had to seek a refuge in France. Nor is this all. To crush Protestant Prussia, the Emperor Napoleon III. was secretly incited by the Vatican into one of the most bloody of ancient or modern wars; and we are not using any unmeaning hyperbole when we say that the prayers of Romish Christendom went up unceasingly for the success of "the second son of the Church," and the corresponding defeat of the old heretic, the Emperor William. But here again Romish blessing was turned into a curse of the most deadly nature; the power of France was crushed into atoms beneath the Protestant King, and the Napoleonic dynasty shattered into a thousand fragments. The very stars in their courses appeared to fight against the French armies, which were driven into their most impregnable fortresses, and then out of them, like so many sheep; until, at last, like a pack of well-whipped curs, they surrendered *en masse* at Sedan. Surely the French, who have vindicated their valour on a thousand bloody fields, were not wanting in soldierly qualities. Then what was the cause of the repeated defeats which they suffered from the victorious Landwehr of Prussia? The cause was this: France, as the conqueror of Germany, would have been the most arrogantly dictatorial Power in Europe; in fact, she would have ordered things pretty much after her own fancy, or as convenience might suggest; but, unquestionably, the restoration of the temporal power of the Pope was one of those measures that such a contingency would have given birth to, and this accounts for the otherwise not very intelligible fact that Roman Catholics almost to a man sympathized with France and against Germany. But here again the prayers of Heaven's self-styled Vicar were abortive, and with the humiliation of Sedan and the exile of the Emperor perished the last hope of the Pope to regain his temporal power and his mischievous influence in European politics. But if the Pope's blessings are nugatory, how much more so are his curses! For example, he kept cursing and excommunicating Victor Emmanuel until people have ceased wondering why the earth did not open and swallow the impious wretch who dared to give to the Italians that first of earthly blessings, " civil and religious liberty." Now, strange as it may appear, from the moment the Pope took to cursing the Italian patriots until the present, nothing but the most marked success has attended them. We might multiply examples, but one more must suffice. Mr. Gladstone went into power a few years ago with perhaps the most overwhelming majority that ever an English Minister possessed, and to-day the Liberal party in Britain has barely an existence. What was the cause of this sudden collapse of a great political party? Answer—ALLIANCE WITH ROME. There is no gainsaying the fact; and Dominion politicians, who, for party purposes, are disposed to coquet with Ultramontanism, will do well to note the fact. On the other hand, the Conservative party were never so strong in the British House of Commons as they are at present. Why? Because they have not hesitated to declare themselves opposed to the intolerant pretensions of the Romish Hierarchy; and furthermore, that they will, as a party, uncompromisingly resist them. Thus it is manifest that the nation, or the political party which forms an alliance with Romish Ultramontanism, is but taking an effectual step towards its own destruction. It was true in the time of James II., and we have seen that it is equally true to-day. Popery, wherever it predominates, exercises a baneful and pernicious influence, even down to the most minute details of every-day life. It drove away, through its cursed intolerance, some of the best workmen in a leading French industry. Go to Ireland, and contrast the state of Protestant Ulster as compared with Popish Connaught. Ulster was an ungenial and sterile wilderness, as compared with the rich pasture lands of other parts of the country; but, notwithstanding its sterility, Protestant industry has made it to blossom like the rose, while the other provinces, cursed by the iron despotism of Popery, are in a state of the most hopeless and abject misery. So obvious is this, that writers without any Irish sympathies—or, if they had any, were sympathies against the Protestant minority—have been compelled to acknowledge the immeasurable superiority of the Protestant peasant over the Roman Catholic. But to come nearer home. Contrast Protestant Ontario with Popish Quebec, and exactly the same state of things is observable; in fact, wherever or whenever you find a people slavishly devoted to the interests of the Papacy, there you will find superstition, ignorance, intolerance, and an absence of that active and industrious energy which is one of the most characteristic features of a Protestant community.

Bearing these facts in mind, we will not be at much loss to account for the signal defeat which overtook the runaway King and his Irish auxiliaries at the Boyne. In discussing the issues of that day on our own times, we can hardly overrate their importance; and well, indeed, will it be if those entrusted with the destinies of this new Dominion keep before them, as steadily as did the Prince of

Orange, those sound political principles which, when faithfully adhered to, must tend inevitably to national prosperity and greatness. It should at the same time be borne in mind that Popery is not alone a huge blot on the religious world; but also, that her political principles are quite as vicious as her religious ones, and so inextricably are they interwoven the one with the other, that it is impossible to speak of them separately. In fact, when Romanism ceases to be political, it must cease to exist entirely; and thus it comes to pass that if a Roman Catholic makes profession of liberal opinions, he is, in proportion to the extent of those opinions, at variance with his Church. If it can be shown that there is any wide divergence amongst Roman Catholics, that section of them which takes ground against the pernicious teachings of Ultramontanism should be encouraged and assisted by all the moral influence which Protestants can bring to bear upon the controversy. Unfortunately, Romanism is not in harmony with sound political maxims, so that to the ordinary Ultramontane mind nothing, for example, can be more obnoxious than Cavour's doctrine, "A free Church in a free State." From the Protestant standpoint, antipathy to such a sound maxim of political economy appears altogether unreasonable; and undoubtedly it is so in truth; but a little reflection will show that, however unreasonable, it is at least perfectly consistent, because, as we may readily gather from the history of the Revolution of 1688, Rome cannot permit the existence of a power co-ordinate with her own. She may, of course, tolerate it, but she will only do so when the ordinary measures which she is so fond of employing are not forthcoming. In Ontario she bows to the inevitable. In Quebec she will enforce her views in every way she possibly can. One distinguishing feature of her policy is this: if the circumstances are very much against her, an immediate recourse is had to various *secret agencies*, and in this way Rome not unfrequently obtains some of her most important conquests, particularly in Protestant countries, where people fancy themselves beyond the reach of her wiles. For example, how many Protestant parents there are who, neglectful of the warnings of the past, send their daughters to be educated in Romish institutions, and find out their mistake when it is too late to apply a remedy. That the work of proselytism may be effectually carried on, these institutions are for the most part perfectly free from Government control or inspection. Such agencies are at work all over this continent, and the ultimate object to be achieved is, not the conversion of so many heretics, but the sapping away of the Protestantism of the country, in order that when some grand attack is made upon our civil rights, we may fall an easy prey into the all-absorbing maw of Romanism. And thus it comes to pass that we have in our midst a system as vicious and disturbing in politics as it is incompatible with the simplicity of the gospel.

James the Second was as great a bungler as he was a coward, and it is extremely fortunate for Europe and the world that he was so. The Pope intended that James should, by a display of constitutional and liberal conduct, so win upon the nation as to cause it to disavow its Protestantism, and again restore to its religious worship the incrustations which the National Church had been at so much pains to lay aside. Rome is not scrupulous as to the means, provided she can accomplish her purpose; and its defeat on this occasion was owing, perhaps, as much to the bungling incapacity of James as to any other assignable cause. The scheme was worthy of the Jesuitical subtlety of Rome, and we are not astonished to know that the Pope was indignant and incensed at the King on account of its failure. Immediately after James had been proclaimed King, he made the following speech before the Privy Council: "I shall preserve the government, both in Church and State, as it is now by law established. I know the principles of the Church of England are for monarchy, and the members of it have shown themselves good and loyal subjects; therefore I shall always take care to defend and support it." But, as already intimated, James was a bungler, and so in the course of a few days he made it sufficiently clear what his intentions on the matter really were. Disguise, if needed, was no longer possible. The Protestants of England felt that a great crisis had arrived in their history, and so they

wisely banded themselves together, adopting the following "Platform," as we would now term it:—
"We whose names are hereunto subscribed, who have now joined the Prince of Orange for the defence of the Protestant religion and for the maintaining the ancient government and laws and liberties of England, Scotland and Ireland, do engage to Almighty God, to His Highness the Prince, and to one another, to stick firm to this cause in the defence of it, and never to depart from it till our religion, laws and liberties are so far secured to us in a free Parliament that they shall be no more in danger of falling under Popery and slavery." This is unquestionably the germ of what subsequently became the Orange Institution, as we shall have occasion to show further on. It is unnecessary to enter into the details of the results which followed; they are matters of history. What we are concerned with just now are the principles involved in the contest, in order that we may see what changes, if any, have since taken place. If we view the Battle of the Boyne as a mere military event, we will be rather surprised to learn that it was, comparatively speaking, of much less importance than a hundred other battles that have since been fought. At best there could hardly have been more than two thousand four hundred men killed out of the combined armies; but, like many other events, its importance is not to be estimated by ordinary standards, and so we come to discover that "the Boyne" was, from

its ultimate effects on the destinies of Europe, one of the most remarkable contests in the history of the world. And in relation to this point, we may notice a charge that is frequently made against the "July celebrations." It is said that such commemorations are in bad taste, because the victory was obtained by one section of Irishmen over another, and that it is consequently unfair, as it is uncharitable, to keep alive such memories. Now, without stopping to discuss the propriety or the impropriety of "celebrations" in the abstract, it will be sufficient to say that those annual displays which take place under the auspices of the Orange Institution are neither intended as an insult to the Roman Catholics personally nor yet to the religion they profess, and, no doubt, conscientiously believe. The victory of the Boyne is not celebrated as a mere feat of arms; if it were, we venture to think that there are few intelligent men who would for a moment hesitate in saying that its perpetuation was unadvisable. When Orangemen speak of the victories that were achieved at "Enniskillen," "Aughrim," "Derry," and the "Boyne," they emphatically re-assert the principles which have rendered the Revolution of 1688-90 for ever memorable; nor need we have the slightest hesitation in saying that if the members of the Roman Catholic Church were candid enough to deal with the subject apart from the intolerable bigotry of their political and religious training, they would.

be the first to confess the deep debt of gratitude they owe to the memory of William III. If, for example, it be asked why are the Roman Catholics of this Province more enlightened and possessed of a greater degree of religious freedom than their co-religionists of Quebec, we say in answer that they owe it to the Revolution of 1688. As we have already intimated, it does not lie within the scope of this Introduction to deal specifically with any of the minute incidents which mark that ever-memorable period in the history of the mother country ; it is only necessary to point out the striking landmarks as we pass ; and most noticeable of all these is, perhaps, what may be termed Rome's change of policy after the defeat which she sustained at the Boyne. It was on that ever-memorable day she was taught at the point of the bayonet that Popish superstition or fanaticism is no match for "free men whom the truth makes free." Rome, as matchless in her craft as she is unscrupulous in her code of morals, saw that it was useless to attempt the destruction of British Protestantism by force of arms, and so, to use a military phrase, she cunningly changed her " base of operations," and proceeded upon an entirely new line of attack. The Gunpowder Plot, the fires of Smithfield, the massacre of 1641, and the innumerable atrocities of which the Romish party had been guilty in Great Britain, naturally caused them to be looked upon not alone with suspicion, but dread, and not unfrequently detestation. Laws were made by men labouring under a strong personal sense of the wrongs done by Popery, and it can hardly be wondered that, in many instances, those enactments were conceived in a harsh and retaliatory spirit. In this connection "the Penal Laws" will at once occur to the mind, but fortunately we are not called upon to justify them, even if we felt disposed to do so. At the same time, it is only right to say that, in view of the course pursued both before and since that unfortunate time, even the Penal Laws are not deserving of the unqualified condemnation which *quasi* Protestant writers heap upon them. It is as certain as anything possibly can be, that if the Romanists of that day had been moderately good citizens, the Penal Laws would never have been enacted. If a Protestant, in 1642, whose friend had been barbarously murdered in the October of the previous year, had been told that Romanism was a heaven-born system of charity which he was bound not alone to tolerate, but to encourage and foster, would it be surprising to find him strongly opposed to do anything of the kind? We suspect not. So long, therefore, as the Protestant population laboured under a keen sense of the wrongs that Popery had inflicted, the guiding spirits in that mischievous system knew perfectly well that they could hope to make but little headway against the liberties of the nation. Rome, however, can always afford to wait, and in this instance, at all events, she pursued this policy to some advantage. Time being on her side, she well knew that by the misrepresentation of facts, the falsification of history (where possible), and the almost innumerable wiles of her Jesuit preachers and writers, a change would ultimately be produced in the aspect of affairs, until at last simple-minded Protestants, who had heretofore looked upon her with detestation, would come to consider her as not being near so black as she had been painted, and that so far from being the embodiment of persecution, tyranny and despotism, Rome was, above all other systems, the most tolerant, forbearing and gentle. It may be convenient for modern Romanists to ignore the facts of history; but, as Protestants, we cannot in justice to ourselves afford to forget them. Not, of course, that we pretend to charge against Roman Catholics, as individuals, any of the wrong-doing of which their Church has been guilty in the name of Religion. The charges we make against the Church of Rome have reference to the denationalizing system of Ultramontanism, which has been comprehensively termed "Vaticanism." Amongst other prerogatives claimed by the audacious Priest of Rome was the right of deposing Sovereigns according to the good pleasure of his will. Anything more monstrous cannot be well imagined ; and yet Cardinal Bellarmin, one of the most distinguished writers of the Romish Church, denounced the denial of this power as heretical. But bad as was the mere deposition of a Sovereign, there was worse yet behind it. Not alone was a King deposed, but from the moment of his deposition he was declared by the Pope to have forfeited his throne; his life was at the mercy of every fanatical Papist in the kingdom, the teaching of the Church of Rome on this point being that such persons may be murdered without fear of temporal or eternal punishment. If to this we add that other maxim of the same Church, namely, that it is perfectly lawful to break faith with heretics, we have a system of religion, or whatever you may wish to call it, so intensely evil, that without question it must owe its origin to the Father of Lies. People are fond of mincing matters in these days, and, as a consequence, both Romanists and Protestants are misled, and not unfrequently deceived, by men whose duty it is to instruct the public mind. It may be fairly asked by the modern Papist, why do you charge against the religion which I profess crimes with which I am not associated, and which I condemn, perhaps, as strongly as you do? Such a question as this is entitled to a straightforward and explicit answer. Your Church claims, without any hesitation, that she is *semper eadem* (always the same)—holding the same principles, teaching the same doctrines, and maintaining with undeviating consistency the identical same ecclesiastical policy. This claim is an inevitable result of her pretensions to "Infallibility." The reasoning proceeds in this way: Rome is infallible to-day; she was infallible when she murdered the Huguenots of France, the Protestants of Ireland, and mercilessly slaughtered the Albigenses and Waldenses; she was infallible when she burnt the heretics in England, or crushed them in the dungeons of the Spanish Inquisition; she was infallible when she excommunicated Queen Elizabeth, and relieved her subjects from all obligations of loyalty—in fact, according to her own theory, there never was a time since the days of the Apostles when she was or could be anything but what she professes to be to-day. The conclusion is inevitable: if it was lawful in Papists to murder deposed Sovereigns three hundred years ago, it is lawful to do so to-day. If Romanists were then under no obligations of loyalty to a Protestant State, it is the merest moonshine to say that they are under such obligations now. If we believe in their loyalty, we are driven to the alternative of supposing that they look upon infallibility as "a sham," and that *semper eadem* is an unmeaning term employed by our theological writers. But as a practical test of this. Are there ten honest Roman Catholics in the whole of Canada who are prepared to adopt the latter alternative? We think not. This then is the ground we take in regard to the Church of Rome, and every candid man must admit that it is perfectly unassailable. Three hundred years ago the public mind was but struggling to free itself from the grasp of the Papacy, the iron of whose despotism had entered into its very soul, and Rome was not then so cautious as she has since become; at that time her principles had, comparatively speaking, free play, but the advance of Bible truth and Protestant liberty rendered a modification of them absolutely necessary. The English Roman Catholics, whose honesty cannot for a moment be questioned, led the way, and so early in 1608, Archpriest Blackwell advocated the adoption of the oath of allegiance. "When the Royal remonstrance of 1661 had been signed by certain Bishops and others in Ireland, it was condemned at Rome, in July, 1662, by the Congregation *de* Propaganda; and in the same month the Papal Nuncio at Brussels, who superintended the affairs of Irish Roman Catholics at that time, denounced it as already condemned by the constitutions of Paul V. and Innocent X., and especially censured the ecclesiastics who, by signing it, had misled the laity." About a century and a quarter afterwards the English Catholics again found it necessary to disavow the teachings of their Church, and on that occasion they emphatically declared that they acknowledged no infallibility in the Pope, and that no ecclesiastical power whatever can, directly or indirectly, affect or interfere with the independence, sovereignty, laws, constitution or government of the realm. Similar protestations were made in Ireland by those who represented the Roman Catholic Church. Dr. Doyle, for example, was examined before Committees both of the Lords and Commons, and was asked this question:

"Does that justify the objection that is made to Catholics, that their allegiance is divided?" In answer he said, "I do not think it does in any way. We are bound to obey the Pope in those things that I have mentioned; but our obedience to the law and the allegiance which we owe the Sovereign are complete, full, perfect and undivided, inasmuch as they extend to all political, legal and civil rights of the King or of his subjects." So late as the year 1823, the Irish Roman Catholic Bishops declared *under oath* that "to believe the Pope infallible was not an article of the Catholic faith." These declarations were all necessary, in order—and we use the word advisedly—to *deceive* the Protestant rulers of Great Britain. The conclusion here is again perfectly irresistible: If the Pope was infallible in 1823, such an important fact must have been known to the Roman Catholic Bishops of Ireland, and yet, for the accomplishment of certain purposes of their own, they do not hesitate to *swear* that the Pope is not "infallible." On the other hand, if they swore to what they knew to be a fact, then the recent dogma of "Infallibility" is a novelty in the Church of Rome, as well as a burlesque upon our common humanity. Roman Catholics may be left to choose whichever horn of the dilemma they like best; in the meantime we proceed to say that, owing to such representations as the above, the "Penal Laws" were relaxed, and finally "Catholic Emancipation" was accomplished, and accompanying it we cannot help thinking that many of the safeguards which surrounded the British Throne were needlessly swept away. Looking at the history of the past fifty years, Protestant statesmen may well ask themselves, what have we been doing? Concession after concession has been made to the demands of the Papacy, but yet, as a spirit of evil, it moves about, ever restless, ever dissatisfied, and thwarting by its unhallowed presence the noblest efforts of man for the improvement of his fellow. What has become of all the guarantees that Popery so freely gave for its good behaviour before Emancipation? Swept away like the chaff before the wind; and if there is any Protestant curious to ascertain the reason, we will call upon that illustrious pervert, the late John Henry Newman, to rise and explain. He says, in his reply to Mr. Gladstone's pamphlet, "NO PLEDGE FROM CATHOLICS IS OF ANY VALUE TO WHICH ROME IS NOT A PARTY." This sentence ought to be printed in legible characters wherever Protestants have intercourse with Romanists, but in no place ought it to be more carefully noted than in the Halls of our Legislative Assemblies and in our Public Schools. Romish Bishops may swear, Romish journalists may explain, and Romish laymen may promise, but unless you have the assurance that Rome herself is a party to the contract, it possesses no value whatever. So says the greatest of modern Romish authorities. Protestants have been always willing to give Roman

Catholics the greatest possible freedom in the exercise of their religious worship, but, unfortunately for the peace of the world, Popery is not satisfied with religious toleration, and it hardly makes pretence to deny that it never can be satisfied with less than complete domination, and that, too, in matters political as well as spiritual; in fact, with the logical Romanist, the one is the natural consequence of the other. To talk about LIBERALISM is simply to insult the "Faith," as the Ultramontanes are pleased to designate their audacious and intolerable pretensions. And that we may not be supposed to misrepresent them in any way, we quote from the recent remarkable Pastoral Letter of Monseigneur Bishop Bourget, dated 1st February, 1876. He says:—

"Liberalism is a false and dangerous sentiment; it is a factious party, which conspires in fact against the Church and against civil society. A Liberal Catholic is a man who, to a certain degree, partakes of this sentiment, whether in this party or in this doctrine; the more sick is he as he is more Liberal; the less sick is he as he is more Catholic. Liberalism always seeks to subordinate the rights of the Church to the rights of the State in the measure of prudence and high wisdom, and even to separate the Church from the State where it desires a free Church in a free State. Liberalism claims that the clergy are called on solely to defend religion, and that the laity have not this mission; since that the

Pope declares, in his Encyclical of 1853, that the laity fulfil in that a filial duty from the moment that they combat under the direction of the clergy. Modern Liberalism pretends that religion should not leave the sacristy, nor go beyond the limits of private piety. But the Pope declares that Catholics can only efficaciously defend their rights and their liberties by actively mixing up in public affairs. By these characteristic traits you will recognize Catholic Liberalism. It is for that we have deemed it our duty to point them out to your serious consideration in order that you may better understand the definition of them which we have given you.

* * * * * *

"In passing through these bad times and living in these days of scandals, attach yourself with all your heart to the practical rules which we trace out for you in the presence of God, and with the sole object of securing your greatest good.

"1st. Hear Jesus Christ in hearing the Church. To this end penetrate the second oracles which fell from the mouth of the Divine Master, 'He who hears you hears Me; and he who does not hear the Church, let him be a heathen or a publican.' Now, here is how we must put this rule into practice. Each one of you can and ought to say in the interior of his soul, 'I hear my Curé; my Curé hears the Bishop; the Bishop hears the Pope; and the Pope hears our Lord Jesus Christ, who aids with His Holy Spirit to render them infallible on the teaching and government of His Church. With this rule so sure I cannot be led astray, and I am certain of marching in the way of justice and of truth.'

" 2nd. Bear a religious respect to all your pastors, fearing that in despising them you incur that terrible anathema pronounced by our Lord, ' He who despises you despises Me.' Oh! and what words; to despise Jesus Christ in despising His priests. They are worthy of attention, and deserve to be seriously considered. As it has just been observed, he who hears the Priest hears the Bishop, and he who hears the Bishop hears the Pope, and he who hears the Pope hears Jesus Christ. He hears then all the clergy, whose chief is Jesus Christ. In the same way, he who despises the Priest despises the Bishop, he who despises the Bishop despises the Pope, and he who despises the Pope despises Jesus Christ. He despises then all the clergy, whose chief is Jesus Christ. After all which has been reproduced above of the instructions given by the Pope and the Bishops against Catholic Liberalism, it is evident that the priests, in their instructions regarding this detestable error, scrupulously attach themselves to the principles which are dictated to them by their pastors. It is then all the clergy who thus speak through the mouth of their members. Thus, to despise this organ of the clergy is to despise Jesus, who made them His ambassadors.

It is to despise the Eternal Father, who sent Jesus Christ, His only Son, into the world, to teach and to save it. But how must we consider him who, upon the hustings, be it at the polls, upon the platform, or in papers, dares to prefer insults to the person and to the character of the priest, to despise or make his words and his conduct to be despised, in order to take away from him, if it be possible, all the estimation and the consideration which he enjoys among the people; and how ought he to be treated ? We invoke, to reply to it, the authority of the Holy See, against which it is not permissible for any one to reply and to make an attack."

Here, then, we have a Roman Catholic Bishop in this Protestant Dominion of Canada setting up an ecclesiastical despotism so absolute that we are actually confounded at the thought of it. But, unfortunately, this is not all. Romanism and Liberty are incompatible; and so by the Encyclical Letter of Gregory XVI. in 1831, and that of Pope Pius IX. in 1864, those who maintain the liberty of the press are condemned as being guilty of an offence against the faith. This statement was recently denied by Roman Catholic writers; but, as we have already shown, it matters little what such people either deny or affirm, because they can hardly call their immortal souls their own, much less the reason with which God has blessed them. Thus speaks the Bishop on the "Liberty of the Press":—

"For about three years the Holy Congregation of the Propaganda, charged with Apostolic superintendence over this country, has been informed that certain papers allowed themselves to publish insults to the ecclesiastical authorities. The Prefect of this Holy Congregation was constrained to write to the Bishops of this Province to impress upon them the necessity of doing all in their power to cause an end to be put to those unhappy discussions, which could only secure the triumph of Protestants. His eminence recommended in his letter the Bishops to compel, if it were necessary, those who were guilty in this particular to submit to this injunction *by forbidding the faithful to read their papers*. 'Curent (Episcopi) ne hujusmodi contentiones per ephemerides et libellos a catholicis exercantur, utque eos qui in hoc delinquerent coërcere et si opus fuerit earumdem ephemeridum lectionem fidelibus prohibere non omittant.' (*Rescript* of 23rd March, 1873.)

"We publish herewith this rule of conduct, and we order all those who have charge of souls to exactly conform themselves to it by refusing admission to the Sacrament to all those who read or efficaciously encourage the newspapers in which they take to task or cover with insults the shepherds of souls, because they oppose the dissemination of erroneous principles, reproved by the Sovereign Pontiff or by the early Fathers, charged by Jesus Christ to teach all people those holy doctrines which are placed in the bosom of the Church. *Especially must the Sacraments be refused to those editors who write such insults, and to those who employ them to edit the newspapers of which they are proprietors."*

Anything more monstrous, more out of harmony with the spirit of the times, more unlike Christianity, more intolerably Popish, has never been attempted against an unfortunate people. Yet this is Romanism undisguised—the identical Romanism that would, if it dare, again imbrue its hands down to the very elbows in the life blood of "those editors" who have dared to "write such insults." Let any intelligent man ask himself what is the meaning of the sentence we have marked in italics. From a Roman Catholic standpoint it is something dreadful. To deprive a man of the Sacraments is simply to consign him to the torments of eternal death; and if Bishop Bourget, in the exercise of that Christian "charity which suffereth long and is kind," can send these unfortunate editors, and printers like Guibord, to the devil with such complaisance, would he not much more quickly send them to the flames or the rack, in order, if possible, to save them from future woes? That Dominion statesmen should have at last become aroused to the importance of this question is, in itself, a gratifying omen.

It will be observed that, as usual with Romish

INTRODUCTION. 39

writers, no attempt has been made to answer the real point at issue, although we have no hesitation in saying that it will be news to many in Lower Canada to learn that there "is no State religion" in that Province. Coming from the Roman Catholic Bishop, we may not unreasonably assume that it is as trustworthy and reliable as the ordinary run of statements from the same source.

Rome is everywhere making strenuous efforts to regain her past ascendancy over the nation. With such a foe to contend against, Protestants must not think that the victory will be an easy one. The events connected with the Revolution of 1688 demonstrate the necessity of that combined and united action which James II. so much dreaded. Men, and especially Orangemen, must be intelligently alive to the issues of the hour.

We cannot close without referring to the persistent efforts that Rome is making to have the education of the country handed over to her precious keeping. We know only too well what such a course would involve. To entrust the Romish priesthood with the education of the people is to have the Bible kicked out of the public schools, and as Protestants we are not just yet prepared to submit to anything of the kind. Yet this is part of Rome's programme.

With these facts in view, it is clear that there cannot be an alliance on the part of the members

C

of the Orange Society with Romish Ultramontanes. The loyal men of Canada must set themselves to oppose vigorously the ever-increasing demands of the Papacy, and at the same time to render as nugatory as possible the concessions already made to the professors of this insatiable system. The safety of our homes, the prosperity and happiness of our country, and the sanctity of our altars demand this; because the Ultramontane doctrine, publicly declared, is: "NO PLEDGE FROM CATHOLICS IS OF ANY VALUE. TO WHICH ROME IS NOT A PARTY."

THE HISTORY

OF THE

HOUSE OF ORANGE:

TO WHICH IS ADDED

THE HISTORY OF

WILLIAM AND MARY,

KING AND QUEEN OF ENGLAND, SCOTLAND, FRANCE, IRELAND,
&c., &c.

BY RICHARD BURTON.

NOTE BY THE PUBLISHER.

THE principal part of this volume having been written during the lifetime of the great and good King William, the plain and somewhat quaint phraseology of that period is perceptible throughout; though in this respect it is likely some modifications were made in our former edition, many years ago, a circumstance which we regret, as we would prefer now to let the sturdy old historian speak in his own words, rather than in those of the present day.

TO THE READER.

I AM very sensible that the greatness of the subject is a sufficient reason to deter me from adventuring to publish my mean endeavours, in relating the glorious and magnanimous achievements of His Majesty's renowned ancestors, as well as to his own; or for the excellent conduct of their Majesties since their happy accession to the throne. But because we have such a furious generation of murmurers, who, if they had their desires, would ruin both themselves and their country, and reduce us to French Popery and slavery, it may seem to be the interest of every man to strive to undeceive those whom these miscreants would delude, since both our eternal and temporal happiness very much depends upon the supporting the present government against all its foreign and domestic enemies. A government founded upon law and justice; a government calculated for the support of the Protestant interest throughout the world, wherein we have a King and Queen of the same excellent religion with ourselves, a happiness which we have been deprived of for almost an age past; Princes of such exemplary virtue and piety that they discourage vice and profaneness, and constantly endeavour to support goodness and modesty, which seem lately designed to be hissed out of the nation.

God grant that our ingratitude and impenitence may never deprive us of such inestimable blessings, and that we do not fall a sacrifice to our stupendous folly and discontent.

THE AUTHOR.

THE HISTORY

OF THE

HOUSE OF ORANGE.

THE family of Nassau, from whom our Gracious Sovereign is descended, is not undeservedly accounted one of the most ancient and honourable in Europe; not only for its great alliances and branches, but also by the advancement of one of this house to the empire of Germany, Adolphus Nassau by name, in the year 1291, and that there has been a succession of the family in a direct line for above a thousand years past; and among them Otho, Count of Nassau, who lived about six hundred years since, and had two wives, with the first of whom he had the province of Gueldres, and with the other that of Zutphen. About three hundred years after, a second Count Otho of Nassau married the Countess of Vranden, whereby he became possessed of several other territories in the Netherlands. In the year 1404, Engilbert, who was his grandchild, married the heiress of the town of Breda and Locke, and was grandfather to Engilbert, second Earl of Nassau, who, in 1491, was by Maximilian, King of the Romans, going into Hungary, made Governor, Lieutenant and Captain-General of Flanders; and afterwards, in 1501, Archduke Philip, going into Spain, constituted him Governor-General of the Netherlands; an experienced Prince both in war and peace, but dying childless left his brother John his large territories. This John had two sons: upon Henry, the eldest, he bestowed all his possessions in the Low Countries, and to his youngest son, William, he bequeathed all his inheritance in Germany. By the earnest endeavours of Henry Nassau, Charles V. was advanced to the empire, against the pretensions of Francis I., the French King, and at his coronation placed the crown on his head, and yet when, upon concluding peace between these two monarchs, Henry was sent by the Emperor to do homage to King Francis for the county of Flanders and Artois, that Prince forgetting former differences, and being fully sensible of his extraordinary merits, married him to Claudia, only sister to Philibert of Chalons, Prince of Orange, by which marriage his only son Revens, of Orange and Chalons, became Prince of Orange.

William, Earl of Nassau, brother to Prince Henry, professed the Protestant religion, and expelled Popery out of his territories, and was father to the great William of Nassau, who attained to be the Prince of Orange, and Lord of all the possessions of the House of Chalons, by the last will of Revens de Nassau, who died childless.

The Emperor Charles V. having a favour for the House of Orange, and received great services from them, was concerned that the young Prince William should be educated in the reformed religion, and therefore took him, with much regret, from his father, and endeavoured to instruct him in the Romish faith, but afterward the former opinions, which he had sucked in with his mother's milk, prevailed upon him so that he became an earnest professor of Protestantism.

William, Count of Nassau, his father, had five

sons and seven daughters, by Juliana Countess of Stolberg.

William, the eldest, was born in 1533, at the castle of Dillemberg, in the county of Nassau, and being taken from his father by the Emperor Charles, as we said, he became a great favourite by his extraordinary wisdom and modesty, so that the Emperor confessed his young Prince often furnished him with notions and hints he should else never have thought of; and upon giving of private audiences to ambassadors, when the Prince would discreetly offer to withdraw, the Emperor mildly reminded him, saying, "Stay Prince," and it was admired by the whole court, that a Prince, not above twenty years old, should be entrusted with all the secrets of the empire and carry the imperial crown upon his resignation to his brother Ferdinand, though the Prince, with some reluctancy, seemed to refuse the employment, by alleging that it was no ways proper for him to carry to another that crown which his uncle Henry of Nassau had set upon his head. Yea, the Emperor had so much confidence in his conduct, that in the absence of the Duke of Savoy, his General of the Low Countries, though the Prince was not above twenty-two years old, yet contrary to the advice of all his Council, rejecting all other experienced generals, he constituted him Generalissimo, who managed that great employ with such discretion and courage, that he caused Philipville and Charlemont to be built in the sight of the French army, which was then commanded by Admiral de Chastillon, that great captain.

These magnanimous actions caused the Emperor to recommend the Prince of Orange to Philip II., his son; but his virtue and courage were so emulated by the Spaniards, that all his most innocent words and actions were misinterpreted, and the King's will and pleasure in defence of their privileges were attributed to his contrivance, which King Philip made him sensible of when he was embarking from Flushing for Spain, charging him with preventing all his private intrigues, with a furious countenance; and when the Prince mildly replied that all had been done by the States themselves, the King shaking him by the wrist, replied, " No, not the States, but you, you are the occasion of it;" which severe reproach in public so disgusted the Prince that he suddenly left the King without further ceremony, only wishing him a good voyage, and so left him in the middle of Flushing, which he knew had much respect for him; and that which increased the Prince's indignation against the Spanish Government was that he saw himself deprived of the government of the Netherlands, which his predecessors always enjoyed, and Cardinal Granville, his implacable adversary, put in his place, which proceedings of King Philip disobliged both the nobility and the people, who hated the pride of Philip as much as they admired the affability of his father Charles, which was much increased when the States (who much dreaded the Spanish insolvency), in a full assembly at Gaunt, desired the King to withdraw his foreign troops out of the provinces, and entrust the natives with the fortified places, and not advance foreign ministers to the government. The King was so far incensed thereat, that he ordered his sister, Margaret of Austria, to set up the Spanish inquisition, and to make divers new bishops. And these were the principal causes of the defection and terrible disorders that followed; for the people, abhorring the name of the inquisition, and the new bishops as members of it, and the nobility being highly incensed at the imperious temper of Granville, after having long suffered under his arrogance, at length the Prince of Orange, Count Horn, and Count Egmont sent King Philip word that "unless he recalled the Cardinal out of the Low Countries, his violent counsels, which were so much abhorred by all, would certainly occasion a revolt in those provinces." This, with much regret, was done; but another, worse than he, was designed in his room, the bloody Duke of Alva, with an army of Spaniards and Italians, which, the Prince and nobility being sensible, was to take revenge for the affront to Granville. The Prince desired the governess to be dismissed from his governments of Holland, Zealand, Utrecht, and Burgundy, which the Duchess refused, but desired him to remove his brother, Count Lodowick, from his person, as being suspected to give him bad counsel, and likewise to take a new oath of allegiance to King Philip; both which he denied, and, as to the last, alleged that "such an oath would oblige him to extirpate heretics, and might compel him to put his own wife to death, who was a Protestant; and that, if he should take another oath, it might be thought he had broken the first."

But the governess being very zealous for settling the inquisition and the new bishops, about four hundred gentlemen, with Prince Lewis of Nassau at the head of them, and several other nobles, presented a petition against it, and were those who were afterwards called gueux, or beggars, so nicknamed for the plain apparel by Count Barlemont, a favourite of the Duchess; which, though given in scorn, did much advance the confederacy that followed, and strengthened the Prince of Orange's party; for their petition being absolutely rejected, these gentlemen caused medals to be made, with the King's picture on one side, and a beggar's dish and wallet on the other, with this inscription, "Faithful to God and the King, even to the carrying of the wallet," intimating that they were better subjects to the King than Barlemont and his adherents; and the Prince of Orange, with the other lords, perceiving their petition slighted, consulted their own safety. Most of them were for taking arms to oppose the landing of the Spaniards in the Netherlands, since, by intercepted letters, they plainly discovered the design was to ruin and destroy them; but Count Egmont, governor of Flanders and Artois, opposed it, and being confident of his own good services, advised them to rely upon the King's clemency and mercy, to which the Prince of Orange replied, that "the King's mercy, upon which he trusted, would be his ruin, and that the Spaniards would make a bridge of him to come into the Low Countries, and then break him;" at which words, embracing the Count, as if foreseeing they should never meet again, they parted with tears in their eyes. The Prince instantly went, with his family, to his town of Breda, only he left his eldest son, Philip, to study in Louvain; and after that to Dillemberg, the ancient seat of the Nassaus.

Soon after, the Duke of Alva, with an army of old Spanish and Italian soldiers came into the Netherlands, and Count Egmont waiting upon him, he said aloud, "Behold the great Lutheran;" yet the Count took no notice of it, but presented him with two fine horses. The Duke, being arrived at Brussels, produced his commission, whereby he was made absolute governor in all causes whatsoever; he then dismissed the assembly of the States, and constituted a court of twelve men, who were to inspect into the troubles. They soon imprisoned a great number of people of all degrees and qualities, and eighteen lords and gentlemen were put to death at Brussels, and the Counts Egmont and Horn imprisoned, and soon after beheaded in the market-place of that city; the first being much pitied by the people for his fond credulity, who rejoiced at the safety of the Prince of Orange; and Cardinal Granville, who was then at Rome, hearing of these proceedings, asked the messenger whether the Duke had taken Silence, which was a name given to the Prince for secrecy and few words: who replying no: "Nay," says Granville, "if that fish has escaped the net, the Duke of Alva's draught is nothing worth."

The cruel and barbarous proceedings of this new governor caused a great many to leave the country, who were summoned to appear before the bloody Council of Twelve at a certain day, and upon their refusal, all their estates were confiscated; among others, the Prince of Orange, Count Culenburgh, and other lords were cited; the Prince refused, alleging that "being of the Order of the Golden Fleece, he could not be judged by any but the King and the companions of that Order. He likewise appealed to the Emperor Maximilian, brother to King Philip, and other German Princes, imploring their aid, who approved of his reasons, and declared their dislike of the proceeding of the Duke of Alva. The time for the Prince's appearing being expired, his principalities were all declared to be forfeited, a Spanish garrison was put into Breda, and his eldest son, Philip William, was sent to Spain to be educated in the Roman religion, and also for an hostage for his father.

And thus King Philip, by these cursed counsels

and the rigorous usage of his subjects, was himself the occasion of the loss of the United Netherlands; who, finding all their privileges violated, and their utter extirpation determined, resolved to throw off this intolerable yoke, and afterwards, in some of their ensigns had this motto, "We will either recover our liberties, or perish in the attempt." And the Prince of Orange observing himself so roughly and unjustly used, being reproached as a public enemy, and exposed to the malice of his implacable adversaries, having his innocent son and his great estate ravished from him, thought it high time to defend his honour and his life by force of arms, and to engage for religion and liberty in the common quarrel of his country. And thereupon he raised an army in Germany, which he sent unto Friesland, under his brothers Lewis and Adolphus of Nassau; and being met by Count Arembergh, with a considerable force, a battle followed, wherein the Nassovians gained a considerable victory, the Spanish army being totally routed, and Aremburgh himself, with the principal commanders, slain, and all their cannon, baggage, and a great sum of money sent to pay the soldiers, taken. This defeat happened in 1568. But Count Lewis enjoyed this victory very little, for the Duke of Alva pursuing him, fell upon him just at the time when the Germans were all in a mutiny for their pay, who rather chose to be miserably slain than to defend themselves; so that six thousand were killed or drowned, Adolphus hardly making his escape.

The Prince, nothing discouraged at this misfortune, raised another army of twenty-eight thousand French and Germans, and published a declaration, wherein he cleared his innocence of those crimes objected against him, charging the Duke and the

Council of Blood with the causes of the war, and then, passing the Rhine by tying his horses together to break the force of the river, the foot arrived silently in the night to the other shore, which so surprised the Duke of Alva that he would not believe it at first, saying, " Sure ye do not think them an army of birds." Arriving thus into Brabant, he offered Alva battle, which the other declined; so after twenty-nine several attempts to engage him to a combat, and the cities not revolting to the Prince as he expected, and the Germans being again ready to mutiny for want of pay, it was thought advisable to dismiss his army, paying part of their arrears by the sale of his plate, artillery, and baggage, and engaging his principality of Orange to his chief officers for the remainder; yet, before their disbanding, he routed eighteen companies of the enemy's foot, and three hundred horse of the Spaniards, near Cambray; most of the commanders being taken prisoners, and the Duke of Alva's son slain.

After this, with only one thousand two hundred horse, the Prince and his two brothers went into France to the assistance of the Protestants against the Duke of Guise and his partizans, where he was successful in several encounters, and at length, by the advice of the great Admiral de Coligny, he gave out commissions to several persons of quality, fugitives of the Low Countries, to infest the Spaniards by sea, by which means he soon became master of all Holland and Zealand. The Germans being driven out of the Netherlands, the Duke of Alva, as if he had conspired to lose these countries, instantly levied new taxes, even the tenths of all goods and estates, which so enraged the people, that were already nearly ruined by the war, that upon the privateers (who were sent abroad by the Prince's commission) taking the town of Brill, a port in Zealand, eight cities in Holland, and all the cities in Zealand except Middleburgh, declared for the Prince of Orange; and Flushing, a considerable city, being animated by the priest at mass, on Easter-day in the morning, turned out the Spanish garrisons in such fury that they hanged Alvares, kinsman to the Duke of Alva. And William, Count of Bergen, at the same time took back several other towns in Friesland, and, which most astonished Alva, Lewis of Nassau, by the assistance of the French, took Mons, the chief city of Hainault.

Meanwhile, the Prince of Orange, with an army of eleven thousand foot and six thousand horse, marched to Louvain, which presented him with sixteen thousand crowns, and was received into Mechlin, and from thence came within sight of Alva's army, which was strongly fortified, yet the Prince resolved to force his intrenchments, or oblige him to a battle, which, whilst he was consulting, he received advice of the horrid massacre at Paris, whereby he lost the Admiral de Chastillon and many other of his dearest friends, together with all hopes of any more relief from France; so that not being able to oblige the Duke to a battle, and doubting the French commanders, who were his chief strength, should desert him upon the news of the bloody massacre, he wrote to his brother Lewis to make terms for delivering up Mons, then besieged by Alva; and then with slow marches retreated to the Rhine, yet with some loss and danger; for a detachment of Spanish horse and foot breaking into his camp in the night, killed and burned all before them as far as his own tent, where he was fast asleep; but a little dog which used to lie on his bed never left barking and scratching his face till he had waked him, so that leaping out of his bed, and perceiving the peril he was in, he hastened to his men, who were now coming to his rescue, and fell upon the Spaniards so furiously that most of the party, which were about a thousand horse and foot, were cut off in their retreat.

After which the Prince dismissed his army and came into Holland, these States, with those of Zealand, having already acknowledged him for their governor, and taken an oath to stand by him with their lives and fortunes.

But though the Prince had the full power of the government in his own hands, yet he acted in all matters in the name of the States, and by his extreme diligence, in four months' time he had provided a fleet of one hundred and fifty sail, well rigged and manned, in the port of Flushing; who for ten years after did unspeakable damage to the Spaniards, and were never but once worsted by them. He likewise banished all Romish superstitions out of the churches, that difference in religion might render them more irreconcilable to their old adversary.

But the Duke of Alva having retaken Mons, sent his son to reduce some other cities in Holland and Guelderland, and because the town of Haarlem had formerly received the Prince of Orange, after the Duke had reduced it by famine, whereof nearly thirteen thousand died, he made a dreadful example of this place, the Spaniards first hanging the governor, and for several days together hanging and drowning the ministers, magistrates and people of the city, to the number of near two thousand, which butcheries made the Hollanders to be more resolved and obstinate against them; so that the other towns made a more vigorous defence for fear of falling into the hands of such cruel bloodhounds. Soon after, the Duke of Alva was recalled out of the Netherlands, and Lewis Requesones, of a milder temper, was sent to succeed him, King Philip now finding that rigour and barbarity did but enrage the Netherlands, and made them more averse to his government. This new governor had the fortune, at his arrival, to be an eye-witness of the defeat of his master's fleet by that of the Prince of Orange; but yet was more fortunate by land; for Prince Lewis of Nassau having brought a fourth army out of Germany, of seven thousand foot and four thousand horse, was defeated by the Spaniards near Nimmeguen; the Germans, according to their usual custom, calling for their pay just as the battle began, and thereby were the ruin of themselves as well as of their general's honour; the Prince Lewis, with his brother, Prince Henry, and the Count Palatine being all three killed in this fight. Upon which victory the Spaniards besieged Leyden, and reduced it to very great extremity, so that they were ready to capitulate; but the Prince having an account of their condition, by letters tied to pigeons and sent into the town, resolved to make the utmost effort possible to relieve it; and having provided two hundred flat-bottomed boats, of fourteen or sixteen oars, and two guns a-piece, which he filled with seamen and provisions, when all things were prepared, the Hollanders broke down the dam that kept out the sea, which thereupon entered with such fury into the country that it was overwhelmed with water, and the camp of the Spaniards was overflowed, so that the city received supplies forty miles off by water; and the Spaniards having sunk their cannon, after four months' fruitless labour were forced to raise the siege, being pursued by the Dutch in their boats, with long grappling irons, wherewith they drowned and destroyed a great number of their enemies. This deliverance from a barbarous and inhuman enemy endeared the Prince of Orange to those of Leyden, who, to recompense their losses by the inundation, erected a university there, which he endowed with ample revenues and privileges.

But to recompense this loss Requesones reduced Zuider Zee; but the Spaniards and Germans falling at variance about their pay, and Requesones dying at the same time, the unruly soldiers fell upon Maestricht and Antwerp, both which towns they plundered and ransacked of an immense treasure, rated at about twenty millions. The robberies of those foreign mutineers caused such an abhorrence and detestation of the government in the people, that those who had hitherto been obedient to the Spanish government now declared the Spaniards enemies to their King and country, and called in the Prince of Orange to their assistance; all the provinces, except Luxembourg, entering into an association, and solemnly swearing to assist each other in delivering their country from Spanish slavery. This happened in 1576, when King Philip, to remedy these disorders, sent Don John of Austria to be governor of the Netherlands, who, by his mild and affable behaviour, wheedled the provinces for a short time to desist from their gallant resolution; and though the Prince of Orange, who saw the bottom of the Spaniards' designs, continually forewarned them not to be deluded with gilded promises, yet Don John having solemnly agreed that the States General should assemble, and that the Spaniards and Germans should depart out of the Netherlands, several of the provinces again submitted to King

Philip; the Prince of Orange, with the States of Holland and Zeeland, protesting against their proceedings, especially as to the articles about religion. But Don John was no sooner settled in his government, being received with much magnificence at Brussels, but he quickly made good the Prince's premonitions, for he seized upon Namur and Charlemont, and sent for the foreign troops. Whereupon, the States finding themselves deluded, they resolved to oppose him by arms, and having demolished the Castle of Antwerp, they joined with the Prince of Orange, and sent to desire his presence at Brussels, where he was received with all kinds of joy and the acclamations of the people, and declared Governor of Brabant and superintendent of the revenues of the provinces.

The States General having declared Don John of Austria the public enemy of their country, he thereupon recalled the Italians and other foreigners, who were banished by the perpetual edict, as it was called, and with them defeated the army of the States at Gemblours, though this loss was recompensed by the surrender of the famous city of Amsterdam eight days after, which was then united to the body of Holland.

In the year 1579 the Prince of Orange laid the foundation of the republic in the Low Countries by the strict union he made between the provinces of Gueldres, Zutphen, Holland, Zeeland, Friesland, and the Ommelands, consisting of twenty-five articles, the chief whereof was, "That these provinces should mutually assist each other against the common enemy, and not treat of war or peace without general consent." This was called the Treaty of Utrecht, because signed in that city; and to show that union was absolutely necessary for their preservation, the

States took this for their motto, "Concordia parvæ res crescunt:" "By concord little things grow great." But the Prince, finding the power of these few provinces not sufficient to defend themselves against other provinces that had reconciled themselves to Spain, nor against that potent crown, he thought it advisable to choose some neighbour Prince to be their protector, and judged none more proper than the Duke of Anjou and Alençon, the only brother of Henry III, King of France; and commissioners being sent to him, it was soon agreed that these six provinces of Holland, Zeeland, Brabant, Flanders, Utrecht, and Friesland, should acknowledge him for their sovereign, upon condition "That he should maintain them in their present privileges and religion; that he should assemble the States General once a year, or oftener if they thought fit; that he should not dispose of any offices or preferments without the consent of the State; lastly, that if he should endeavour to infringe or violate this treaty he should immediately forfeit his sovereignty, and they be fully absolved from any allegiance to him, and be at liberty to choose another sovereign."

This agreement being made, Archduke Matthias, brother to Rudolf, Emperor of Germany, who had been sent for some time before by some factious Lords (who envied the virtue and glory of the Prince of Orange), finding that the States sought for a more powerful protector, took his leave and retired into Germany, though not without large acknowledgments and presents from the State General. The Prince of Orange hastened the march of the Duke of Alençon, whose presence he knew was very considerable, especially since in this year, 1580, the King of Spain had published a most bloody prosecution against him, "reproaching him with the favours bestowed on him by his father, Charles V., and declaring him to be a rebel, heretic, hypocrite, like to Cain and Judas, of an obdurate conscience, a villain, the head of the Netherland troubles, a plague to Christendom, and an enemy of all mankind;" declaring further, "That he did prosecute and banish him out of his countries and estates, forbidding any of his subjects to converse with or relieve him, giving all his estate to those that would take it, promising, upon the word of a King, and as the minister of Almighty God, that if any would deliver him alive or dead, or else take away his life, he would give to him or his heirs five thousand crowns of gold, and the free pardon of all the crimes that he had before been guilty of; and if they were not noble to make them so, and to reward all that shall assist them therein; and likewise that all his adherents should be banished, and their lives and estates given for a prey to any that would take them."

The Prince of Orange made a very smart apology in answer hereunto, wherein he fully vindicates himself from all the crimes objected against him. proving at large, "That all the miseries of the Netherlands ought to be imputed to the Council of Spain, who endeavoured to reduce those countries to absolute slavery, both as to religion and civil liberties, and acting more like madmen than politicians, and like that foolish King Rehoboam, following the silly advice of a weak woman, and Cardinal Granville, the Pope's creature, telling the King that his father had chastised the people with whips, but the son ought to whip them with scorpions, and therefore they endeavoured to bring in the inquisition, and the new bishops which were the occasion of all these commotions. And as to his taking arms against his sovereign, he showeth that Henry Bastard, of

Castile, the King's great grandfather, had with his own hands slain the King Don Pedro the cruel, his lawful brother, and possessed his kingdom, whose successor King Philip was, and enjoyed it to this day. And that there was a reciprocal bond between a Prince and a subject, and if the Prince infringes his oath the subject is free from his allegiance; that the King of Spain was admitted to be Duke of Brabant upon certain conditions which he had sworn to maintain, and yet had notoriously violated; and if the nobility did not endeavour by arms (since no other means was to be found) to preserve and defend their liberties, they ought to be counted guilty of perjury, treachery, and rebellion to the States of the country. And whereas the King had offered money to take away his life, he did not doubt of God's protection, yet certainly he could never be accounted a gentleman by persons of honour, who would be so wicked and infamous to murder a man for money, except they were such Spaniards who, being descended from the Moors and Jews, might retain that quality from their ancestors, who offered money to Judas to betray our Lord and Saviour Jesus Christ into their hands, that they might crucify Him."

The Prince concluded his apology by telling the States General, "That since their peace and quiet seemed to depend upon his death, he was willing to lay down his life to free them from the calamities under which they suffered, having already for their sakes lost his estate, his brethren, yea, and his own son, and that his head, over which no Prince or potentate on earth had any power, was yet at their command, and that he would be a willing sacrifice to procure their tranquillity; but if they thought fit still to use his service, he would employ his life, counsel, and all he had in the world, for the defence and preservation of the Netherlands."

In answer to this the States declare that they are fully satisfied that the crimes and slanders charged upon the Prince are altogether false and malicious, and that all the honours that had been conferred on him were so far from being sought for or desired by him, that he only accepted them at their earnest request and entreaty, with the full consent and by the free election of the country, and therefore they humbly entreated him still to continue his administration, and likewise to accept of a guard for his person against any villainous attempts upon his life.

The States General of the united provinces perceiving that, notwithstanding the intercession both of the Emperor, the French King, the Queen of England, and other Princes and States of Christendom to King Philip on their behalf, yet he still continued obstinately resolved to yield to nothing but what might reduce their country absolutely to Popery and slavery; thereupon, in 1581, they published an edict of renunciation against him, wherein they declare, "That it being acknowledged by all mankind that a Prince is ordained of God to preserve his subjects from all injuries and violence, even as a shepherd defends his sheep, and that the people were never created to be bondmen and slaves to his will and pleasure, whether his commands are right or wrong, but that he is advanced to that dignity to govern them by equity and reason, and to cherish them as a father doth his children, even with the peril of his life. If a King, therefore, fail therein, and instead of protecting his subjects shall strive to destroy them and deprive them of their ancient laws and privileges, and endeavour to make them bond slaves, his subjects are thereupon discharged from all subjection to such a Sovereign, and are to reckon and esteem him a tyrant, and that he is absolutely fallen from his former dignity and sovereignty; and the Estates of the country may lawfully and freely abandon him, and elect another Prince to protect and defend them in his place; especially when his subjects neither by prayers nor petitions can mollify his heart, nor divert him from his tyrannical and abitrary courses, since they have no other way to preserve their ancient liberties, lives, wives, children and estates, which, according to the laws of God and nature, they are bound to defend, and which hath been practised in divers countries, especially in those where the King was obliged, by oath, to govern according to law, and was admitted to the sovereignty upon certain conditions and special contracts.

"Now, it being apparent to all the world that Philip, King of Spain, giving ear to certain wicked counsellors, hath in every particular broken all the oaths and obligations which he hath entered into for the defence of these provinces, and hath determined to enslave, ruin and destroy them, and all their interest therein, etc., We, the States General, being pressed by extreme necessities, do, by general resolution and consent, declare the King of Spain to be fallen from the government, dominion, and jurisdiction of these countries, and we are resolved never hereafter to acknowledge him for our Prince and Sovereign Lord, but do hereby declare ourselves and all the inhabitants of these provinces to be for ever discharged from all manner of oaths and allegiance to the said King, etc. In witness whereof, we have caused our seals to be hereunto annexed. July 26th, 1581."

The Duke of Anjou having been in England to make a visit to Queen Elizabeth returned again to Antwerp, after three months' splendid entertainment in the English Court, the Queen, at his departure, earnestly recommending to him to govern the people with mildness and to endeavour to gain their affections, which would be the most durable foundation that he could lay for the security of his government. The Duke was received at Antwerp with all kind of magnificence, being made Duke of Brabant with much solemnity, and having taken an oath to protect and defend them in all their rights; afterwards the nobility and gentry swore allegiance to him as their Prince and Governor.

Soon after a plot was laid to kill the Prince of Orange, which was thus managed: Gaspard de Anestro, a Spanish merchant living at Antwerp, finding his affairs in a very low condition, by reason of the many debts he had contracted and was not able to pay, he bethought himself of the great reward promised by the King of Spain to the murderers of the Prince of Orange; and being greedy of this prey, which he thought might again retrieve his credit, he consulted with the Governor of Gravelin how to put this act in question, and at length concluded to employ a wicked boy he had, called Joanille, to perpetrate it, who no sooner was acquainted with it but he readily undertook it. The day appointed for this execrable deed was on a Sunday, when, the Duke of Anjou making a great feast, the Prince of Orange was present. The boy accordingly came to the house, where he was confessed by a Jacobin friar, and promised the pardon of all his sins; the priest likewise deluding him and saying that he should go invisible, having given him some characters in papers, with frogs' bones and other trifles, which were found in his pocket. Being thus strengthened in his resolution he drank a glass or two of wine, and the ghostly father having given him his blessing at the stairs foot, left him. Joanille went into the room, where the prince and several lords were at dinner, clad like a Frenchman, and was thought to be a servant of one of the French noblemen; he endeavoured to come near the prince, having charged his pistol with two bullets, designing to shoot him behind, as he had been instructed, but was still hindered. The prince, having dined, went towards his withdrawing room, showing by the way to a nobleman the cruelties of the Spaniards in the Netherlands, wrought in tapestry. The murderer, having placed himself in a window of the hall, discharged his pistol at the hinder part of his head, but, the Prince turning his face at the same instant, the bullet entered in at the throat, it being so near that the fire entered with the wound, burning his ruff and his beard, and breaking one of his teeth; the bullet came out of his left cheek, near the nose, without hurting his tongue. This terrible blow being given, all present were amazed, and one of the halberdiers in a rage thrust the villain through, and a page presently after dispatched him. The boy was quickly known to belong to Anastro, who was imprisoned, together with the monk. The first was released, but the friar, together with the carcase of the murderer, were both hanged and afterwards quartered. The prince's wound was somewhat dangerous, for the bleeding of the jugular vien could by no art or means be stopped, till they contrived that for nine days together several persons appointed should hold their thumbs upon the wound night and day, so that at length it closed and the danger was over. At first the French were thought to have committed the act; but the Prince of Orange, though weak, writing in his own hand to the magistrates of Antwerp, to let them know it was a Spaniard, they at length were satisfied. The grief of the great city was extraordinary upon the Prince being wounded, the magistrates commanding fasts to be kept to pray for his recovery, and their joy was great when they heard that he was out of danger. The Prince of Parma, governor of the Spanish Netherlands, concluded he was dead, and sent mild letters to several cities to surrender to him.

After this the Duke of Anjou, envying the power of the Prince of Orange, which he thought eclipsed his own, and not enduring to be a Sovereign only in name, with such a limited authority, by the advice of some of his young counsellors, he resolved to seize upon the principal places in the Netherlands—that is, Antwerp, Bruges, Dunkirk and Dendermond—upon pretence that the people of Antwerp had encompassed his palace with design to murder him. The two last he took possession of, but the citizens of Bruges and Antwerp defended themselves with so much courage, that the French were killed in such heaps before the gates as prevented those without from entering in to their relief. The Flemings had some suspicions the Prince was concerned in the attempt, which was somewhat occasioned by his fourth marriage with Louise de Coligny, a French lady; but he perceiving it, and that the States party grew every day weaker in the Walloon provinces, retired into Holland, where he thought himself more secure, and his life less exposed to the bigoted Papists, and settled at the city of Delph, where Henry Frederick, grandfather to our present gracious Sovereign, was born.

The Duke of Anjou's party being defeated, he was obliged to restore those places of which he had made himself master, and, returning into France, died soon after, some say of poison, others of mere vexation for this inglorious enterprise.

The Spaniards, thinking they had no greater enemy in the world than the Prince of Orange, and that he being gone they should attain their full purposes for enslaving the Netherlands, they used all manner of base and treacherous practices to murder and destroy him, which they too successfully effected in the manner following. In May, 1584, a young man, of about twenty-seven, coming to the Prince's Court at Delph, delivered him a letter as he passed along; the Prince demanding whence it came, the youth, being of a seeming innocent countenance, replied that it was his own letter, and contained matter of concernment for the service of the country; it was subscribed "Francis Guyon." The Prince went away, and the next day the fellow desiring a counsellor of the Prince's that he might be heard and receive an answer of his letter, and that he had several other things of importance to discover both concerning the country and religion, the Prince, having notice of it, commanded one of his council to examine him, to whom he gave a large account of his pretended adventures, and that he had procured several blanks (which he produced) with Count Mansfieldt's seal, which were given him for the use of passports for victuallers, but might be serviceable to the Prince upon other occasions. The Prince recovered the blank passports, intending to try some experiment with them, and by this means he became so familiar at Court, that the Prince, some days after, having an account of the death of the Duke of Anjou, he sent for this villain into his chamber, to inquire something of him, while he was in bed, and the wretch afterwards confessed in prison that if he had had a dagger or penknife he would have certainly slain him then. After this he came constantly to prayers and sermons, and was observed to read Du Barth's works, particularly the history of Judith and Holofernes, where there are certain persuasions and encouragements to cut off tyrants; sometimes he borrowed a Bible of the porter upon pretense of religion, so that at last he went about the Court without suspicion. Awhile after the Prince ordered him to be sent to Count Biron into France, to try if he could make any advantage of the passports, upon which he desired money to buy shoes and stockings, being in an ill condition. The Prince ordered him ten or twelve crowns. Next day he bought a pistol of one of the guard, but finding it did not shoot true he bought two more, which were according to his mind. After this he watched when the Prince went down to the hall to dinner, and demanded a passport of him, but in such a hollow and confused voice that the Princess asked what he was, for she did not like his countenance. The Prince told her his business. After dinner, the Prince going out of the hall, the villain stood behind a pillar in the gallery, with his cloak on one shoulder, having two pistols under his left arm, holding in his right hand a paper like a passport, as if to have the Prince sign it. As the Prince passed along, having one foot upon the first step of the stairs, the traitor, advancing, drew forth one of his pistols so suddenly that he was not perceived till the blow was given; the three bullets wherewith the pistol was charged entering in at his left side and coming out of his right, through the stomach and vital parts. The Prince, feeling himself hurt, said only thus: "O, my God, take pity of my soul; I am sore wounded; my God, take pity of my soul and of this poor people;" after which he began to stagger, but his gentleman usher supported him, and set him upon the stairs. The Countess of Swartzenburg, his sister, asked him if he did not recommend his soul to Jesus Christ. He answered "Yes," and never spoke a word more, dying in a few minutes after. The murderer endeavoured to escape, but being taken and told he was a wicked traitor to endeavour to kill the Prince, "I am no traitor," said he, "but have done what the King of Spain commanded me, and if I have not slain him, cursed be my ill-fortune." After this he freely confessed the whole matter, and that he had done it by the instigation of the Jesuits and the encouragement of the Prince of Parma, who assured him of the reward promised to the assassinator by the King of Spain.

For this horrid crime a particular and tremendous sentence was pronounced against him by the judges —"That Baltazar Gerrard (which he confessed was his true name) should be laid upon a scaffold in the market-place of Delph, to have his right hand, wherewith he committed that execrable deed, torn with two burning hot pincers, and the like to be done in six several parts of his body, as his arms, thighs, and several other fleshy parts; his privy members to be cut off, and he to be quartered alive; to have his heart plucked out and thrown in his face; and, lastly, his head to be cut off and to be set upon a pole upon the watch-tower behind the Prince's lodgings; his four quarters to be hanged upon gibbets upon the four bulwarks of the town." "This sentence," said the judges, "we think fit to pronounce against this wicked murderer, for having (to the great grief and sorrow of all good men) committed a most execrable crime and abominable treason upon the person of so famous and renowned a Prince as the Prince of Orange was, for which he ought in nowise to remain unpunished, but rather, with all rigour and severity, to be made an example to future ages."

Having notice of his death, he was first astonished, cursing the hour of his birth, and wishing he had never learned the wicked principles of the Jesuits at Dole, but had still been a mean tradesman, and not fallen into this folly; "but since it is done," said he, "there is no remedy, and I must now suffer for it." This dreadful sentence was fully executed; and yet in all his torments he never cried out, nor seemed to be in any pain; yea, smiled at an accident that happened in the midst of his tortures, having often boasted that he would not show the least sign of fear.

Thus died the renowned William, Prince of Orange, at fifty-one years of age. He was of an active spirit and strong memory, and his wisdom, constancy, magnanimity, his courage, patience, and labours, were all so extraordinary, that they are rather to be admired than described; a person in whom concurred a solid judgment to undertake so great and difficult an enterprise, and an unparalleled courage to carry it on, and a very great constancy to finish the freedom of his country against the mighty power of Spain, and the treacheries of many of his own countrymen; so that the States and the people of the Netherlands, who had so often experienced his conduct and magnanimity in their most pressing extremities, admired his virtues, which scarce ever before met in one person, bewailing him as if no greater loss could have befallen them in this world, and solemnized his funeral with all imaginable magnificence, that being the last honour they could pay to his glorious memory. He had four wives, by whom he had four sons and eight daughters.

Philip William of Nassau was eldest son to the great William Prince of Orange, Philip II., King of Spain, being his godfather, who, when his father was compelled to take arms in his own defence, was a student at the university of Louvain, and was taken thence by force, to the infringement of the liberties of the place, notwithstanding all the protestations of the rector to the contrary, and the complaints of the Prince, his father, who publicly exclaimed against the cruelty of the Spaniards, since no privilege nor innocence of age could secure any from their tyranny and injustice. He was carried from thence into Spain at thirteen years of age, and educated in the Roman Catholic religion, where he continued a prisoner about thirty years, during which his gaoler presuming to speak abusively of the proceedings of his father, the Prince, who inherited his gallant temper, not enduring his insolent discourse, took him round the middle, and, throwing him out of the window, broke his neck. The King of Spain consulted with his Council what punishment to inflict for this great action; but at length by the interposing of a generous young Spaniard, who was present, and affirmed that the captain's ill conduct was the occasion of his death, it was passed over.

But at length, in hope to create some jealousies between his brother Maurice and himself, King Philip released him and sent him into Flanders, where he lived in great state with the Spanish governor of the Netherlands, at Brussels, and was employed by the King to conduct into the Netherlands his bride and spouse that was to be, the Infanta Isabella, to whom King Philip had given in dowry the sovereignty of the seventeen provinces. This was a very astonishing policy to all the Netherlands, that the son of a Prince who was so abhorred by the Spaniards should be chosen for this honourable employment, and caused such a jealousy in the States of the United Provinces towards him (the King of Spain having likewise restored to him all his estate in the Spanish Low Countries and the Franche Comté), that they would not allow him to make any visit, much less to reside, in any of their provinces, though he was very desirous so to do; and though his younger brother, Prince Maurice, out of his generous temper, surrendered up all the great estate that belonged to Philip, his elder brother, at Breda and other places, yet, to prevent his being suspected by the States General, he declined seeing him in person, rendering his respects to him constantly by persons deputed thereunto. He married Eleonora de Bourbon, sister of the Prince of Condé, and, by matching with a Princess of the blood, he was reinstated in his principality of Orange, and died, without children, at Brussels, in 1618, leaving his inheritance and title to his brother.

Maurice of Nassau, Prince of Orange, successor to his father, both in conduct, courage and success, who being but seventeen years old at the death of his father was yet called to the government, and was no ways discouraged at the great successes of Alexander Farnese, Duke of Parma, who, in a very short time, had reduced several cities and towns to the Crown of Spain, nor with the insolence of the Earl of Leicester, who, at the desire of the States General, was sent by Queen Elizabeth to be their governor, though, by his insupportable pride and ambition, he more endamaged the Low Countries than the succours he brought relieved them, so that for four years together that commonwealth laboured under dreadful convulsions, occasioned by the intrigues of the Earl of Leicester and the policies of the Spaniards, till at length, by the fortunate and total destruction of the nicknamed invincible Spanish Armada, designed to have devoured all England, the Prince of Parma lost all his reputation at once; Prince Maurice, about the same time, obliging him, to his everlasting shame, to rise and run away from the siege of Bergen-op-Zoom, and for twenty years after, even till the time of the truce, fortune was so favourable to the Prince that victory seemed to attend him, insomuch that he recovered near forty cities and many more fortresses, and in three pitched battles defeated the forces of the King of Spain, besides the victories his admirals obtained at sea upon the coast of Flanders and Spain. The stratagem by which he surprised Breda was very remarkable, for the garrison of that town being Italians, and greedy of fuel in that cold country, they very readily assisted the boatmen to draw his bark of turfs over the ice within the castle walls, under which the Prince had laid several armed soldiers, who, suddenly starting up, surprised and soon seized the guards, taking possession of the castle, with the loss only of one man, though it were an action of such danger and importance. Soon after the town of Gertrudenberg was surrendered to the Prince in view of the Spanish army, consisting of thirty thousand men, commanded by Count Mansfieldt, an experienced general, who could not force the Prince out of his trenches, though he daily provoked him; so that Prince Maurice, having sent a trumpeter to the Count, he asked him how his master, being a young and fiery Prince, could contain himself within his trenches after such fair provocations. The trumpeter replied that the Prince of Nassau was a young Prince, but as old and experienced a general as his Excellency.

The next year the Prince took Groning, the capital city of that Province; also Rhineburg, Meurs and Grave, and gained great reputation by the defense of Ostend; for the Spaniards having made themselves masters of it after a siege of three years, with a loss of sixty thousand men, and the expense of above a hundred millions of treasure, they were possessed of nothing but a heap of ruins, more like a burying-place than a city; and the Prince soon after gained Sluce, a place of far greater importance. And at the battle of Newport he had such great success against far more numerous forces than his own, that the Archduke Albert, with several other persons of quality, were wounded; all the Spaniards' cannon, with above one hundred cornets and ensigns, falling into the victor's hands, with the slaughter of six thousand of the enemy upon the place; the Prince having before the fight sent away all the ships that transported his men into Flanders, telling them that now there was no way to escape, but they must either march over the bellies of their enemies, or else drink salt water. After several other successes against the Prince of Parma and other Spanish generals, whereby he raised up the sinking republic of the united Netherlands, he died in 1625. He was never married, and left his titles and large possessions to his younger brother, Henry Frederick of Nassau, Prince of Orange, who was third son to the renowned William, Prince of Orange. He was born in 1584, and was an excellent general, not in the least degenerating from the courage and gallantry of that heroic family, being every way equal in fame to his brother, Prince Maurice, taking the famous cities of Odousel and Groll, in despite of the Spanish general, who, with a numerous army, was not able to relieve it; nor was he less successful at sea, his Vice-Admiral Hein taking a fleet of the Spaniards near Cuba, in the West Indies, valued at about twenty millions. After this he took Bois-le-Duc, which had withstood all the attempts of his brother Maurice, and would not be drawn away till he had reduced it, though Count Henry of Bergnes, the Spanish general, made an incursion into the province of Utrecht to divert him, and afterwards happily surprised the city of Wessel, where the magazine of provisions, and all the great artillery of the Spanish army, were laid up.

About this time, Count John of Nassau, his kinsman, upon some discontent revolting to the Spaniards, was defeated by one of the Prince's captains near the Rhine, in the open field, with half his number of men, himself being carried prisoner to Wessel, from whence he could not be redeemed without the payment of eighteen thousand rix dollars; to revenge which dishonour, Count John, when at liberty, endeavoured with a strong navy of ships to seize the town of Williamstadt, but was totally defeated by the Hollanders and four thousand prisoners taken, and the rest either killed or drowned, he himself and the Prince of Brabançon hardly escaping.

The States General, to testify their gratitude to Henry, Prince of Orange, for the great services he had performed, about this time, by a public edict, declared that all the dignities, honours and employments which he then enjoyed shall descend to his eldest son, Prince William; the instruments whereof, being drawn up and sealed by the States, were presented to the young Prince in a box of gold. After this, Prince Henry continued still more successful, taking the towns of Ruremond, Vuelo and Strall; and, lastly, undertaking the siege of Maestricht, where he surrounded his trenches with such strong circumvallations that both the Spanish and German forces were obliged to march away with dishonour, and leave him the honour of reducing so important a place.

Divers other prosperous attempts he made, at his retaking the fort of Skink Scans, and regaining the castle and city of Breda, which the Marquis Spinola had been a whole year in taking, with vast loss and expense, and yet the Prince now reduced it, to his immortal honour, in four months; and as favourable was his fortune at sea, where Admiral Tromp, falling upon a numerous fleet of the Spaniards in the Downs, of sixty-seven men of war, destroyed the greatest part of them, to the number of forty ships sunk, wherein about seven thousand men were lost and two thousand carried prisoners into Holland, amongst whom was the great gallion of Portugal, called "Maria Theresa," carrying eight hundred men, whereof not one escaped.

In 1641, Prince William, only son of the Prince of Orange, married the Princess Mary, eldest daughter to King Charles I., and soon after Prince Henry gained the strong fort of Hulst, in Flanders, which the Spaniards were not able to relieve. Thus it may be observed that William, Prince of Orange, laid the foundations of the commonwealth of Holland; Prince Maurice, his son, fixed and strengthened them by his victories; and Henry Frederick, the younger brother, by continuing his conquest and enlarging their territories, at length compelled the Spaniard to renounce his pretended right over them, and to acknowledge them an independent State, treating with them by the title of the High and Mighty States General of the United Provinces; so that by the swords of the illustrious House of Orange this potent republic was first founded, which is now arrived to that grandeur so as to send ambassadors upon equal terms with the most potent Princes of Christendom, even to the King of Spain himself, whose subjects they were not above one hundred years ago, and whose revolt had proved a great advantage to that Crown, they having been so many years a barrier to the Spanish Netherlands against the excessive power and ambition of France, which, without their assistance, had long since swallowed them up.

Prince Henry married the daughter of John Albert, Count of Solms, who came with the Queen of Bohemia into Holland: a lady of excellent beauty, modesty, and prudence, by whom he had one son and four daughters; the eldest, named Lovison, was married to Frederick William, Prince Elector of Brandenburg, by whom he had several children; the second, Henrietta, was married to the Count of Nassau; the third, Catharine, was espoused to John George, Duke of Anhalt; the fourth was married to the Duke of Simeren. Prince Henry died March 12, 1647, and was succeeded by William of Nassau, Prince of Orange, who was born in 1626—a Prince of worthy hopes and courage, but was suddenly taken away by death in the twenty-fourth year of his age, having been married nine years to the Princess Mary, daughter of King Charles I., by whom he had Prince William Henry, who was born November 4, 1650, some few days after his father's death, the Lords States General of Holland and

Zealand, and of the cities of Delft, Leyden, and Amsterdam, being his godfathers.

William Henry of Nassau, Prince of Orange, was endowed with all the noble and virtuous qualities of his ancestors of the illustrious House of Orange, which seemed designed by Heaven to be the protectors of religion and liberty for several ages, His Majesty's glorious predecessors being the founders and establishers, and himself the restorer, of the half-ruined Batavian republic, as well as the deliverer of those three kingdoms from the utmost danger of Popery and slavery. This excellent Prince suffered many affronts by Barneval's party, revived in the persons of the De Witts expecting, with inimitable patience, the advancement to those honours and dignities which of right belonged to his family, and which, by the decree of a prevailing faction, he was deprived of presently after the death of his father.

But King Lewis, his inveterate enemy, did, accidentally, very much to contribute to his exaltation; for having in 1672, like a rapid torrent, overrun the flourishing Batavian republic, he thereby gave opportunity to the Prince to discover to the world the spirit of his ancestors, in recovering the united provinces from the ruin which seemed to attend them by the success of that King, even beyond his hopes, nay, almost his wishes: which put that people into such a consternation as occasioned them to complain of the unhappy conduct of Cornelius and John De Witt, who had then the sole management of all affairs, and to believe that none but the glorious House of Nassau was capable to support their tottering state in this age against their potent French enemies, as they had formerly rescued them from the tyranny of Spain.

Neither was the grandmother of the Prince wanting to engage the favourers of that family to endeavour to remove that eclipse under which it had so suffered, which her Highness managed with a courage and magnanimity above her sex, so that being awakened by her remonstrances they began to consider how they themselves had of late been slighted and neglected, whilst all the great employments of the commonwealth were bestowed upon the sons of burgomasters; and being seconded by the rage of the commonalty, who were dreadfully terrified to see a victorious army in the very bowels of their country, they obliged the States General, in the beginning of 1672, to depute Monsieur Beverning, John De Witt, and Jasper Fagel, to invest his Highness the Prince of Orange in the dignities belonging to his ancestors, of captain and admiral-general of the united provinces, who, having accepted the same, and taken his oath, presently went upon action against the French; but the province of Holland still suspected the fidelity of their magistrates, seeing their frontier towns and garrisons fall daily into the hands of their victorious enemies, and at Dort they raised a dangerous mutiny, and resolved that his Highness the Prince of Orange should be advanced to the stadtholdership also, as judging it absolutely necessary for the public good; upon which an Act was instantly drawn up, and read in the public hall by the secretary, wherein the magistrates declared his Highness the Prince of Orange stadtholder, captain and admiral-general of all their forces by sea and land, with the same power and authority that his ancestors of glorious memory had formerly enjoyed; which occasioned great rejoicing in that city.

But Cornelius De Witt, an ancient burgomaster of the town, returning at the same time indisposed from the fleet, and being desired to sign the Act, replied "he would never do it;" nor could all the persuasions of his friends, nor the menaces of the multitude, who were ready to break into his house, nor the tears of his wife, who was sensible of his danger, prevail upon his obstinate temper, till she threatened to show herself to the people and declare her own and children's innocency, and abandon him to the fury of the ungoverned populace, which soon after occasioned his tragical death; for they being fully persuaded that he and his brother John were real enemies to the Prince, and a certain surgeon having charged Cornelius that he had made a private proposal to him to take away his Highness's life, he was thereupon imprisoned, and upon trial was sentenced to forfeit all his dignities and employments, and to be for ever banished out of the territories of Holland and West Friesland.

The people, who accounted the Prince to be their protector and deliverer, believed his judges to be partial in punishing so great a crime with so easy a judgment, and the trained bands at the Hague being in arms, they presently ran to the prison, where, while they were got together, it happened that John De Witt came in his coach to fetch his brother out of prison; upon which one of the burgesses cried out, "Now the two traitors are got together, and it is our fault if they escape us." This had been enough to inflame the multitude, but a greater motive happened; for while they were all expecting the coming down of the two De Witts, an unhappy report was raised that above a thousand peasants and fishermen were upon their march to plunder the Hague, upon which another burgher cried out, "Come, gentlemen, let us pull these traitors out by the ears; do but follow me and I will lead the way." These words, with their great affection to their Prince, and the ruin of their country, to both which they accounted the De Witts to be the greatest enemies, completed their rage, so that they immediately broke open the prison doors and forced down the two brothers into the street, where they were soon dispatched by the multitude, who, after they had laid the pensionary John De Witt sprawling on the ground, cried out, "See there the traitor that has betrayed his country." Thus fell John and Cornelius DeWitt, two violent enemies of the House of Orange. It is said that John was the contriver of those acts whereby his Highness was precluded from all the great employments which were due to him from his predecessors, and that a certain ambassador being in private discourse with him, said, "Most illustrious sir, I have heard much of your singular prudence and unwearied diligence, but far less than what I now observe; from whence I dare assuredly pronounce that either you will be the ruin of the Prince, or else that one day, for his sake, you will come to destruction." It is likewise reported, that when he was a youth of about eighteen years old, a certain advocate being desired by his father to examine him, gave this account of him: "That he found in him those great parts and that ripeness of wit which was rarely to be seen in others;" and afterwards, when he was made pensioner of Holland and Dort, the same advocate presaged of him that "he would never die a natural death." "Thus," saith a worthy parson, "ended one of the greatest lives of any subject of our times, in the forty-seventh year of his age, after having administered in that state as pensioner of Holland for about eighteen years, with great honour to his country and himself."

It must be remarked that the present war with the States General was commenced in concert between the French King and Charles II., in a time of the greatest peace and security on the Dutch side; so that, when the English fell upon their Smyrna fleet, no clap of thunder in a frosty morning could be more surprising, both to the Hollanders and the rest of Christendom; yea, the Court of France itself could scarce believe that he would run as great an adventure, though our Court had obliged themselves thereto, and though in the declaration of war which the King published the Dutch are charged with making abusive pictures, and denying the right of the flag, which was an undoubted prerogative of the Crown of England, yet the Parliament and people were of opinion that this war was made in pursuance of the instructions of the French King, sent over to Dover by the Duchess of Orleans; whereby the destruction of the commonwealth of Holland is declared to be the only means to settle arbitrary government and Popery in these three nations.

Upon our declaration of war the French King began to march with his vast army into the Netherlands, which he overran with such a rapid motion that the people were astonished, and the States knew not what course to take to prevent it, which occasioned those commotions aforementioned; but his Highness the Prince of Orange being advanced to the stadtholdership, the face of affairs began to alter, and their courage was revived. Monsieur Fagel succeeded De Witt as pensioner, and the Prince presently resolved to be upon action, rejecting all the applications made to him by the two Kings, of making him sovereign of the provinces, with such disdain and greatness of soul as is scarce to be matched, always declaring that "he would never betray a trust that was given him, nor ever sell the liberties of his country, that his ancestors had so long defended."

In pursuance of this generous resolution, his Highness took command of the army upon him, who were more animated at the thoughts of being under the conduct of so gallant a general; so that at Bodegrave a handful of men twice repulsed above five thousand of the French from the walls of Ardenberg, and, besides the slain, took five hundred prisoners, with several commanders and persons of quality, through the extraordinary valour of no more than two hundred burghers and one hundred garrison soldiers, only that they were assisted by the women and children, the women filling the bandileers, and the children brought bullets to their parents.

Soon after, the siege of Groningen, which had been besieged with near three thousand men by the Bishop of Munster, was, by the courage of the citizens, raised, with the loss of half the enemy's army, and a prodigious quantity of ammunition spent in vain, in reducing thereof; to which His Highness' care in furnishing them with all necessaries for defence was highly contributing.

About the same time, the Prince resolving to dislodge the outguards of the French, gave a strong alarm to them, and without moving from his saddle all night, drove them to their trenches before Utrecht, and carried several lords prisoners to Amsterdam. His Highness then resolved to attempt the reducing of Woerden, and after a bloody and obstinate fight, wherein above two thousand of the French were slain, and not above seven hundred of the Dutch, his Highness, finding the garrison relieved with such a numerous supply, drew off his men, and retreated to his quarters; after which was held a council of war of the principal officers of the army, which being ended, a certain colonel would needs be impertinently inquisitive of the Prince, to know what was his great design against the French at that time. His Highness demanded of him whether he would discover to any other what he should declare to him? The colonel said, "No, he would not." "Then," said the Prince, "my tongue is also endued from heaven with the same grace," an answer becoming the wisdom of a Prince and the reservedness of a great commander.

His Highness being with the army at Maestricht, sent out a party to reduce the strong castle of Walcheren, which was soon surrendered with a great quantity of wheat and other provisions. During this time the Duke of Luxembourg, with fourteen thousand horse and foot, resolved to invade the province of Holland, in hope to plunder Leyden and the Hague, and marched from Woerden over the ice with three thousand five hundred of the lightest of the infantry, of which attempt His Highness having notice, marched with all speed towards the French, who in the meantime had taken Swamerdam, and by the retiring of Colonel Paine Vin from his post at Niewerbourg had a free passage open for their retreat, who must have perished in the waters or surrendered by reason of the sudden thaw. The Duke himself was like to have been lost by a fall into the thawed water, losing in his slippery expedition about six hundred of his best soldiers. The French committed horrid ravages at Swamerdam, ravishing women, stripping and wounding the aged and decrepit, and throwing infants that smiled in their faces into the fire.

And now the strong city of Coverden, the key of the province of Friesland and Groning, which in that fatal year, 1672, fell into the hands of the Bishop of Munster, with great loss of men and a long siege, was retaken in an hour, and not above sixty men slain, and of the enemy one hundred and fifty killed, and four hundred and thirty prisoners; it was furnished by the Bishop with a prodigious quantity of warlike ammunition. This success highly encouraged the Dutch, and so surprised the enemy that they instantly quitted several other garrisons, and much advanced the honour of the Prince, to whose prudent management of affairs they attributed this happy alteration in the future of their country; which his Highness likewise extended to pacify the dissension between the old and new magistrates of Friesland, who acted contrary to each other; but upon his Highness appearing in their assembly all discords vanished, and all things were settled for the defence of the Netherlands, by his visiting the frontier fortifications of Flushing, Sluce, Ardenburgh (where the keys of the town were delivered him in a silver basin by the young virgins of that city, decked with garlands of several flowers), and several other strong places.

In 1673, the Dutch were hotly assailed, on the one side by the French King, with a puissant army, while Condé and Luxembourg lay at Utrecht with powerful forces, to watch an opportunity to invade the very centre of their territories; and by sea, the King of England vigorously attacked them with his own and the French fleet, so that the Prince of Orange was obliged not to stir abroad, but to observe their designs, and prevent the threatened descent of the English. In May, the King of France with an army of forty-two thousand men, sat down before Maestricht; the garrison consisted of about four thousand foot and nine hundred horse, under Monsieur Farieux, a resolute and experienced commander, as appeared by the stout resistance he made against this mighty force; so that, though the French gained the place, yet it was with such a deluge of blood—no less than nine thousand of their bravest soldiers being slain in the siege, with an incredible number of his choicest officers—that the purchase was sufficiently dear; and, after three weeks' valiant defence, with the loss of half the garrison by innumerable assaults, batteries, and storming of fresh assailants night and day. The courageous governor would still have held it out had not the petitions of the magistrates and ecclesiastics obliged him to surrender, of whose worthy conduct the Prince of Orange was so well satisfied, that he instantly preferred him to be Major-General of the Army; and the French King was so mortified, that, when he had taken the town, he broke up his army and returned to Paris, sending part of them to Turenne, to enable him to harass the country of Treves, because that Elector had assisted the Emperor against him.

The French army being thus dispersed, and the English fleet, since the engagement of May 28 (when both sides claimed the victory), being retired from the coast of Holland, his Highness, now more at liberty, resolved not to lie still; so that calling off his forces which lay for the defence of Zealand, to join with the rest of the army, he sat down before Naerden with twenty-five thousand men, upon which the Duke of Luxembourg with ten thousand, and four regiments of Munster horse, advanced within view of the Prince's entrenchments, but not daring to attempt the relief of the town;

the Prince, after three hours' resistance, beat the French from their works, and forced them to retire in great confusion into the city, and the next day they surrendered it up. The garrison marching out, the governor made a profound reverence to the Prince, and, it is said, assured him that "he had reasons sufficient to surrender the town so soon;" but it seems the King did not think them so, for he was condemned to perpetual imprisonment, and had his sword broken over his head at Utrecht, for the garrison consisted of near three thousand men, and wanted neither ammunition nor provisions, and the French had much strengthened the fortifications, yet the Prince took it in four days, and lost not above a hundred men, and two hundred wounded.

And now his Highness, to avoid so many sieges as the towns they had lost would cost to recover, resolved upon a gallant action, the boldness of which amazed all men, but the success extolled the prudence, as well as the bravery, of it; for the King of Spain and the Emperor having joined in a confederacy with the States General for mutual defence against the French, as the common enemy of both, the Prince, that he might perform something remarkable before the approaching winter, marched directly with his army out of the Netherlands, and joining with the confederates, he resolved to besiege Bonne, which had been put into the hands of the French at the beginning of the war, wherein the Elector of Cologne and the Bishop of Munster had entered jointly with France. It had a garrison of two thousand men, and was well furnished with all provisions, and eighty great guns mounted on their walls and bulwarks. The Marshal de Humières, with seven thousand horse, faced the Leaguer, but durst not

F

venture to succour it; so that the confederates, having finished their batteries and brought three mines to perfection, prepared for a general storm; but willing to save their men, sent a summons to the governor to surrender the town, since they were without relief, and, if they pleased, might send out some to see what mines were ready to play upon their refusal, which would be followed by putting to the sword all in arms, if taken by storm. This so affrighted them that the next day they capitulated, and fifteen hundred French marched out of the town, the rest being either dead or wounded.

This successful expedition of his Highness put the French into such a consternation to see the reverse of their fortune, that they who lately, with insulting pride, threatened the ruin of others, were now at their wits' end to save themselves; so that, upon the loss of so many men as had lately died by sickness and the sword, they were compelled to abandon all their conquests in the Netherlands in less time than they gained them, retaining only Maestricht and the Grave, of all they lately possessed belonging to this republic. Woerden was the first that felt the tyranny and was first evacuated, but the Duke of Luxembourg extorted sixteen thousand livres of them, to save the town from burning, by the King's order. Harderwick paid twelve thousand livres; Crevecœur, three thousand pistoles; Bommel, a strong fortress, on which the King of France had bestowed sixty thousand livres, gave hostages to pay thirty-six thousand livres to spare their houses. Utrecht was obliged to give a hundred thousand crowns; and the French all departing in one day, the burgomasters absolved each other from their oaths which they had taken against the restoration of his Highness the Prince of Orange, to whom they sent their deputies to acknowledge him their Stadtholder, in the name of the whole province of Utrecht. Thus his Highness may, in some sense, seem to have outdone Cæsar himself, for he vanquished even where he neither saw nor came, but only by the terror of his arms and victories. In consideration of this happy turn of affairs, occasioned by the prudence and conduct of his Highness, the States General, in February following, published a decree to declare their gratitude, confirming the charge of Stadtholders of the province of Holland and West Friesland on the person of his Highness during life, and also on the heirs male of his body, as a standing monument of his surpassing merits; and that very day the States of Zealand likewise conferred the same dignities upon his Highness, and made him withal hereditary noble of their province.

In the beginning of the year 1674, the Parliament and people of England being weary of the war with Holland, which was entered into without their consent or liking, were very desirous of a peace, so that the French Court party, having little hope of wheedling the House of Commons to give any more money to carry on their black designs against the religion and liberties of the nation, under the pretence of this war, they were obliged to make a separate peace with the Dutch, exclusive of the French King, though to their great regret that they were forced to abandon their dear ally, from whom they had drawn such great sums of money for secret service. Upon the strength and heart of this peace, his Highness the Prince of Orange concerted with the German and Spanish troops to begin an offensive war, and, at the head of an army of forty thousand men, to march into France. In pursuance hereof, the three armies being joined, arrived at Nivelle the beginning of August, 1674, where they continued for some days; but finding the Prince of Condé, who lay not far off, encamped with an army of fifty thousand, unwilling to come forth and hazard a battle in the open field, they endeavoured by all ways imaginable to provoke and draw him out of his trenches; but all proving ineffectual, they resolved to besiege some place of importance, believing that Condé would endeavour to relieve it; whereupon his Highness marched from Seneffe toward Brinch, General Souches, with the imperial forces, leading the van. Count Waldeck commanded the main battle with the Holland army; and Count de Monterey the rear with the Spaniards; the Prince of Orange commanded the whole confederate army.

The Prince of Condé having notice of their movement, and being sensible of the difficulty and straitness of the passages, put his men in order, and letting the vanguard pass, and the greatest part of the main body some leagues before, he then fell in upon the rear-guard of the Spanish horse and dragoons, consisting of four thousand, commanded by the Prince de Vaudemont, and broke them with great slaughter, and not much resistance, taking several prisoners of quality, with the baggage, which the Prince of Orange having notice of, he sent three battalions of infantry to their relief. Condé warmed with success, drew his whole army out of their trenches, and fell with much fury upon the Dutch squadron, breaking them to pieces, killing or taking all their commanders, and gaining several standards; and here his Highness the Prince of Orange gave particular testimonies of his undaunted bravery, throwing himself, with his sword in his hand, before the daunted fugitives, endeavoring, by all means imaginable, to stop their flight, and by his own example encouraging them to renew the battle, so that he was often in danger either of being slain or taken prisoner; but at length his Highness joining the rest of the Dutch, who stood firm, whom he made the right wing, with the Imperialists and Spaniards on the left, the fight was renewed with more fury and vigour than ever, both armies being animated with the hope of victory, and seeming equally resolved rather to die than be overcome. His Highness omitted no pains on this important occasion, so animating his soldiers that they strove with emulation to outdo one another, and both armies fought till night, with an obstinacy on both sides hardly to be paralleled, though the fields were all strewn over with the bodies of the slain and wounded, while the combatants, covered with blood and sweat, encouraged each other the more by that dismal spectacle. Thus the fury of the French, which at first carried all before them, about ten o'clock at night began to abate; the French infantry, of which they had lost a considerable part, drawing off at a distance, notwithstanding all the endeavours of the Prince of Condé to have brought them back again, who thereupon fearing some further mischief might befall his army, ordered the horse also to retire, leaving the victory by this means to his Highness the Prince of Orange, who, two hours after the retreat of the French, drew off his army likewise to their appointed quarters.

Thus ended this bloody battle, wherein at first the French prevailed, but at length lost the victory, having seven thousand men slain outright, besides the wounded, of whom the Prince of Condé left above fifteen hundred in the villages about his quarters at Picton. On the Confederates' side, the slain, wounded and deserters amounted to about six thousand five hundred in all. It is said that a letter was intercepted from the Prince of Condé to the French King, giving him an account, "That upon a general review of his army he found himself but in an ill condition, having lost the flower of his infantry and the best part of his horse, and therefore did not think himself strong enough to venture a second battle;" having likewise lost a great number of officers and persons of quality, and several standards, among which was one called the White Standard of France, which was afterward hung up with great solemnity in the church of the Carmelites at Brussels, richly embroidered with gold and silver, with the sun in the middle passing through the zodiac, with this haughty motto, " Nil obstabit eunti :" " Nothing can stop his course." But the principal honour of this victory ought, next under God, to be ascribed to his Highness the Prince of Orange, of whom General Souches gives the following account in a letter to the States General: "I have endeavoured to discharge my duty in attending his Highness the Prince of Orange during the bloody and famous battle between the Confederate army and that of the Christian King, the happy issue of which has proved so much to the glory of the Prince of Orange, who showed upon that occasion the prudence of an aged captain, the courage of a Cæsar, and the undaunted bravery of a Marius, all which, my lords, I speak without flattery, as being contrary to my nature." And as the friends, so the enemies of his Highness agreed to give him equal glory for this adventure, the Prince of Condé himself declaring that " he had done in all things like an old captain, but only in venturing himself too much like a young man;" though this old general had done the same in this day's action, charging into the thickest troops like a young cavalier.

The next day after the fight his Highness marched, with his whole army, near Mons, and took up his headquarters at St. Gilaine, till they had recovered their disorders in the late battle, and then began to think of further action. At length it was concluded to besiege Oudenard, to draw the Prince of Condé out of his cautious marches to relieve it. The Confederates made their approaches to the town, and were already masters of the counterscarp, when Condé decamped from Beumont, with his whole army of forty thousand men, either to relieve or give the Confederates battle. His Highness advised that they should immediately fall upon the enemy, wearied and tired with a long march, but General Souches prevented the execution of this magnanimous resolution; for instead of ranging his men in battle array, he crossed the river in so much haste that he left some pieces of cannon behind him, and thereby left a way open for the Prince of Condé to enter the town with part of his army, who, thinking he had done enough in relieving it, avoided coming to a battle; so that his Highness, finding no more good to be done, resolved to march back to Grave, where his presence would be more necessary, leaving Count Waldeck the command of the army in his absence. The siege of this place had been undertaken some time before by General Rabenhaupt; the garrison consisted of four thousand foot and nine hundred horse, of which the Marquis of Chamilly, a valiant and expert captain, was governor, wherein were four hundred and fifty pieces of cannon, of which one hundred were mounted upon the bulwarks, besides a vast quantity of powder, corn, grenadoes, and all manner of warlike ammunition, for the French had made a magazine there of all that they had brought away from their deserted conquests. Rabenhaupt sat down before it with about twenty regiments of foot and some horse, and was afterwards reinforced by the troops of the Prince of Courland and the Elector of Brandenburg, who summoned the city on every side, assaulting it with much violence, but was as vigorously defended by those within, though they were reduced to drink water. His Highness arrived there on the 9th of October, with sixty cornets of horse, whose presence revived the courage of the besiegers; yet the French held out till the 25th, when Chamilly, finding such large breaches made in the fortifications, much widened by the fortunate blowing up of a mine, which almost destroyed a covert way, so that it was impossible for him to hold out against the general storm designed the next day, he surrendered the town upon honourable articles.

The following winter was spent in preparing for an early campaign the next year, 1675, in the beginning whereof the Hollanders made grateful acknowledgments to his Highness the Prince of Orange for his signal conduct and services in redeeming them from the calamities which they had suffered under a cruel foreign enemy, offering him the title of Duke of Guelderland; but to convince the world of the sincerity of his intentions, and how little ambitious he was to aggrandize himself by the war, his Highness refused those honours; but being at the same time offered the command of Governor Hereditary of the same province, he readily accepted it, and in the management thereof discovered his excellent prudence in civil as well as military affairs.

But whilst his Highness was intent to oppose the designs of the French for the ruin of his country, he was visited with the small-pox, which struck a great damp to the progress of affairs, and was the more lamented as having proved fatal to his family in the persons of his father, mother, and his uncle, the Duke of Gloucester; but it pleased God that by the care and skill of an able physician, and certain peculiar remedies sent him by the Duke of Brandenburgh, his Highness recovered, and within twenty days was abroad again, and hastened to the general rendezvous of his army at Rosendael, in order to the relief of Limburgh, then besieged by the Marquis of Rochefort. The King of France, with an army under the Prince of Condé, posted himself advantageously for covering the siege; but such was the slowness of the Germans, and the weakness and disorder of the Spanish troops, that the besieged, having little hopes of relief, and unable to oppose the great numbers of the French troops, surrendered sooner than was expected; after which, having wasted a great part of the adjoining country, the King returned to Paris, being prevented from doing further mischief by the diligence of his Highness and the Duke de Villa Hermosa.

Soon after, the great General Turenne being killed by a cannon bullet in Alsatia, the Prince of Condé was sent thither as general, and the Count de Montmorency was left to command the French army, who, though a captain no less wary than his predecessor, yet his Highness kept him so upon his guard that he could not disturb the siege of Treves, which, after the fatal overthrow of Monsieur Crequi, fell into the hands of the Imperialists; so that Montmorency was unwilling to hazard a battle with the Prince, after two such great losses, for fear of a third; insomuch that he suffered Binch to surrender to his Highness at discretion, it being a garrison of three hundred and fifty men, and had great quantities of provisions, even in the sight of his army; but it appeared afterwards that the Count had positive orders not to engage the Confederates, so that his Highness, finding winter approaching, broke up his army and returned to the Hague.

The King of France at this time seemed very desirous of peace, his subjects being wearied and ruined with the charge of the war, and several Princes offered to interpose in the matter, and the King of England continuing still in the French interests, seemed very zealous therein, and took upon him to be a mediator between the King and his enemies. At length, in 1676, a treaty was begun at Nimeguen, whither the plenipotentiaries from all parts repaired as to the general rendezvous; but the preparations for war went on as vigourously as ever, and his Highness was thoroughly employed to get his army ready early in the spring, considering the formidable musters the French made under Marshal Crequi, near Charleville; and Marshal de Humieères, having got together a body of fifteen thousand men, fell into the country of Aloft, and the Spaniards being too weak to resist him, put all the country under contribution. Hereupon his Highness marched with all speed to join the Duke of Villa Hermosa at Cambron, which he did on the 26th of April; but before this Marshal Crequi had surrounded the city of Condé with sixteen thousand men, and the King of France and the Duke of Orleans, upon notice thereof, joined him with ten thousand more, who incessantly battered the town four days together with much fury, insomuch that they were forced to surrender at discretion, though his Highness was marched as far as Granville for their relief. After this the King of France sent the Duke of Orleans to besiege Bouchain with some of his troops, it being a strong fortress of considerable consequence, the King posting his army so as to hinder the Prince from relieving it; but his Highness, struggling through all difficulties of the season, and want of provisions and magazines in Flanders, marched with his army in view of the French King, facing him several days together, and was at length resolved to have attacked him with a detachment of twelve thousand men, and to endeavour to have relieved the town, but understanding the place was taken he altered his resolution; nor would his Highness stir till the French King first decamped, leaving to the Prince the honour of having dared the whole power and fortune of France; so that if the Confederates lost a small town, the French lost the greater honour of accepting so brave a challenge.

The King of France returning home, and leaving his army under the command of Marshal Schomberg, his Highness concluded with the Spaniards and the German Princes of the Lower Rhine to set down before Maestricht, which, though strong before, yet had been extremely fortified since possessed by the French, and had now a garrison of eight thousand choice men, under Calvo, a resolute Catalonian. To divert this siege, Schomberg sent the Marshal de Humières, with fifteen thousand men, to besiege Aire, a city in the province of Artois, and strongly encompassed on three sides by a marsh, the only way to approach it being defended by a strong fort, with five bastions and a moat; but the fort not having men sufficient to defend it against the great number of the French, who likewise threw bombs incessantly into the town, and fired the houses, the townsmen grew so impatient that they beat a parley, and the articles were soon agreed to by the French, because they heard the Duke of Villa Hermosa was coming to relieve it, and the Governor was forced to surrender the town.

His Highness continued the siege of Maestricht all this while with much vigour, and the latter end of July the trenches were opened, his Highness assigning to every one their quarters; and among the rest, the English, under three colonels, Fenwick, Widrington and Ashly, consisting of two thousand five hundred men, besides reformades and volunteers, who presented a petition to his Highness, wherein they humbly desired "That all of their nation might be assigned a particular quarter, and be commanded apart; that if they behaved themselves like men they might have the honour due to their courage, but if they did ill, that they only might bear the disgrace of their cowardice; there being no reason why they should suffer for the miscarriages of others." The Prince readily granted their request, and ordered them a separate post under Fenwick, the eldest colonel, and they accordingly signalized their valour during the siege, which was carried on with the utmost conduct and resolution, his Highness continually animating his soldiers by his presence, and teaching them by his example to contemn danger. Many of the outworks were taken with great slaughter on both sides, but were again supplied by the unwearied industry of the besieged. In one of these assaults, his Highness, who continually exposed his person, received a musket-shot in the arm; but to prevent his men from being discouraged, he plucked off his hat with the same arm, and waved it about his head. But the Confederate army being weakened both by sickness and the many attacks against the town, and the Germans not bringing in their promised supplies, a council of war was called in the Prince's camp, and there being advice that Monsieur Schomberg was coming with all the French forces for the relief of the town, it was concluded to raise the siege; and so this campaign ended without success, occasioned by the weakness of the Spaniards, and the uncertainty of the German councils; and soon after, his Highness finding that Schomberg was satisfied with relieving Maestricht, and not to be brought to a battle, he returned back to the Hague, where, in a general assembly of the States, he gave an account of the summer's expedition, so much to their satisfaction that he received their congratulations, and new returns of thanks for the many toils, hardships and dangers to which he had exposed his person for the preservation of his country. In September following, his Highness received an account that the Imperial army had taken Philipsburg, for want of being well provided, which was as unexpected as the raising of the siege of Maestricht.

The following winter was spent in treating for the peace at Nimeguen, which the common people of Holland were very desirous of, the war being a great hindrance to their trade; but the French insisted upon such high terms, that his Highness opposed it to the utmost, though King Charles II. was still very earnest to bring his dear ally out of his troubles. But still the French pursued the war with their usual application; for in February, 1677, though it were in the depth of winter, their forces marched into the Spanish Netherlands, and having provided sufficient magazines, they in a manner blocked up Valenciennes, Cambray and St. Omer at a distance, giving out they would be masters of two, if not three, places before the Confederates could take the field. The French, at the same time, broke into Germany on the other side of the Rhine, ravaging, burning and ruining these countries with a barbarity peculiar to the most Christian King; soon after the city of Valenciennes was surrounded with an army of forty or fifty thousand men under the Duke of Luxembourg, wherein was a garrison of two thousand foot and one thousand horse and dragoons, and the French King being arrived in the camp, commanded that the besieged should be kept awake all night by flinging bombs, grenades and firepots into the town, and the next morning, when they were tired with the night's toil and gone to their repose, so that few were left to guard the works, the assailants carried all before them, and turned the great guns upon the town, which so terrified the besieged that they presently surrendered at discretion.

Animated with this success, the French King immediately sat down before Cambray, a town of great trade, and had been in the Spaniards' hands about eighty years; it had a garrison of one thousand four hundred horse and four regiments of foot, and after a few days' siege, this city was, like the other Spanish towns, surrendered upon articles; and at the same time St. Omer was besieged by the Duke of Orleans, with a very great army. The news of this sudden progress of the French so alarmed the Netherlands that his Highness the Prince of Orange was resolved to take the field, the Dutch having received their payments from Spain, and concluded to continue the war another campaign, being brought to this resolution by the vigour and courage of his Highness, who had begun to prepare his troops to march upon the first motion of the French; but by the usual delays and neglects of the Spaniards, though the Prince used the utmost diligence and application, yet he could not arrive soon enough to succour Valenciennes and Cambray, but was now resolved to venture a battle to endeavour the relief of St. Omer. At Mount Cassal both armies met, where, after a sharp encounter, wherein his Highness showed the utmost bravery, the French themselves confessing that the Prince that day withstood no less than thirty-nine battalions of foot and a hundred squadrons of horse, he made such an honourable retreat as wanted little of a victory, which was occasioned by the plain flight of his men, whom he was forced to resist like enemies; of which the States General were so sensible, that in answer to his letter, wherein his Highness gave them an account of what had passed, they sent him another, returning their unfeigned thanks to his Highness for his indefatigable pains and care, not sparing his own person; of which they besought him to be more tender for the future, considering the great importance thereof for the preservation of his country. After this followed the surrender of the citadel of Cambray, which had held out till now, though the town was taken, and likewise St. Omer, which, after a vigorous resistance, wherein the French lost many considerable officers, was surrendered upon articles.

After this the French King returned to Paris, leaving Crequi to oppose the Duke of Lorraine, and Luxembourg to observe the motions of the Prince of Orange, who, July 23, 1677, having recruited his own army, and received several auxiliary supplies from the German princes, marched in at the head of them (for the Confederates had all submitted to his conduct), from Alost, to attack the French, lying under the walls of Aeth, but finding Luxembourg so advantageously posted between two rivers that he could not be forced to a battle, he marched to Charleroy, and instantly beleaguered that town, which had a garrison of four or five thousand French, under the command of Count Montal, who, mistrusting the design, had furnished it with all manner of ammunition and provision, and such a number of great guns that he had sent away a great part of them. The Duke of Luxembourg, hearing his Highness was sat down before the city, drained all the garrisons of the French conquests, and having made up a body of forty thousand men, posted himself so strongly, having a wood upon his right wing and a river before him, that there was no forcing his trenches, neither could the Confederates fetch any forage from the country beyond the Sambre, from whence they used to be supplied; all which his Highness considering, drew off and marched to Sembreef, thereby to preserve his army, wherein consisted the safety of his country; though no man was ever more daring when there was any probability of prevailing. His Highness, finding the French were resolved not to come to a battle, but to be upon the defensive, and secure what they had gotten, leaving the army near Brussels, under Count Waldeck, returned to the Hague, and had the thanks of the States returned him a second time for his wary and prudent conduct.

In October this year his Highness went over into England, at the invitation of King Charles, in hopes that his presence would much contribute to a general peace between France and the Confederates, which the King seemed very solicitous to have concluded, by the instigation, as it was thought, of the French Court, who were willing to put an end to the war for the present. The Prince, October 19, arrived at Harwich, and went post to Newmarket, where the Court then was, which in two or three days returned to Whitehall, where his Highness, having a sight of the Princess, was so pleased therewith that he immediately made suit to the King and Duke that she might be his bride, which they seemed well pleased with if a peace was first concluded; but his Highness absolutely refusing that condition, the King, being very well satisfied of his Highness's excellent merits, resolved to grant his request, and the next day declared in council his design of marrying the Prince of Orange with the Princess Mary; upon which the whole Council went in a body to compliment the Prince and Princess, and the news was received in both city and country with bells, bonfires, and other signs of extraordinary joy and satisfaction, and they were married accordingly, November, 4, 1677, being his Highness's birthday.

Yet, amidst these nuptial joys and caresses, his Highness, knowing how necessary his presence was in Holland, made haste to return; so that he departed from London, November, 29, with his Princess, and arriving at Homslaerdike, stayed there till they made their public entry at the Hague, which they did in a few days, in as magnificent a manner as both the magistrates and people could express to declare their joy and satisfaction for these happy nuptials.

In 1678, even in January, the French King made such mighty preparations for the ensuing campaign as alarmed all Europe, but more especially the Dutch and their allies; so that the King of England sent the Earl of Faversham with a project of peace to the French King consisting of several heads, which, if he should refuse to accept of that, then King Charles

G

and the States General would unite their forces to compel him to reason. The French rejected the King's propositions, continuing their mighty warlike preparations; upon which King Charles recalled his forces out of the French service, who had often occasioned his gaining many considerable victories; and the Parliament meeting soon after, the King acquainted them that he had made an alliance with Holland to compel the King of France to a reasonable peace; upon which the Commons gave money for raising thirty thousand land soldiers and a fleet of ninety men-of-war; but it appeared afterward the Court never intended any war, but to have used these forces to far worse purposes, even to the advancing arbitrary government and Popery in these kingdoms; of which the Dutch were so sensible, that much doubting the sincerity of King Charles' negotiations, they were at last constrained to make peace with the French, upon disadvantageous terms, to pacify the factions and discontents of the people.

The French King, in March this year, came before Gaunt with an army of eighty thousand men, and by incessant batteries and stormings took it in nine days' time—having drawn the Spanish forces towards Mons under pretence of besieging it—and then fell upon Ipre with such rapid violence, that he soon reduced that likewise, though with such loss of officers and soldiers that he put his army into garrisons, and then returned to Paris. This gave such a mighty alarm to the Hollanders, that all things drove on violently for a peace; which the French King being sensible of, and having now gained his point in Flanders, to prevent the English from being in earnest against him, he sent an imperious project of a peace, declaring he would admit of these conditions and no other, which the Dutch were obliged to accept of, since they could obtain no better. But before the peace was ratified, the French made several pretensions and delays in performing even what themselves had agreed to, as his Highness the Prince of Orange foresaw and foretold they would do, insomuch that they blocked up the City of Mons, a chief frontier of Flanders, upon which his Highness resolved to march to the relief of it, great preparations being made to that purpose; and understanding that the Confederates had joined the Holland and Spanish forces, that lay near the canal of Brussels, he departed by night from the Hague, and marching toward Mons with his army, being accompanied by the Duke of Monmouth, he fell upon the Duke of Luxembourg with such fury that he forced him to retire; and animating his soldiers, with his eyes sparkling like fire, they despised all dangers by their gallant general's example, who in the midst of fire and smoke, and bullets flying thick as hail, had ventured so far that he had been in imminent danger, had not Monsieur Overkirk opposed himself against a daring captain that was just ready to charge the Prince with full career, laying him dead on the place. The horse all this while were lookers on, not being able to advance into the narrow passages and deep descents, so that all the weight lay on the foot and dragoons. Night coming on, the Duke of Luxembourg drew off in great silence and confusion, leaving to his Highness, as certain marks of victory, the field of battle, his tents, baggage, wounded men, store of powder and other ammunition. The States General appointed commissioners to congratulate his Highness for this victory gained with so much reputation and glory, beseeching him withal to be careful of his illustrious person, considering the tranquillity of his country and the repose of the Church and Protestant religion depended so much thereon.

The very day this memorable battle was fought the peace between the Dutch and French was signed at Nimeguen, of which intelligence was brought to his Highness the next morning, who would else have pursued the advantages he had gained to the full relief of the town, having already, in spite of so many disadvantages from an army so suddenly drawn together, and so hasty a march as that of the Dutch, taken divers posts, fortified with so much skill and industry by the French, and attacked them with a resolution and vigour that at first surprised them, and after an obstinate and bloody fight so disordered them that though the night prevented the end of the action, yet it was verily believed that if the Prince had been at liberty next day to pursue it, with seven or eight thousand English, which were ready to join his army, he must, in all appearance, not only have relieved Mons, but made such an impression into France as had often been designed, but never attempted, since the war began; upon which a French officer present said, "That he esteemed this the only heroic action that had been done in the whole course and progress of it." The prince having received advice of the peace sent a deputy with the news to the Duke of Luxembourg, who desired to see the Prince, and accordingly met him in the field, at the head of his chief officers, where all civilities passed between them proper for the occasion; and the French with great curiosity crowded about this young Prince, who had the day before engaged in such a desperate action as that of St. Denis was esteemed to be; so that his Highness could not have ended the war with greater glory, nor with greater spite, to see such a great occasion wrested out of his hand by the sudden and unexpected signing of the peace, which he had assured himself the States General would not have consented to without the Spaniards; yet upon the certain news of it he drew back his army, returned to the Hague, and left the States to pursue their own measures in order to finish the treaty betwixt France and Spain.

During which the King of England sent over a person of honour to the States General, to acquaint them how much he was surprised at the news of their signing a particular treaty with France, even without the inclusion of Spain; declaring, that if they would refuse to ratify what their Ministers had signed at Nimeguen, his Majesty would immediately declare war against France, and carry it on with all vigour, pursuant to the treaty lately entered into with them. All men were much amazed at this sudden turn of the Court of England, and the Prince complained "That nothing was ever more hot and cold, nor any councils ever more unsteady, than those of England, since if this despatch had come twenty days before it might have changed the face of affairs in Christendom, and have obliged the French to such terms of peace as should have left the world in quiet for many years to come, but would now have no effect at all;" which happened accordingly, for at last it appeared to proceed only from the discovery of the Popish plot, which extremely alarmed the people and Parliament, who were much disturbed at the treacherous designs of our Court in promoting the Popish and French interest, and thereby forcing the Dutch to comply with that King almost upon his own terms; and therefore, to divert the humour, King Charles pretended to be in earnest for engaging in a war against France, which for some time hindered the ratification of the treaty, and English forces were daily transported into Flanders, as if the war were really to have been carried on, which encouraged those that were against the peace in Holland, and occasioned the Spaniards to use their utmost endeavours to prevent the concluding it.

But the French King, being unwilling to lose the great advantages he had obtained by this treaty, resolved to remove all difficulties, and satisfy the States in their demands; yea, he despatched ambassadors to the Hague with full authority to remit all the differences about the treaty with Spain and himself to their determination, which raised in the States such a good opinion of the sincerity of that King's proceedings, that they quickly adjusted all matters in contest between the two crowns; so that the treaty was signed September 20, 1678. The other Confederates, as the Emperor, the King of Denmark, the Duke of Brandenburg, etc., were very much enraged that they were left to treat singly with their potent enemy, who demanded very severe conditions from them; so that the ratification of the treaty with Spain being hereby delayed, the French King, to quicken it, sent Marshal d'Humiéres with a great army into Flanders, plundering and burning all before them, and putting these countries under contribution with so much fury and insolence that the common people complained heavily of the calamities and miseries which they undeservedly suffered by the slowness of the Spanish council; so that at length both the Spaniards and Emperor were obliged to comply with the offers of France who else threatened in a few days to make the terms much higher. The other Prince though they very much resented this sudden conclusion of a peace at such disadvantage, yet knowing their own inability were forced to be contented to make a separate peace for themselves. The King of England, observing that he could not hinder it, sent his plenipotentiaries again to Nimeguen, to sign the general treaty; but in the interval, some new pretences arising between the Spaniards and French, the States General were very diligent to compose them, the transactions being seldom managed by them but in the presence of his Highness the Prince of Orange, whose prudence was still consulted in matters of the greatest difficulty; he himself discovering an extraordinary generosity, that while others preferred points of honour before the public peace, his Highness quitted his own interest in postponing his demands for reparation of the devastations in his own estates and territories, so as not to impede the tranquility of his country, many of his lands being ruined and destroyed in the Spanish Netherlands, and other adjacent parts; of which, and several other injustices in seizing upon his large possessions in other places, though the provinces of Guelderland, Zealand and Utrecht made loud complaints against the French in his Highness's behalf, yet could the Prince obtain no satisfaction; but the States and their subjects being quite tired out with the war, the general peace was signed in January, 1678; and the English mediators were called home by that King, who was fully employed at home about the matter of the Popish plot, which both Houses of Parliament and the generality of the nation believed to be real, though the King and some of the Court credited no more of it than what themselves were concerned in, and the Prince of Orange at that time told a public Minister 'that he had reason to be confident that the

King was a Roman Catholic, though he durst not profess it."

Thus Europe, for the present, was left in a general peace, though the French King soon after made such shameful pretences to the dependencies upon his late conquests, both in Flanders and Germany, that he gained more after the peace than by his arms in the war, no Prince or State being either willing or able to oppose him therein. These disputes began in 1681, and continued some years, at which time that King likewise began to raise a violent persecution against his own Protestant subjects, proceeding from the perfidiousness and ingratitude peculiar to Louis XIV.; for it is well known that for the signal services which they performed to Henry IV., his grandfather, in asserting the rights of the Crown against the Papists, who were then in rebellion against him, that great Prince, in acknowledgment thereof, confirmed to them an edict for the free exercise of their religion, which was called the Edict of Nantes, whereby they were to enjoy all liberties and privileges, both in religious and civil matters, and to be as capable of all offices and employments as his other subjects. This he declared should be inviolable, and it was accordingly confirmed both by his son, Louis XIII., and likewise by the present King, upon a very remarkable occasion; for he being very young when he ascended the throne, the Prince of Condé soon after raised a civil war in the kingdom against him, but the Protestants, by their unshaken loyalty to him, defeated the designs of his enemies, and settled that crown upon his head which he wears this day, of which eminent service he seemed to be so sensible that in 1652 he made a public declaration of it at St. Germain's, and every one endeavoured to exceed in proclaiming the merits of the Protestants, the Queen Mother herself acknowledging that they had preserved the State; but since by the maxims of the Roman religion no faith is to be kept with heretics, the Jesuits and Ministers of State endeavoured to instil into the King's mind this treacherous notion, that since the Protestants were so potent as to advance the King, they might likewise, upon another occasion, remove him again. From this infernal reasoning, without their having given the least umbrage or suspicion of disloyalty, it was resolved they must be suppressed and ruined.

Therefore, as soon as the kingdom was settled in peace, the Protestant towns of Rochelle, Montauban, &c., which had showed the greatest zeal for the King's service, were plundered by the soldiers and otherwise impoverished; then their churches and exercises of religion were prohibited them, under false pretences that they exceeded the grants allowed them; yea, in matters of law, religion was urged by the advocates at the instigation of the priests, so that they cried out, "I plead against a heretic, an enemy to the State and to the King's religion, whom he would have to be destroyed;" so that the judge dared not do them justice, for fear of being counted a favourer of heretics, and upon complaint they were told, "You have your remedy in your own hands; why do you not turn Catholics?" This was succeeded by processes throughout the kingdom, to inquire what the Protestants had said or done for twenty years past about religion, or other matters, and there being no want of perjured villains to swear what was absolutely false, the judges, though sensible of it, encouraging them therein, the prisons were soon filled, and many innocent and virtuous persons were whipped and sent to the galleys for slaves. Next they were deprived of all public offices and employments, contrary to an express article in the Edict of Nantes; yea, were forbid to exercise several arts and trades for maintaining their families.

This was in 1669, and in 1680 all lords and gentlemen were commanded to discharge their Protestant officers and servants; nay, they would not suffer Protestant midwives to do their office, but expressly ordained that no woman should receive any assistance in that condition but from Popish midwives; and to consummate their miseries they were forbid, under severe penalties, to go out of France to get their bread in other countries, whereby they were under the horrible necessity of perishing for hunger in their own. They laid severe taxes upon them, raising the sum from forty or fifty livres to seven or eight hundred, and quartered dragoons upon them till it was paid. Then an edict was published that children of seven years old should abjure their religion, forcing their parents to give them allowances beyond their abilities, taking them away, and suffering them to see them no more; even persons of the best quality were thus used. Protestant schoolmasters were prohibited, and three universities suppressed, though absolutely granted by the Edict of Nantes; Papists were forbid to marry Protestants, or ministers to hinder people, directly or indirectly, from turning Papists. These and a multitude of other cruel and barbarous oppressions they groaned under, when the Elector of Brandenburg being pleased to intercede on their behalf, the King assured him " he was very well satisfied with the behaviour of his Protestant subjects, and that so long as he lived no wrong should be done them," and yet at the same instant, with his usual sincerity, he gave orders for demolishing several of their churches and shutting up others, imprisoning their ministers, and using divers manifest injustices against those he pretended to protect.

At this time some of the persecuted people sent their children to Orange, as being a sovereign principality, to finish the course of their studies in security; but this so displeased the King, that he sent a body of two thousand men, under his Lieutenant-General, into Languedoc, who positively commanded the Prince of Orange's magistrates to send away all the children home again, and not to receive any more for the future into their university or schools; which, though it appeared very unreasonable, yet the magistrates, to prevent further mischief, complied therewith, and thought they had thereby given full satisfaction to his demands; but were strangely surprised to hear that during the capitulation the Lieutenant-General still approached with his forces nearer the city, and that he had absolute orders to demolish their walls. In short, he advanced, and quartered eight companies of dragoons in the citizens' houses, where they committed many disorders, constraining as well all the inhabitants, as the other subjects of his Highness in the villages round about, to assist at the ruin of their own walls and towers, which were blown up, at which the people laboured the more earnestly to be the sooner rid of those arbitrary guests, who were said to have already vitiated several virgins. The Prince, having news thereof, represented their case to the States General, as a breach of the last peace, desiring them to signify their just resentment of these unreasonable proceedings of the French King, and to demand reparation for such horrid violations instantly upon concluding a general peace, and without the least provocation given.

The States accordingly, by their ambassador, represented it as an infraction of the peace of Nimeguen, and required satisfaction for the damages which the Prince and his subjects had so illegally and contrary to the faith of treaties and leagues sustained, but could only have this answer from the French Court, that as to the money extorted from the inhabitants it was done without the King's order, and he had commanded restitution to be made; that upon the submission of the people to his will and pleasure he had withdrawn his forces out of the principality, and restored free commerce to the inhabitants, according to their desires; and for the rest, he had reason for what he had done.

After the peace was concluded, his Highness applied himself to reform the government of Utrecht and other towns, and likewise to concert matters with the States General for the future security of his country against the treacheries and false pretensions of France; the Prince being unusually present in the principal debates of the Assembly, both as to peace and war, who always appeared no less prudent and vigilant to prevent disorders at home than to repel foreign hostility. In July, 1681, his Highness came over into England, and arriving at Whitehall dined at Sir Stephen Foxe's, and then went to Windsor, where the Court then was, and having continued here about ten days returned back to Holland.

In the interval of affairs his Highness retired to Dieren, or Soestdyke, to divert himself, and at other times made progresses to take a review of the frontier towns belonging to the State, who in 1682 had ordered the towns of Breda, Grave and Naarden to be strongly fortified; and it was proposed in the Assembly of the States to raise sixteen thousand men and incorporate them with the old regiments, and to add a new squadron of twenty-four men-of-war, both to prevent any sudden insults of the French upon their territories and to assist the Spaniards, if they should commit any act of hostility, which was much to be suspected, considering the shameful pretensions that King set up of dependencies in the Spanish Netherlands.

In 1682 the Marquis of Grana was made Governor of Flanders, of which he gave notice to the States General and the Prince, and soon after his Highness had an interview with the Marquis between Breda and Antwerp, where they entered into conferences about their future management of affairs; his Highness likewise visiting the fortified places in Flanders belonging to the States, being accompanied by the Princes, who were received with all kind of respect and splendour by the cities of Brussels, Antwerp, etc. About this time the Count d'Avaux, the French Ambassador, arriving at the Hague, put in a memorial to the Assembly of the manner how he expected to receive audience, but the States replied that the things which he desired were wholly new and never practised before, and therefore they could in nowise comply with them; whereupon his audience was put off till he was willing to receive it upon the former terms. In November this year the Envoy of Muscovy came to wait upon the Prince, then at Soestdyke, to give an account that the great Czar was dead, and that the two Princes now reigning were advanced to the throne.

In the end of 1683, the King of Spain being no longer able to suffer the continual invasions of the French upon his cities and towns in Flanders, and his cruel treatment of his subjects for not paying unjust and unreasonable contributions, he proclaimed war against him both by sea and land, and ordered all the effects of the French merchants in his dominions to be seized and sent to the States General, to assist him in this just defensive war, who thereupon concluded to raise a considerable force, both for his aid and their own security, and accordingly his Highness gave out several commissions, and sent eight thousand men toward Flanders. In the meantime the French King, according to his usual method, having ordered great detachments to be sent from all the conquered places toward Valenciennes, in April, 1684, he himself, accompanied by the Dauphin and Dauphiness, came from Paris thither. The Prince was very desirous to have perfected the new levies, and to have marched at the head of them to oppose him, but the obstinacy of Amsterdam and some other towns, which refused to allow their quota for maintaining him, prevented his Highness's worthy designs. The French King having mustered his army between Condé and Valenciennes, he immediately invested the city of Luxembourg; and though the governor made a very notable defence, and the French lost a considerable number of men, yet the greatness of their army, which was posted so as to prevent any relief, at length obliged the town to capitulate, and on the 7th of June following it was surrendered upon articles; and soon after, a truce being made with Spain, they were forced to suffer the loss of this city with the same temper as they had done many before.

And as the French King continued thus tyrannically to injure his neighbours, so he treacherously proceeded to exercise horrid cruelties upon his own Protestant subjects; for though he had resolved upon their destruction, yet at the same time he declared that he had not the least intention to infringe the Edict of Nantes, and accordingly, in 1684, he absolutely concluded to cancel and make void that edict, and to banish all the ministers out of the kingdom, and several young priests were sent about the country to inflame the mobile against the Protestants! and it was declared in print that "the Catholic faith must be planted by fire and sword, alleging the example of a King of Norway, who converted the nobles of his country by threatening them to slay their children before their eyes, if they would not consent to have them baptised, and to be baptised themselves." The Protestants were very sensible of the mischiefs designed against them, and exposed their grievances to the King with all humility and submission, which produced no other effect upon his tyrannical temper than to hasten their destruction by open force and violence, in so terrible a manner as is scarce to be paralleled. At first they quartered troops of bloody and desperate dragoons upon them, who loudly bellowed that "the King would no longer suffer any Protestants in his kingdom, and that they must resolve to change their religion, or else to suffer the utmost cruelty that could be inflicted upon them;" to which these innocent souls replied that "they were ready to sacrifice their lives and estates for the King's service, but their consciences, being God's, they could not in the same manner dispose of them." This answer did but enrage their hellish adversaries, so that the first seized their goods and then fell upon their persons, inflicting all the barbarities imaginable to induce them to renounce their religion. They hung up men and women by the hair of the head, or by the feet, within their chimneys, smoking them with wisps of wet straw; they threw them into great fires, and plucked them thence half roasted; they tied them on the rack, and poured wine down their throats till the fume had deprived them of their reason, and then made them say they would be Catholics; they stripped them stark naked, and larded them all over with pins from head to foot; they kept them from sleeping seven or eight days and nights together; they tied parents to bed-posts and ravished their daughters before their eyes; they plucked off the nails from the hands and toes of others, with the most intolerable pain; and after these and a thousand other horrid indignities, if they refused to abjure their religion, they threw them into close, dark and stinking dungeons, exercising upon them all sorts of inhumanity; and yet, after all these barbarous usages, they compelled those wretched people who had not courage and constancy enough to persist in the faith, and therefore turned Catholic, or new converts, as they called them, to acknowledge that "they had embraced the Roman religion of their own accord," and had the impudence to declare, even against the evidence of millions of witnesses, "that force and violence had no share in the conversions, but that they were soft, calm and voluntary, and that if there were any dragoons concerned therein, it was because the Protestants themselves devised them, that they might have a handsome pretence to change their religion." In the meantime their houses were demolished, their lands destroyed, their woods cut down, and their wives and children seized and put into monasteries; and an edict was published for plucking down all the Protestant churches in the kingdom—and all for promoting the Catholic religion. Yea, the mischief did not terminate here, for the French King, being too potent to be resisted by the Duke of Savoy, he compelled that Prince to publish an edict for prohibiting the poor Waldenses and

Vaudois to exercise their religion on pain of death, and being assisted with a great number of French troops under Monsieur de Catinat, the soldiers committed the like violences and barbarities against them as they had done in France.

His Highness the Prince of Orange highly disapproved of these proceedings, and was a silent mourner for the miseries of the Protestant Church, which now seemed to be threatened more than ever; for King Charles II. dying in February, 1685, the Duke of York succeeded him, who instantly declared himself a Roman Catholic; and on the 10th of June following the Duke of Monmouth landed, with one hundred and fifty men, at Lyme, in Dorsetshire, declaring—

"That he had taken arms for the defence and vindication of the Protestant religion, and the laws, rights, and privileges of England, from the invasion made upon them, and for delivering the kingdom from the tyranny of James, Duke of York." About the same time the Earl of Argyle, setting sail from the Vlye, in Holland, landed in the west of Scotland, publishing a declaration to the same purpose; but, either by weakness or treachery, they were soon defeated and both beheaded, and a multitude of their followers executed; for which great success King James published a proclamation for thanksgiving, and among other expressions says, that "nothing now remained which could possibly disturb the future quiet of his reign;" in confidence whereof, he, with the advice of his Popish councillors and their adherents, proceeded to commit several open violations upon the laws of the land and the properties of his subjects.

Some time before, his Highness, returning from Homslaerdike to the Hague, gave audience to several foreign Ministers, and parted thence to visit the garrisons of Maestricht, Bois-le-Duc and other places, and on his return was met by the Princess at Loo, having, in his progress, given all necessary orders for the well governing and strengthening of those places. In December, 1687, the Marquis d'Abbeville, Envoy Extraordinary from the King of England, had audience of his Highness and the States of Holland; and about the same time the States, considering the danger that might arise from the great number of foreign Popish priests (notwithstanding the intercession of the Envoy of the Emperor of Germany on their behalf), they made a decree, commanding them to retire out of the Netherlands and never to return again, promising a reward of one hundred ducatoons to any that should make discovery, and laying a penalty of six hundred florins upon those that should harbour or conceal any of them, for the first offence, twelve hundred for the second, and corporeal punishment for the third; whereupon many of them went over to England, where their hopes and expectations of having their religion settled daily increased.

The King of England being unwilling to afford any assistance to the heretical States, against his dear ally the French King, published a proclamation in March, 1687, commanding the return of all subjects then in the service of the States General, either by sea or land, with no other allegation but that the King thought it fit for his service. The States raised some dispute with the Marquis d'Abbeville about this matter, refusing to let them return into England, insomuch that the Marquis soon after delivered in a memorial to the States, by express orders from the King, signifying "That his master was much surprised to find that their lordships persisted in their resolutions in refusing to leave his subjects to return into England, and that whereas their lordships alleged that there was nothing so agreeable to nature as that he who was born free should have the right and liberty to settle himself wherever he should think it most advantageous to him, and that it was in his power to be naturalized and become a subject to them under whose sovereignty he submits his person, and that the Government receiving him thereby acquire over him the same right it has over its own proper and natural subjects." The Marquis replied, "That this pretended natural liberty could not subsist after obedience and dominion had been introduced, so that the rights of sovereignty and obedience were now only to be considered, and that in virtue of those rights it had been the common opinion in all times that no natural subject could withdraw himself from the obedience he owed to his lawful Prince, from whence it was that the Kings of Great Britain had, in all times, prohibited their subjects to engage in any foreign service, and had recalled them from it when and as often as they thought fit." The Marquis further instanced a capitulation made between the Earl of Ossory and his Highness the Prince of Orange, "That in case the King of Great Britain should recall his subjects in the service of the States, they should be permitted to retire; by virtue of which capitulation, and his reasons alleged, the Marquis demanded their dismission, from which the King would never depart; neither was he willing to doubt of their lordships' compliance with it." But it seems few or none were willing, for very few returned, judging, it may be, that they might do more service where they were, for the interest of their country, than in fighting at home against their own countrymen and fellow-Protestants; and as their unwillingness justified the resolution of the States General, so it rendered the endeavours of the Marquis ineffectual; for the States having disbanded them, the greatest part enlisted themselves again under their command, as well officers as soldiers, though the King had ordered the masters and captains of ships and vessels to give such as would return free passage, with promise of advancement when they came to England.

In May, 1688, the Prince Elector of Saxony was splendidly entertained by his Highness the Prince of Orange, at Homslaerdike; and the next day his Highness accompanied him to Scheveling, where they went on board a small vessel that carried them to a squadron of seventeen men-of-war, which arrived from Schouvelt, under the command of Vice-Admiral Allemond, who upon their approach sent two light frigates and a shallop to meet them, and they were saluted with the cannon of all the ships; when having dined on board the Vice-Admiral, they returned to Scheveling, and from thence his Electoral Highness went to visit Delft, Rotterdam, Dort, Maestricht, Leige, Aix and Cologne, and so returned home by the way of Frankfort; about which time the Envoy of Brandenburg acquainted the Prince of Orange and the States with the death of the Elector, his master, a Prince extremely firm to the Protestant interest, and whose death was much regretted by the Protestant Princes and States, the Prince and States sending a gentleman with compliments of condolence to his son and successor.

The King of England having obtained the opinion of his judges for the dispensing power, soon made use of it; for first he employed Popish officers, and put them into chief command; the Earl of Clarendon being recalled from the government of Ireland and the Earl of Tyrconnel, a Papist, sent to succeed him, to the great terror of the Protestants of that kingdom. The Earl of Castlemaine was sent Ambassador to Rome; an army was raised and mustered at Hounslow Heath; the Lord Bishop of London was convened before a new and illegal court of judicature for ecclesiastical affairs, and suspended from his office for refusing to suspend the Rev. Dr. Sharpe, under pretence that he had uttered seditious words in his sermons; then a declaration was published for liberty of conscience, and suspending all the penal laws in matters of religion, and acquitting all persons from taking the oaths of allegiance and supremacy, both in England, Scotland and Ireland; the Pope's Nuncio arrived in England, being received with much respect by the King, and dined with the King and the Lord Mayor at Guildhall; Popish Chapels were erected in several places in London and other cities and towns in England; the charters of several corporations that were yet unseized were now taken away; these and divers other illegal proceedings put the nation into a ferment, and they were enraged at the authors of them; nay, they do not stop here for after this the King again renewed his declaration for liberty of conscience, with a peremptory order to command all the clergy to read it in their several churches and chapels throughout the kingdom, and that the Bishops should distribute them throughout their several dioceses; but the rigorous proceedings against the Lord Bishop of London the last year, and against the Vice-Chancellor of Cambridge and the Fellows of Magdalen College Oxford this year, were such evident breaches of his indulgence to tender consciences, that it gave still geater dissatisfaction to the nation and portended some sudden alteration; the Vice-Chancellor of Cambridge being deprived of his office and suspended of his headship for refusing to admit one Alban Francis, a Benedictine monk, to be Master of Arts without taking the oaths by virtue of the dispensing power, though contrary to the statutes which he had sworn to maintain; and the Fellows in Magdalen College, in Oxford, being twenty-six in number, for refusing to admit one Farmer, a scandalous Popish priest, to the presidentship of that college, and electing Dr. Hough were pronounced guilty of disobedience to His Majesty's commands and deprived and expelled from their respective fellowships; and the Bishops, judging that their distributing the declaration would be an owning and asserting the King's assumed dispensing power, and foreseeing the pernicious consequences thereof, the Archbishop of Canterbury and six others drew up a petition in behalf of themselves and their brethren, setting forth the reasons why they could not comply therewith. This was so ill resented by the King and his Popish councillors that the petition was judged tumultuary, and all the seven Bishops were commited prisoners to the Tower. And now the Jesuits acted their masterpiece of policy, as they imagined, though it proved very fatal to them: for, knowing that the King grew old, and that on his life the hopes of restoring their religion depended, since the heir-apparent was a Protestant, who would soon ruin all their machinations, they resolved, if possible, to advance a Popish successor, and thereby ensure Popery and slavery to the nation. Hereupon they raised a report, some time before, that the Queen was with child, though the people did not believe it, and several lampoons were made upon that subject; and the Bishops being now secured, this was thought the propper time for the Queen to fall in labour, and accordingly June 10th, 1688, it was published that she was delivered of a Prince, for which the King ordered all signs of rejoicing to be made, and a day of thanksgiving was appointed, as being a thing of mighty consequence for advancing the Catholic cause; though the joy was somewhat abated by the acquittal of the seven Bishops, five days after, who, being tried at the King's Bench bar, were brought in not guilty, at which the people, yea, the King's own army at Hounslow Heath shouted for joy, to the severe mortification of the Court.

The King having declared that he intended to call a Parliament to turn his declaration of liberty of conscience into a law, and likewise to abrogate all the penal laws and tests, both against the Dissenters and Roman Catholics, the Jesuits had a great desire to sound the intentions and thoughts of their Highnesses the Prince and Princess of Orange upon that subject; to which purpose, Mr. James Steward undertook to write a letter to pensionary Fagel, not without the knowledge and approbation of the King, which occasioned Mynheer Fagel's answer to this effect:

"That their Highnesses had often declared, as they did more particularly to the Marquis d'Abbeville, His Majesty's envoy extraordinary to the States, that it is their opinion that no Christian ought to be persecuted for his conscience, or be ill-used because he differs from the public and established religion; and therefore they could be content that even the Papists in England, Scotland, and Ireland might be suffered to continue in their religion with as much liberty as is allowed them by the States of the United Provinces; and as for the Protestant Dissenters, their Highnesses did not only consent, but heartily approved of their having an entire liberty or the full exercise of their religion without any trouble or hindrance. That their Highnesses were ready, in case his Majesty of England should desire it, to declare their willingness to concur in the settling and confirming this liberty, as far as it lay in them; and were ready, if desired, to concur in repealing the laws, provided always that those laws remain still in their full force and vigour, whereby the Roman Catholics are excluded out of both Houses of Parliament, and out of all public employments, ecclesiastical, civil, and military, as likewise all those other laws which confirm the Protestant religion, and which secure it against all the attempts of the Roman Catholics. But that their Highnesses could not agree to the repealing of the tests, or those penal laws that tend to the security of the Protestant religion, since the Roman Catholics received no other prejudice from these than the being excluded from the Parliament or from public employments; and that by them the Protestant religion is covered from all the designs of the Roman Catholics against it, or against the public safety, and neither the tests nor those other laws can be said to carry in them any severity against the Roman Catholics, upon account of their consciences, they being only provisions qualifying men to be Members of Parliament, or to be capable of bearing offices, by which they must declare before God and man that they are for the Protestant religion; so that all this amounts to no more than a securing the Protestant religion from any prejudice that it may receive from the Roman Catholics. That their Highnesses have thought, and do still think, that more than this ought not to be asked nor expected from them; since by these means, the Roman Catholics and their posterity would be for ever secured from all troubles in their persons or estates, or in the exercise of their religion; and that the Roman Catholics ought to be satisfied with this, and not to disquiet the kingdom because they cannot sit in Parliament, or to be in employment; or, because those laws, wherein the security of the Protestant religion chiefly consists, are not repealed, by which they may be in condition to overturn it; that their Highnesses also believed that the Dissenters would be for ever satisfied when they should be for ever covered from all danger of being disturbed or punished for the free exercise of their religion, under any pretence whatsoever."

This was the substance of the letter written by that great Minister of State, as discovering the just sentiments of their Highnesses, which did noways please the Papists, who had high expectations of carrying all before them; and, therefore, Mr. Steward, in his second letter to the pensioner, awhile after, says: "That the court was quite beyond it, and had taken other measures," and what they were soon after appeared; namely, to defeat their Royal Highnesses of their just interest and right to the succession of the Crown, by pretending that the Queen was delivered of a Prince of Wales.

But the nobility and gentry of England, beholding the deplorable state of the nation, and foreseeing the subversion of their ancient laws and established religion to be designed by him who had largely promised the protection of both, and at the same time seeing Popery and arbitrary power hovering over their heads, and ready to seize on their liberties and properties, and that both were designed to be perpetuated and entailed upon them and their posterity by a succession of Popish Princes; Mrs. Cellier having declared in print, before the pretended birth, that it would be a Prince, and that the Queen would likewise bring forth a Duke of York and a Duke of Gloucester; after several consultations whither to fly for succour, at length they resolved to apply themselves to his Highness the Prince of Orange, to whose illustrious family it had been an inherent glory for some ages, to relieve the distressed, and support the Protestant cause. His Highness, they saw, inherited all the surpassing qualities of his ancestors; their matchless prudence, justice, courage, their truth and magnanimity; and besides all these excellent endowments, they were well assured of the fair title he had to the Crown itself. To him, therefore, the Lords spiritual and temporal, with a great number of the chiefest of the gentry of the kingdom, make their application, and in an humble memorial represent their grievances to their Highnesses to this effect:

"That their Highnesses cannot be ignorant that the Protestants of England, who continue true to the government and religion, have been many ways troubled and vexed by many devices and machinations of the Papists, carried on under pretence of royal authority, and things required of them answerable before God and man; several ecclesiastical benefices of churches taken from them, without any other reason given than the King's pleasure; themselves summoned and sentenced by commissioners, appointed contrary to express law; deprived of their free choice of magistrates; divers corporations dissolved; the legal security of their religion and liberty, established by King and Parliament, abolished and taken away by a pretended dispensing power; new and unheard-of maxims broached, that subjects have no right but what is found and derived from the King's will and pleasure; the militia put into the hands of persons unqualified by law, and a Popish mercenary army maintained in the kingdom in times of peace, directly contrary to law; executing of ancient laws against several crimes and misdemeanors obstructed and prohibited, and the statutes against corresponding with the Court of Rome, against Papal jurisdictions, and Popish priests suspended in the courts of justice; those judges displaced who acquit any whom the Court would have condemned, as happened to the Judges Holloway and Powel, for acquitting the seven bishops; the free choice of members of parliament wholly taken away, notwithstanding all the care and provision made by the law in that behalf, by the Quo Warranto against charters, and proposing ensnaring questions; all things levelled at the propagation of Popery, for which the Courts of England and France have now for a long time so strenuously bestirred themselves; endeavours and practices used to persuade their Highnesses to consent to the abolishing the penal laws and tests (though herein disappointed.) The Queen being with child first proclaimed and divulged by Popish priests, and in the sequel thereof a child produced without any clear proof or evidence of sufficient and unsuspected witness; besides that it cannot be believed that the said child was ever born of the Queen, by reason of her known sickness and indisposition, and many other arguments, as not being confirmed by any certain foregoing signs of conception; the place of her lying-in being often changed, and pretended delivery celebrated in the absence of the Princess of Denmark, and while the English ladies were at church, in a bedstead which was provided with a convenient passage in the side of it, by which means the child was conveyed to the Queen by the Ladies L'Abadie and Taurarier; that these be matters left to the discretion of a free parliament, and that in the name of your Highnesses, and the whole nation, the Queen may be desired to prove the real birth of the pretended Prince of Wales, by a competent number of credible witnesses of both sexes; or in case of a failure herein, that the reports of any such birth may be suppressed for the time to come. That they humbly crave the protection of their Highnesses in this matter, as well as with respect to the abolition and suspension of the laws made to maintain the Protestant religion, their civil rights, fundamental liberties, and free government; and that their Highnesses would be pleased to insist that, besides the business of the child, the government of England according to law may be restored; the laws against Papal jurisdiction, priests, &c., be put in execution; the suspending and dispensing power be declared null and void, and the privileges of the City of London, free choice of magistrates, and all other liberties, as well as that of other corporations, be restored and maintained."

Their Highnesses, with no less willingness than generosity, and out of their zeal for the Protestant religion, and compassion of the oppressed, listened to their complaints. And his Highness, well weighing the justness of their requests and the reality of their grievances, instantly began to take measures in order to their deliverance. And soon after his Highness went to meet the Elector of Brandenburg, and some other princes and noblemen of Germany, at Minden, which so alarmed the French King that Monsieur d'Avaux, his ambassador, presented a memorial to the States General, intimating that the King, his master, being informed of the motions and conferences that were made and held towards the frontiers of Cologne, against the Cardinal of Furstemburgh and the Chapter, he was resolved to maintain the Cardinal and their privileges against all those who should go about to trouble them: but herein the politics of King Lewis failed him, his Highness the Prince of Orange managing his affairs with such exact secrecy, that neither the King nor his sagacious council could penetrate into the design till it was upon the point of execution, and out of danger of being defeated. For upon his Highness's return from that conference at Loe, orders were given for drawing the forces the States had raised for his Highness's assistance and encamping them upon the Mocker Hyde, and the forces of those Princes whom his Highness had engaged to aid him in this glorious expedition had orders to be upon their march, as those of Brandenburg, Hesse-Cassel, &c. And the States General assembled at the Hague, when his Highness was present, and their debates and consultations having been kept very private for some days, at length they published the following manifesto:—

"That the States had resolved with their ships and men to assist the Prince of Orange, who being invited by the reiterated importunities of the nobility and gentry of England, to oppose that arbitrary government which his Britannic Majesty is designing to introduce into that kingdom, has fully determined to go over to that country, as well for that reason as to save the English religion, which his Majesty has also resolved to destroy. Both which enterprises being so contrary to the laws of God and man, and particularly those of the kingdom of which they threatened the utter subversion, the Prince of Orange, instigated by motives of his own innate piety which will not permit him to suffer the ruin of religion, nor the overturning of so fair a kingdom, has resolved to call a free parliament, &c., for which reasons, and because the design of the King of England is manifestly apparent by the strict alliance which he has contracted with the most Christian King, who now bears no goodwill to the United Provinces, and whose proceedings are justly, therefore, by them to be suspected; so that if his Britannic Majesty should be suffered to become absolute in his dominions the United Provinces could be no longer in security; and, therefore, it being their interest that the fundamental laws of that kingdom and the English religion should be preserved, they hoped that God would bless the Prince of Orange with happy success."

King James, though at first he would not believe that the vast preparations in Holland concerned him, though the French King had given him notice of them some time before, was now fully convinced thereof by this manifesto; and all of a sudden the bells began to ring backward at Whitehall, and the first news we heard of their disturbance was a proclamation, September 28, 1688, by which it was intimated that "the King had received undoubted intelligence that a great and sudden invasion from Holland was to be speedily made in a hostile manner upon his kingdoms, under the false pretences of liberty, property and religion; but that an absolute conquest of his kingdoms, and the subduing him and his dominions to a foreign power, &c. However, relying upon the ancient courage, faith and allegiance of his people, as he had formerly ventured his life for the honour and safety of the nation, so he was now resolved to live and die in defence thereof, against all enemies whatsoever," &c. After this the King published a proclamation of general pardon, with some few exceptions; restored the injured gentlemen of Oxford and Cambridge to their rights; dissolved the ecclesiastical commissions; vacated the Quo Warranto against the City of London, and issued forth a proclamation for restoring all corporations to their ancient charters, liberties, rights and franchises, in short, he undid almost in one day all that he had been doing since his first coming to the crown.

Yet such was the folly of the Romish party in the midst of this consternation, that the show of the Prince of Wales still went on, and October 15 the child was christened: the Pope, represented by his nuncio, being godfather, and the Queen-dowager, godmother; and two days after, the King, to secure his territories, commanded his lord and deputy-lieutenants, and all other officers concerned, to cause the coasts to be strictly guarded, and that upon the first approach of the enemy, all the oxen, horses and cattle which might be fit for draught should be driven twenty miles from the place where the enemy should attempt to land.

October 22, the King commanded a particular assembly of his Privy Council, and sent for all such peers, spiritual and temporal, as were in town, together with the Lord Mayor and aldermen of the City of London, the judges, and several of his counsel learned in the law, telling them that "he had called them together upon a very extraordinary occasion, but that extraordinary diseases must have extraordinary remedies; that the malicious endeavours of his adversaries had so poisoned the minds of some of his subjects, that very many of them did not believe that the child wherewith God had blessed him was his, but a supposed child; however, he could say, that by a particular providence scarce ever any Prince was born where there were so many persons present; that he had taken time to have the matter heard and examined, expecting that the Prince of Orange, with the first easterly wind, would invade the kingdom; and, therefore, as he had often ventured his life for the nation before he came to the crown, so he thought himself more obliged to do the same being King, and did intend to go against him in person, by which, in regard he might be exposed to various accidents, he therefore thought it necessary to have this done first, to satisfy his subjects, and prevent the kingdom's being engaged in blood and confusion after his death."

After this, the affidavits of several ladies were produced, in which some swore that they saw milk upon Her Majesty's smock (for they did not think fit to mince the matter); others, that they saw the midwife take the child out of the bed; another, that she stood by the bedside when Her Majesty was delivered of the Prince; another swore, that having had the honour to put on Her Majesty's smock, she saw the Queen's milk; another deposed that she saw the Queen in labour, and heard her cry out much; another, that she saw the midwife give the Prince three drops of the blood of the navel-string mixed with black cherry water, with a great deal of other nauseous stuff. Then the affidavits of the Lords were produced, among whom one swore that he saw Mrs. Labadie carry the child into another room, hither he followed her, and saw the child when she first opened it, and that it was black and reeking; another swore that he saw the child, and that it had the marks of being new born; another, that he heard the Queen make three groans, or squeaks, and that at the last of the three the

Queen was delivered of a child. The physicians swore what was proper, but not fit to be repeated; however, the whole was at length published, to the shame and scandal of all modest eyes and ears.

"And now, my Lords," said the King, after all the depositions were read, "although I did not question but that every person here present was satisfied before, yet, by what you have heard, you will be the better able to satisfy others; besides, could I and the Queen have been thought so wicked as to impose a child upon the nation, we saw how impossible it would have been; neither could I myself have been imposed upon, having constantly been with the Queen during her being with child, and the whole time of her labour, and, therefore, there is none of you but will easily believe that I, who have suffered so much for conscience sake, cannot be capable of so great a villain, to the prejudice of my own children. I thank God that those who know me know well that it is my principle to do as I would be done by, and that I would rather die a thousand deaths than do the least wrong to any of my children."

Yet this zealous harangue had but little influence upon the Generality of the people (with whom the King, by his late actions, had wholly forfeited his reputation), who daily discovered, as far as they dared, their longing desires for the arrival of His Highness the Prince of Orange, to deliver them from the apparent mischiefs that impended over the nation.

His Highness's preparations for his expedition went on apace, and the Marquis of Albeville, King James's ambassador at the Hague, presented a memorial to the deputies of the States General upon that subject; but while he expected an answer the troops embarked, and his Highness and the Marshal Schomberg came to the Hague, and on Friday, October 16, the fleet, consisting of six hundred and thirty-five men-of-war, fire-ships, tenders, &c., for the carriage of horses, foot, arms and ammunition, sailed about four in the afternoon from the Flats near the Brill, with the wind at S. W. and by S. The Prince embarked in a vessel of between twenty-eight and thirty guns, with Count Solmes, Count Stirum, the Sieur Bentwick, with Sieur Overkirk, Marshal Schomberg, Count Charles his son, with several others, as well English noblemen as strangers, who were in the fleet. Next day they came in sight of Schevelinge, but meeting with a very terrible storm, which continued for two days and nights together, were forced to put into harbour again, some ships and small vessels on which the horses were aboard suffering some prejudice. Upon their return the Prince immediately gave an account to the States General of the condition of the fleet, which was not so much damaged as was published in the English *Gazette*, but rather turned to the advantage of his Highness as the affair was managed; for, to make the English Court more remiss in their preparations, the Haarlem and Amsterdam *Gazettes* told a most lamentable story of what had happened, as "that the Prince was returned with his fleet so miserably torn and shattered, that he had lost nine of his men-of-war and several lesser vessels; that one thousand of his horse were utterly lost; that a calenture was got among the seamen; that Dr. Burnet and several of the Prince's chief ministers were drowned; and that the States had an ill opinion of the expedition in general, so that it was a thing almost impossible that the Prince should be in a condition to pursue his design till next spring.

The stratagem had some effect upon the Court, for the Papists' hopes hereupon began so to revive, that the King ordered the restoring the charters and the fellows of Magdalen College, the vacating the ecclesiastical commission, and the other grants which he had newly made to be suspended, till he heard the Prince was again put to sea, and thereby made the whole nation sensible how little trust or credit was to be given to his most solemn promises and declarations. But all hands being at work, the damage that had been sustained was repaired in eight days' time, so that on November 3, about ten in the morning, upon a signal given, the whole fleet once more set sail. About midnight an advice boat brought intelligence that the English fleet, consisting of thirty-three sails, lay to the westward of the Prince's, upon which the Prince fired a gun, which caused a great consternation throughout the whole fleet; but a small advice boat cruising for more certain intelligence brought news that instead of the English fleet which had given the alarm, it was only Admiral Herbert, with a part of the Dutch fleet which had been for some hours separated from the main body. In the morning the Prince gave a signal for the Admirals to come aboard of him, and soon after the fleet was got into the North Forelands, at which time the fleet was ordered to close up in a body, fourteen or fifteen deep, his Highness leading the van in the ship called the Brill, carrying a flag with English colours, with this motto, "The Protestant religion and liberties of England," and underneath, "I will maintain it." In the meantime the council of war sent two small frigates into the mouth of the Thames, who, returning, brought news that the English fleet lay at the buoy in the Oar, about thirty-four sail, the wind contrary at E.N.E.; upon which the Prince gave orders for stretching the whole fleet between Dover and Calais, seventy-five deep, which extended in breadth within a league of each place, the flank and rear being guarded by men-of-war, the trumpets sounding and drums beating at least three hours together; after which, the Prince giving the signal for the fleet to close, they sailed that night as far as Beachy, and the next morning came in view of the Isle of Wight, and then orders were given to extend the fleet in a line as before. The next morning they made directly for Torbay. Upon his Highness's arrival, the people, flocking in great numbers to the shore, signified their welcome in loud acclamations of joy. Soon after, the Prince gave two signals for the Admirals to come on board, and then the whole fleet cast anchor, and preparation was made for landing, whilst the Admirals stood out to sea as a guard, and the small men-of-war attended for the defence of those that landed, besides six men-of-war that were ordered to run in and guard the bay itself. It is remarkable that his Highness had a brisk east and north-easterly wind for two days, which brought them directly towards Torbay, and the wind then turning westerly carried them into the bay, which otherwise might have been very troublesome and dangerous.

The Prince now displayed a red flag at the mizen yard-arm, while General Mackay, with six regiments of foot, was the first that set foot on shore, under the protection of the "Little Porpoise," which was ordered to run herself aground to secure their landing. This was upon November 5th, a day memorable to the English before, but now doubly remarkable for a second deliverance from the bloody designs of the Papists. But the people were so far from making opposition that they only stood there to welcome their guests with all manner of provisions and refreshments; so that his Highness safely landed his whole army, consisting of ten thousand six hundred and ninety-two foot, and three thousand six hundred and sixty horse—in all fourteen thousand three hundred and fifty-two.

The news of the Prince's being landed was carried to the Earl of Bath at Exeter, and Captain Hicks going thither, the people flocked to him in great numbers to list themselves in the service of the Prince of Orange, for which the mayor of the city would have sent him to prison, but was prevented by the people. The next day the Lord Mordaunt with Dr. Burnet came thither, with three or four troops of horse, and, commanding the gates to be opened, released the captain, and going to the mayor, asked him if he would wait upon the Prince at his entrance, who pleading his obligation of an oath to King James, and desiring that his conscience might not be imposed on, was excused. The next day the Prince, with his guards, marched into the city, and went to the Dean's house, where he resided during his stay at Exeter; after whom followed the whole body of his army, who were quartered about Tiverton, Culhampton, Honyton and other places. The Sunday following his Highness went to the cathedral, where his Highness's declaration of reasons inducing him to appear in arms in the kingdom of England, for preserving the Protestant religion, and for restoring the liberties of England, Scotland and Ireland, was read by Dr. Burnet before a numerous auditory, the substance whereof was:

"That it was certain and evident to all men that the public peace and happiness of any kingdom and state could not be preserved where the laws, liberties, and customs established by the lawful authority in it were openly transgressed and annulled, more especially where the alteration of religion was endeavoured, and a religion contrary to law designed to be introduced, whereas they who were most immediately concerned therein were indispensably bound to preserve the established laws, liberties, and customs, and, above all, the religion and worship of God established among them, and to take effectual care that the inhabitants of such state or kingdom might neither be deprived of their religion nor ousted of their civil rights, more especially since the greatness of kings, royal families, and all in authority, as well as the happiness of their subjects and people, depended in a more especial manner upon an exact observation of those their laws, liberties and customs; upon which ground his Highness further declared that he could no longer forbear to let the world know how apparently he saw with regret that they who had then the chief credit with the King had overturned the religion, laws, and liberties of these realms, and subjected them in all things relating to their consciences, liberties, and properties to arbitrary government, and that not only by secret and indirect ways, but in an open and undisguised manner; that those evil counsellors, for advancing and covering this with some plausible pretences, did invent and set on foot the King's dispensing power, by virtue of which they pretend that, according to law, he can suspend and dispense with the execution of those laws that have been enacted by the authority of King and Parliament for the security and happiness of the subject, and to render these laws of no effect, but it is most certain that they cannot be suspended but by the same authority that made them; for, though the King may pardon the punishment of a transgressor in cases of treason and felony, yet it cannot, with any colour of reason, be thence inferred that he can entirely suspend the execution of those laws unless he has such an arbitrary power that the laws, liberties, honours and estates of the subjects depend wholly upon his good-will and pleasure; and though they have obtained a sentence for asserting this dispensing power to be a right depending on the Crown, yet it cannot be imagined that it should be put in the power of twelve judges to offer up the laws, rights, and liberties of the whole nation to the arbitrary will of the King, especially such as are first advanced, and then threatened to be turned out if they do not comply therein; and some Papists, who are incapable by law, are made judges.

"That the King, though known to be a Papist, was yet received and acknowledged by the people to be their King, and did so solemnly swear and promise at his coronation that he would maintain their laws and liberties, and the Church of England, as it was established by law; and though several laws have been lately made for preserving their liberties and the Protestant religion, and to prevent all Papists from being put into employment, yet these evil counsellors have in effect annulled and abolished all those laws, and in direct opposition thereto have set up an illegal commission, for ecclesiastical affairs, in which one of the King's ministers, who is a Papist, sits and acts, though by law incapable of any public employment; that these Commissioners have suspended the Bishop of London, only for refusing to obey an order to suspend a worthy divine without citation or process; they have turned out the President and Fellows of Magdalen College, without citing them before any legal court or competent judge, only for refusing to choose for their legal president a person recommended by these evil counsellors, contrary to the right of free election, and contrary to Magna Charta, 'That no man shall lose life or goods but by the law of the land;' and afterward put the College wholly into the hands of Papists. They have cited before them all the chancellors and archdeacons of England, to certify the names of the clergy, who did not read the King's declaration for liberty of conscience, though the reading of it was not enjoined them by the Bishops, who are their ordinaries. These evil counsellors have procured orders for building several Popish churches, chapels, monasteries, colleges of Jesuits for corrupting of youth, and raised one to be a privy councillor and minister of State, contrary to several express laws, by the rules of which they evidently show that they are no way restrained, and wherein they are served and seconded by these ecclesiastical commissioners.

"They have also followed the same methods in civil affairs, by procuring orders to examine all lord-lieutenants, deputy-lieutenants, sheriffs, justices of peace, and all others that were in any public employment, whether they were for taking away the penal laws and tests, and those who in conscience could not comply were turned out, and divers unqualified persons put in their rooms; they have seized upon the charters of several towns, and procured the surrender of others, which elect parliament men; and placed new magistrates, many of them

Papists in divers corporations. They have removed such judges, as would not, in all things, conform to their designs, and put in others whose compliance they discerned beforehand; whereby much blood had been shed in many places of the kingdom against all the forms and rules of law, without suffering the persons accused to plead in their own defence. They have put the administration of justice into the hads of Papists, though all their sentences are null and void in law, and have disposed of all military employments, in the same manner both by sea and land, to strangers as well as natives, and Irish as well as English, to maintain and execute their wicked designs of enslaving the nation, by their assistance. In Ireland, the whole government is put into the hands of Papists, so that the Protestants through terror have in great number left that kingdom, and abandoned their estates in it, remembering well that cruel and bloody massacre in 1641. In Scotland the King has declared himself clothed with such an absolute power as to be obeyed without reserve.

"These great oppressions, and open contempts of all laws, being insufferable, have put the subjects under great fears, and to look out for such lawful remedies as are allowed of in all nations; but to deter them from endeavouring to preserve their lives and estates by petition, or other means authorized by law, the evil counsellors proceeded with rigour against those who used those methods, particularly the Archbishop of Canterbury, and others, who humbly offering their reasons, why they could not order the declaration of liberty of conscience to be read in the churches, were sent to prison, and after trial, as if guilty of some enormous crime, and obliged to appear before proposed Papists, and those judges that gave their opinion in their favour were turned out. They have also treated a peer of the realm as a criminal, for saying, that the subjects were not bound to obey the orders of a Popish justice of the peace, because they were put into employments contrary to the law.

"That his Highness, and his dearest and most beloved consort, the Princess, have signified to the King, in terms full of respect, the just and deep regret these proceedings have given them, and, in compliance with his desires, have declared their thoughts about repealing the penal laws and tests, whereby they hoped there might have been a happy agreement among the subjects of all persuasions, which yet these evil counsellors have so misrepresented, as to endeavour to alienate the King more and more from them, as if they designed to disturb the quiet and happiness of the kingdom; and the last and great remedy for all these great evils being the calling of a parliament, for securing the nation against the practices of these evil counsellors, cannot be easily brought about, since by a parliament duly chosen, they doubt to be called to account for all their open violations of the laws, their plots and conspiracies against the Protestant religion, and the lives and liberties of the subjects, their designing, under the specious pretence of liberty of conscience, to sow divisions among Protestants, and from their mutual quarrels to carry on their own designs, to prèvent which, the electors and elected for parliament men, are to be beforehand engaged to comply with their wicked designs, and the returns are to be made by Popish sheriffs and mayors of towns, so that this only remedy of a free parliament is hereby made impracticable.

"And to crown all, there are great and violent presumptions, inducing their Highnesses to believe that these evil counsellors to gain more time to carry on their ill designs for encouraging their accomplices, and discouraging all the good subjects, they have published that the Queen hath brought forth a son, though there appeared, both during the Queen's pretended bigness, and in the manner in which the birth was managed, so many just and visible grounds of suspicion, that not only their Highnesses, but all the good subjects of this kingdom, vehemently suspect that the pretended Prince of Wales was not born of the Queen; and since their Highnesses have both so great an interest in this matter, and such a right, as all the world knows, to the succession of the crown, and since the English nation had ever testified a most particular affection and esteem to them both; their Highnesses cannot excuse themselves from espousing their interests in a matter of such high consequence, and from contributing all that in them lies, for the maintaining of the Protestant religion, and to the laws and liberties of those kingdoms, and for securing to them the continual enjoyment of all their just rights: to the doing of which, his Highness is most earnestly solicited by a great many lords, both spiritual and temporal, and by many gentlemen and other subjects of all ranks.

"Therefore it is, that his Highhess hath thought fit to go over into England, and to carry over a force sufficient, by the blessing of God, to defend him from violence of those evil counsellors; his Highness declaring that this expedition is intended for no other design, but to have a free and lawful parliament assembled as soon as it is possible, and that, in order thereto, all the late charter, limiting of elections, contrary to custom, shall be considered as null and of no force, and all magistrates to return to their former employment, and particularly the ancient charter of London, to be again in force; and none to be suffered to choose or be chosen parliament men, but those qualified by law; and that the members of parliament so chosen shall sit in full freedom for making laws to secure the Protestant religion, and to establish a good agreement between the Church of England and all Protestant Dissenters; as also, for the securing and covering of Papists, and all others, who will live peaceably from all persecution for religion, and for doing all other things, which the two Houses of Parliament shall find necessary for the peace, honour and safety of the nation, so that there may be no more danger of the nation's falling at any time hereafter under arbitrary government; to which parliament his Highness will also refer the inquiry into the birth of the pretended Prince of Wales, and of all things relating to it, and the right of succession.

"And his Highness declares that for his part he will concur in everything that may produce the peace and happiness of the nation, which a free and lawful parliament shall determine, since his Highness hath nothing before his eyes in this his undertaking, but the preservation of the Protestant religion, the covering of all men from persecution for their consciences, and the securing to the whole nation the free enjoyments of all their laws, rights and liberties under a just and legal government.

His Highness further declares that this is the design he has proposed in appearing upon this occasion in arms; in the conduct of which his Highness would keep the forces under his command, under all the strictness of martial discipline, and take a special care that the people of the countries through which he shall march, shall not suffer by their means; and, as soon as the state of the nation will permit it, his Highness promises that he will send back all those foreign troops that he hath brought along with him; his Highness does therefore hope that all the people will judge rightly of his proceedings; though he does chiefly rely on the blessing of God for the success of this his undertaking, in which he places his whole and only confidence.

"Lastly, his Highness doth invite and require all persons whatsoever, all the peers of the realm, both spiritual and temporal, all lords-lieutenants, deputy-lieutenants, and all gentlemen, citizens and other commons of all ranks, to come and assist him, in order to the executing of this his design, against all such as shall endeavour to oppose him; that so, all those miseries which must need follow, upon the nations being kept under arbitrary government and slavery, may be prevented, and that all the violences and disorders which have overturned the whole consitution of the English government, may be fully redressed in a free and legal parliament. His Highness likewise resolving that as soon as the nations are brought to a state of quiet, he will take care that a parliament will be called in Scotland, for restoring the ancient constitution of that kingdom, and for bringing the matters of religion to such a settlement that the people may be easy and happy; for putting an end to all the unjust violences that have been, in a course of so many years, committed there : and that his Highness will also study to bring the kingdom of Ireland to such a state that the settlement there may be religiously observed, and that the Protestant and British interests may be secured, and will endeavour, by all possible means, to procure such an establishment in all the three kingdoms, that they may all live in a happy union and correspondence together, and that the Protestant religion, and the peace and happiness of these nations, may be established upon lasting foundations."

Soon after, his Highness published an additional declaration to this effect:

"That after he had prepared and printed the former declaration, his Highness understood that the subverters of the religion and laws of the kingdom, hearing of this preparation to assist the people against them, had begun to retract some of their arbitrary and despotic powers, and vacated some unjust judgments and decrees, occasioned by the sense of their guilt, and the distrust of their force, hoping thereby to quiet the people, and divert them from demanding the re-establishment of their religion and laws, under the shelter of his Highness' arms; and do also give out that his Highness intended to conquer and enslave the nation: though his Highness is confident that no person can have such hard thoughts of him as to imagine that he hath any other design in this undertaking than to procure a settlement of religion, of the liberties and properties of the subjects upon so sure a foundation, that there may be no danger of the nations relapsing into the like miseries at any time hereafter, and as the forces that his Highness brought along with him are utterly disproportioned to the wicked design of conquering the nation, if he were capable of intending it; so the great number of the principal nobility and gentry that are men of eminent quality and estates, and of known integrity and zeal for the religion and government of England who do accompany, and have earnestly solicited his Highness to this expedition, will cover him from all such malicious insinuations; since it cannot be imagined that these should join in a wicked attempt of conquest, to make void their own lawful titles to their honours, estates and interests. His Highness is likewise confident that all men see how little weight is to be laid on the promises and engagements that can be now made, since there has been so little regard had to them in times past; and the imperfect redress that is now offered, as it is a plain confession of the violations of the government, which his Highness hath set forth, so the defect thereof appears, since they lay down nothing but what they can take up at pleasure, still reserving entire their claims and pretences to that absolute power which has been the root of all their oppression and the subversion of the government; and it is plain there can be no remedy, no redress but in parliament, by a declaration of the rights of the subjects that have been invaded, and not by any pretended Acts of Grace, to which the extremity of their affairs has driven them; therefore it is that his Highness has thought fit to declare that he will refer all to a free assembly of the nation in a lawful parliament."

His Highness likewise sent the following letter to all the offcers and seamen of the English fleet :— "Gentlemem and friends, we have published a declaration, containing a full and true account of our intentions in this expedition: since it is evident that the Papists have resolved the total extirpation of the Protestant religion in Great Britain, and will infallibly reduce you to the same condition in which you see France, if they get once the upper hand. Yor are now at last sensible that you are made use of only as instruments to bring this nation under Popery and slavery by means of the Irish and other foreigners that are assembling for your destruction. Therefore we hope that the Almighty God will inspire you with such thoughts as may facilitate your deliverance, and preserve your country and religion from all these impending miseries, and whereas, in all probability, this can never be effected unless you join with us, who labour for your deliverance, we do expect your assistance herein; and shall always remember," &c.

The Prince sent a letter also to the King's army to the same purpose, intimating to them what they might expect both form the cashiering of all the Protestant and English officers and soldiers in Ireland, and by the Irish being brought over to be put in their places, when it should be thought convenient for themselves to be turned out; hoping withal that they would not be abused by a false notion of honour, but would consider what they owed to God, their religion and their country, themselves and their posterity, which were to be preferred before all private considerations and engagements whatsoever.

Whilst his Highness continued at Exeter, the King seemed very resolute at London to oppose him in person, mustering his army at Hounslow Heath, and beating up for volunteers in the streets, though with little success; he then sent for the Bishops, whom he had so lately contemptuously used, to advise him what measures to take in this exigency, who accordingly came in a body, and the Archbishop of Canterbury, in the name of the rest, delivered himself to this effect:—"That it was necessary for him to restore all things to the State wherein he found them when he came to the crown, by committing all offices of trust to those qualified by law, and to redress such grievances as were generally complained of: to put an effectual stop to all dispensations, and recall and cancel those which had been obtained of him: to dissolve the ecclesiastical commission, and promise the people never to erect the like for the future: to restore the universities to their legal state, particularly both the Magdalen colleges, and not to permit any to enjoy preferment but those qualified by the statutes of the university and the laws of the land: to suppress the Jesuits' schools, and grant no more licences to scuh, being apparently against law and his own interests: to send inhibitions after those four Roman bishops who, under the title of apostolic vicars, presumed to exercise illegal jurisdiction within the kingdom: to suffer no more Quo Warrantos against corporations and to restore those charters which had been taken away: to fill up the vacant bishoprics with persons qualified by law: to act no more by virtue of a dispensing power, but permit it to be settled by Act of Parliament. That upon the restoration of corporations he would call a free Parliament, and suffer them to sit to redress grievances. Lastly, to permit the bishops to lay such motives and arguments before him as, by the blessing of God, might bring him back to the communion of the Church of England, into whose Catholic faith he had been baptized." Not long after the Lords spiritual and temporal presented the King the following petition:—

"We, your Majesty's most loyal subjects, in a deep sense of the miseries of a war now breaking forth in the bowels of this your kingdom, and of the danger to which your Majesty's sacred person is thereby like to be exposed, and also of the distractions of your people, by reason of their present grievances, do think ourselves bound in conscience of the duty we owe to God and our holy religion, to your

Majesty and our country, most humbly to offer to your Majesty that, in our opinion, the only visible way to preserve your Majesty, and this your kingdom, would be the calling of a parliament, regular and free in all its circumstances. We, therefore, do most earnestly beseech your Majesty that you would be graciously pleased, with all speed, to call such a Parliament, wherein we shall be most ready to promote such counsels, and resolutions of peace, and settlements in Church and State, as many conduce to your Majesty's honour and safety, and to the quieting the minds of your people.

"We do likewise humbly beseech your Majesty, in the meantime, to use such means for the preventing the effusion of Christian blood as to your Majesty shall seem most meet.

"And your petitioners shall ever pray, &c.

"W. Cant,	Nom. Ebor.,
Grafton,	W. Asaph,
Ormond,	Fran. Erly,
Dorset,	Tho. Roffen,
Clare,	Th. Petriburg,
Clarendon,	T. Oxon,
Burlington,	Paget,
Anglesey,	Chandos,
Rochester,	Osulston."
Newport,	

Presented by the Archbishop of Canterbury, the Archbishop of York elect, the Bishop of Ely, and the Bishop of Rochester, the 17th of November, 1688. To which the King returned the following answer:—

"My Lords,

"What you ask of me I most passionately desire, and I promise you, upon the faith of a King, that I will have a Parliament, and such a one as you ask for, as soon as the Prince of Orange has quitted this realm; for how is it possible a Parliament should be free in all its circumstances, as you petition for, whilst an enemy is in the kingdom, and can make a return of near a hundred voices?"

His Highness lay some days at Exeter, expecting that such gentlemen as resided nearest his court should have come to him sooner than those at a distance, but finding something of an unexpected slowness, he could not forbear to signify some little resentment to some of the principal gentlemen of Somersetshire and Devonshire, that came to join him, on the 15th of November, 1688, in the following speech:—

"Though we know not all your persons, yet we have a catalogue of all your names, and remember the character of your worth and interest in your country. You see we are come according to your invitation and our promise. Our duty to God obliges us to protect the Protestant religion, and our love to mankind your liberties and properties. We expected you that dwelt so near the place of our landing would have joined us sooner; not that it is now too late, nor that we want your military assistance, so much as your countenance and presence to justify our declared pretensions, rather than accomplish our good and gracious designs. Though we have brought both a fleet and a good army to render these kingdoms happy, by rescuing all Protestants from Popery, slavery and arbitrary power; by restoring them to their rights and properties established by law; and by promoting of peace and trade, which is the soul of government, and the very life-blood of a nation; yet we rely more on the goodness of God and the justice of our cause than on any human force and power whatever, yet since God has pleased we shall make use of human means, and not expect miracles, for our preservation and happiness, let us not neglect making use of this gracious opportunity, but, with prudence and courage put in execution our honourable purposes. Therefore, gentlemen, friends and fellow-Protestants, we bid you and all your followers most heartily welcome to our court and camp. Let the whole world now judge if our pretensions are not just, generous, sincere, and above price, since we might have even a bridge of gold to return back; but It is our principle and resolution rather to die in a good cause than live in a bad one, well knowing that virtue and true honour is its own reward, and the happiness of mankind our great and only design."

But quickly after, his Highness found the English nobility and gentry no less faithful to him than he had been to them, and that his several declarations had the wished effect. The Lord Wharton and the Lord Colchester, with a strong party, marched through Oxford to his Highness's camp without opposition. The Lord Lovelace, with another party out of Oxfordshire, got as far as Cirencester, but were opposed, and himself taken prisoner by the county militia; yet his whole party, except four or five that were slain or maimed in the skirmish, broke their way through, and his lordship was soon after released out of Gloucester prison by young gentlemen of that county, who took up arms for the Prince, and drove out all the Popish crew that were settled in that city. The Lord Delamere, having raised a considerable force in Cheshire, advanced to Nottingham to join the gentlemen of that county, who were ready to receive him; and on the 22nd of November, at the rendezvous there, the following declaration was published:

"We, the nobility, gentry, and commonalty of these northern counties, assembled together at Nottingham, for the defence of the laws, religion and properties, according to those free-born liberties and privileges descended to us from our ancestors, as the undoubted birthright of the subjects of this kingdom of England (not doubting but the infringers and invaders of our rights will represent us to the rest of the nations in the most malicious dress they can put upon us), do here unanimously think it our duty to declare to the rest of our Protestant fellow-subjects the ground of our present undertaking.

"We are, by innumerable grievances, made sensible that the very fundamentals of our religion, liberties and properties are about to be rooted out by our late Jesuitical Privy Council, as hath been of late too apparent. 1. By the King's dispensing with all the established laws at his pleasure. 2. By displacing all officers out of all offices of trust and advantage, and placing others in their room that are known Papists, deservedly made incapable by the established laws of our land. 3. By destroying the charters of most corporations in the land. 4. By discouraging all persons who are not Papists, preferring such as turn to Popery. 5. By displacing all honest and conscientious judges, unless they would, contrary to their consciences, declare that to be law which was merely arbitrary. 6. By branding all men with the name of rebels that but offered to justify the laws, in a legal course, against the arbitrary proceedings of the King, or any of his corrupt ministers. 7. By burdening the nation with an army to maintain the violation of the rights of the subjects. 8. By discountenancing the established reformed religion. 9. By forbidding the subjects the benefit of petitioning, and constructing them libellers, so rendering the laws a nose of wax to serve their arbitrary ends; and many more such like, too long here to enumerate.

"We being thus made sadly sensible of the arbitrary and tyrannical government that is, by the influence of Jesuitical counsels, coming upon us, do unanimously declare that not being willing to deliver our posterity over to such a condition of Popery and slavery as the aforesaid oppressions inevitably threaten, we will, to the utmost of our power, oppose the same by joining with the Prince of Orange (whom we hope God Almighty hath sent to rescue us from the oppressions aforesaid); will use our utmost endeavours for the recovery of our almost ruined laws, liberties and religion; and herein we hope all good Protestant subjects will, with their lives and fortunes, be assistant to us, and not be bugbeared with the opprobrious terms of rebels, by which they would fright us to become perfect slaves to their tyrannical insolences and usurpations; for we assure ourselves that no rational and unbiassed person will judge it rebellion to defend our laws and religion, which all our Princes have sworn at their coronations; which oath, how well it hath been observed of late, we desire a free Parliament may have the consideration of.

"We own it rebellion to resist a King that governs by law; but he was always accounted a tyrant that made his will the law; and to resist such a one we justly esteem no rebellion, but a necessary defence; and in this consideration we doubt not of all honest men's assistance, and humbly hope for and implore the great God's protection, that turneth the hearts of His people as pleaseth Him best, it having been observed that people can never be of one mind without his inspiration, which hath in all ages confirmed that observation, 'Vox populi est vox Dei.'

"The present restoring of charters, and reversing the oppressing and unjust judgment given on Magdalen College Fellows, is plain are but to still the people, like plums to children, by deceiving them for a while; but if they shall by this stratagem be fooled till this present storm that threatens the Papists be passed, as soon as they shall be resettled, the former oppression will be put on with greater vigour; but we hope in vain is the net spread in the sight of the bird, for—1. The Papists' old rule is, that faith is not to be kept with heretics, as they term Protestants, though the Popish religion is the greatest heresy; and 2. Queen Mary's so ill observing her promises to the Suffolk men that helped her to her throne; and above all, 3. The Pope's dispensing with the breach of oaths, treaties or promises, at his pleasure, when it makes for the service of the holy church, as they term it. These, we say, are such convincing reasons to hinder us from giving credit to the aforesaid mock shows of redress, that we think ourselves bound in conscience to rest on no security that shall not be approved by a freely elected Parliament, to whom, under God, we refer our cause."

The Lord Delamere, being assured of the resolution and courageous zeal of his followers, continued awhile in those parts to watch the motions of the Papists in Lancashire, who began to take arms under the Lord Molineux, and for a time assisted to guard Chester for the King; but upon the surprisal of that garrison for the Prince, were soon after beaten, or, rather, ran away out of the town, and disbanded of themselves. In the north the Earl of Danby, the Lord Fairfax, and other persons of quality seized upon the city of York, and turned out the Lord Mayor and other magistrates that were Papists and ill-affected. Colonel Copley, the Deputy-Governor of Hull, seized upon all the guards of that garrison, and, with the assistance of some of the townsmen and some seamen, made the Lord Langdale, the Governor, and the Lord Montgomery, the Marquis of Powis, his sons, prisoners, till he had secured the citadel, wherein was a plentiful magazine of powder and all sorts of provisions, with a train of artillery ready fixed to be drawn out into the field. Plymouth, also, with the Earl of Huntington and all the Popish officers and soldiers, were seized by the Earl of Bath for his Highness, and at the same time all the chief seaport towns in Cornwall declared for the Prince, so that there was no enemy behind him to disturb the rear of his advancing army.

But the King, being as yet in hopes to force his way through all the great opposition made him by the whole kingdom, having sent his army before to Salisbury, went thither to them; yet, before he went, he thought it requisite to provide for the safety of the pretended Prince of Wales, and not daring to trust to the validity of the aforementioned affidavits, for more security he sent him away with a strong guard to Portsmouth, that, if things went ill, he should be conveyed over to France. When the King came to Salisbury he began to bleed at the nose and was observed to continue bleeding for some time, which seemed at that time ominous to him; but, in the midst of these surprises, more ill news arrived to increase his astonishment; for besides the Lord Cornbury, who had carried off a considerable party of horse to the Prince some time before, several other regiments of foot had now deserted and were gone the same way. Upon his arrival near to Salisbury he was met by the Duke of Berwick, the Earl of Feversham, and several other officers on horseback, and by them attended to the gates of the town, being met by the mayor and aldermen in their formalities, and conducted to the bishop's palace; but these flattering appearances soon vanished, he quickly perceiving that his English forces were generally dissatisfied and seemed unwilling to engage in civil bloodshed against their own countrymen and of their own religion, which was to fight with their bodies against their consciences, and likewise discovered the discontents of the people, who supplied the machels very sparingly for his army, so that not judging himself safe among them, and upon a false alarm that Marshal Schomberg was within thirty or twenty miles of him, he returned back in all haste to Windsor, and from thence to London, being extremely discouraged that Prince George and the Lord Churchill were both gone to the Prince, and that the Princess Anne of Denmark was also retired from the Court. The Prince of Denmark and the Lord Churchill left each of them the following letters behind them, directed to the King:—

" Sir,

" With a heart full of grief I am forced to write what prudence will not permit me to say to your face; and may I ever find credit with your Majesty, and protection from heaven, as what I now do is free from passion, vanity or design, with which actions of this nature are too often accompanied. I am not ignorant of the frequent mischiefs wrought in the world by factious pretences of religion; but were not religion the most justifiable cause, it would be made the most specious pretence; and your Majesty has always shown too uninterested a sense of religion to doubt the just effects of it in one whose practices have, I hope, never given the world cause to censure his real conviction of it or his backwardness to perform what his honour and conscience prompt him to. How then can I longer disguise my just concern for that religion in which I have been so happily educated, which my judgment thoroughly convinces me to be the best, and for the support of which I am so highly interested in my native country; and is not England now, by the most endearing tie, become so?

"Whilst the restless spirits of the enemies of the reformed religion, backed by the cruel zeal of France, justly alarm and unite all the Protestant Princes of Christendom, and engage them in so vast an expense for the support of it, can I act so degenerate and mean a part as to deny my concurrence to such worthy endeavours for disabusing of your Majesty by the reinforcement of those laws, and establishment of that government, on which alone depends the well-being of your Majesty and the Protestant religion in Europe? This, sir, is that irresistible and only cause that could come in competition with my duty and obligations with your Majesty, and be able to tear me from you, whilst the same affectionate desire of serving you continues in me. Could I secure your person by the hazard of my life, I should think it could not be better employed; and would to God these your distracted kingdoms might yet receive that satisfactory compliance from your Majesty in all their justifiable pretensions, as might, upon the only sure foundation, that of love and interests of your subjects, establish your government, and as strongly unite the hearts of all your subjects to you, as is that of, sir, your Majesty's most humble and most obedient son and servant."

The Lord Churchill's letter ran thus:

"Sir,

"Men are seldom suspected of sincerity when they act contrary to their interests; and though my dutiful behaviour to your Majesty in the worst of times (for which I acknowledge my poor services much overpaid) may not be sufficient to incline you to a charitable interpretation of my actions, yet I hope the great advantage I enjoy under your Majesty which I can never expect in any other change of government, may reasonably convince your Majesty and the world that I am actuated by a higher principle, when I offer that violence to my inclination and interest as to desert your Majesty at a time when your affairs seem to challenge the strictest obedience from all your subjects, much more from one who lies under the greatest personal obligations imaginable to your Majesty. This, sir, could proceed from nothing but the inviolable dictates of my conscience, and necessary concern for my religion (which no good man can oppose), and with which, I am instructed, nothing ought to come in competition. Heaven knows with what partiality my dutiful opinion of your Majesty hath hitherto represented those unhappy designs which inconsiderate and self-interested men have framed against your Majesty's true interest and the Protestant religion. But as I can no longer join with such to give a pretence by conquest to bring them to effect, so will I always with the hazard of my life and fortune (so much your Majesty's due) endeavour to preserve your royal person and lawful rights, with all the tender concern and dutiful respect that becomes, sir, your Majesty's most dutiful and most obliged subject and servant."

The Princess Anne of Denmark likewise directed the following letter to the Queen, upon her withdrawing:—

"Madame,

"I beg your pardon if I am so deeply affected with the surprising news of the Prince's being gone, as not to be able to see you, but to leave this paper to express my humble duty to the King and yourself; and to let you know that I am gone to absent myself to avoid the King's displeasure, which I am not able to bear either against the Prince or myself; and I shall stay at so great a distance as not to return before I hear the happy news of reconcilement; and as I am confident the Prince did not leave the King with any other design than to use all possible means for his preservation, so I hope you will do me the justice to believe that I am incapable of following him for any other end. Never was any one in such an unhappy condition, so divided between duty and affection to a father and a husband; and therefore I know not what to do but to follow one and preserve the other. I see the general falling off of the nobility and gentry, who avow to have no other end than to prevail with the King to secure their religion which they saw in so much danger by the violent counsels of the priests, who, to promote their own religion, did not care to what dangers they exposed the King. I am fully persuaded that the Prince of Orange designs the King's safety and preservation, and hope all things may be composed without more bloodshed, by the calling a Parliament. God grant a happy end to these troubles, that the King's reign may be prosperous, and that I may shortly meet you in perfect peace and safety; till when, let me beg you to continue the same favourable opinion that you have hitherto had of your most obedient daughter and servant,

"ANNE."

The King now issued out a proclamation of pardon to all his subjects that had taken up arms under the Prince, if they returned within twenty days; but very few or none came back, and about the same time, a party of the Prince's men being abroad, and advancing beyond their strength, were pursued and charged by Colonel Sarsfield, with seventy horse and thirty dragoons and grenadiers, who overtaking them at Wincanton, they posted themselves behind the hedges; whereupon the King's party dismounted and marched up to them, and they began to fire briskly, several being killed and wounded; but Colonel Sarsfield getting into the field with his horse, and charging them in the rear, they were most of them killed or taken prisoners; Lieutenant Campbell, who commanded them, being slain, and of the King's party four were killed, and Cornet Webb mortally wounded. This slender success was soon damped by an address from the fleet for a free Parliament, which now began to grow cold in his service, and the continual desertions of his army; so that the King not thinking it convenient to hazard a battle with them, upon the approach of the Prince's forces, with whom now were a great part of the nobility, he recalled the remainder of them, with his train of artillery; and upon his return to Whitehall he appointed Colonel Beril Skelton to be Lieutenant of the Tower, in the place of Sir Edward

Hales; and in pursuance of the advice of the Lords spiritual and temporal, ordered the Chancellor Jeffries to issue out writs for summoning a Parliament to sit Jan. 15th following. The Bishop of Exeter, who left the city upon the approach of the Prince, was likewise nominated Archbishop of York, which had been vacant for some time, and was thought to have been designated for Father Peters, if things had gone on. But the King's affairs growing daily more desperate, and the Prince of Orange marching forward with his army, and being advanced to Hungerford, after a consultation with the Queen and the Jesuits, it was resolved to send the following proposals of accommodation to his Highness, which were soon after published, with the Prince's answer thereto:

"Whereas, on the 8th of December, 1688, at Hungerford, a paper signed by the Marquis of Halifax, the Earl of Nottingham, and the Lord Godolphin, Commissioners sent unto us from his Majesty, was delivered to us in these words following, viz.:

"'Sir,

"'The King commandeth us to acquaint you that he observeth all the differences and causes of complaint alleged by your Highness, seem to be referred to a free Parliament. His Majesty, as he hath already declared, was resolved before this to call one, but thought that, in the present state of affairs, it was advisable to defer it till things were more composed. Yet seeing that his people continue to desire it, he hath put forth his proclamation in order to it, and hath issued forth his writs for the calling of it. And to prevent any cause of interruption in it, he will consent to anything that can be reasonably required for the security of all those who shall come to it. His Majesty hath therefore sent us to attend your Highness for the adjusting of all matters that shall be agreed to be necessary to the freedom of elections, and the security of sitting, and is ready immediately to enter into a treaty, in order to it. His Majesty proposeth, that in the meantime the respective armies may be retained within such limits, and at such a distance from London, as may prevent the apprehensions that the Parliament may in any kind be disturbed, being desirous that the meeting of it may be no longer delayed than it must be by the usual and necessary forms.

(Signed)   "'HALIFAX,
"'NOTTINGHAM,
"'GODOLPHIN.'

"We, with the advice of the lords and gentlemen assembled with us, have, in answer to the same, made these proposals: 1. That all Papists and such persons as are not qualified by law, be disarmed, disbanded, and removed from all employments, civil and military. 2. That all proclamations which reflect upon us or any that have come to us, or declared for us to be recalled; and that if any persons, for having so assisted, have been committed, that they be forthwith set at liberty. 3. That for the security and safety of the City of London, the custody and government of the Tower be immediately put in the hands of the said city. 4. That if His Majesty shall think fit to be at London during the sitting of the Parliament we may be there also, with an equal number of our guards; or if His Majesty shall please to be in any place from London, at whatever distance he thinks fit, that we may be at a place at the same distance. And that the respective armies do remove from London thirty miles, and that no more foreign forces be brought into the kingdom. 5. That for the security of the City of London and their trade, Tilbury Fort be put into the hands of the said city. 6. That to prevent the landing of French or other foreign troops, Portsmouth may be put into such hands as by your Majesty and us shall be agreed upon. 7. That some sufficient part of the public revenue be assigned us, for the maintaining of our forces, until the meeting of a free Parliament.

But these proposals of the Prince proving of too hard digestion at Whitehall, the offer of accommodation was thought to be designed only to gain time; and the Romish counsellors perceiving that this would not obtain, began to think of other measures; so that the child being sent for back from Portsmouth to Whitehall in great haste, the Queen having made up her equipage, December 10, took her solemn leave of the King, with the pretended Prince of Wales and her attendants, whereof it is said that Father Peters was one—but it was thought with a large proportion of treasure and jewels—she crossed the water to Lambeth, where three coaches with six horses awaited them, and with a strong guard went to Greenwich, and so to Gravesend, where she and her retinue embarked in a yacht for France, and landed the next day about four o'clock in the afternoon. The Queen and several courtiers being gone, the Popish priests began to shift for themselves; and the same night the King called an extraordinary council, and sent for the Lord Mayor and Sheriffs of London, charging them to preserve the place and quiet of the city as much as in them lay, after which they were dismissed; but the council continued their debates upon the present exigency of affairs a great while longer, and were ordered to meet again the next morning, when, to the surprise of the city and kingdom, about three o'clock in the morning the King took barge at the privy stairs with a small equipage, and went down the river, without being so much as known to many of the officers of his household who were then in waiting; whose sudden departure may be supposed to be occasioned by the news that alarmed the Court the day before, that the Prince's forces had made their way through Reading, and gained the pass of Twyford Bridge, without any considerable resistance; for about fifteen hundred horse and three troops of dragoons being quartered in the town of Reading, they had noticed that a detachment of the Prince's army were marching up towards them, which put them into such a consternation that, not finding themselves strong enough to maintain the town, the officers, upon consultation, concluded to draw off and make good their post at Twyford Bridge; but their scouts coming in with news that the roads were clear, the commander ordered a Scotch regiment of horse and the Irish dragoons to march back and repossess themselves of Reading, which they did, and were placed in the market-place and other posts, continuing on horseback the most part of the night, to prevent surprise; yet, hearing no more of the Prince's advanced party, their officers ordered them to alight and refresh themselves and their horses; but about ten in the morning the trumpets sounded to horse, the Prince's forces being at the town's end almost before they were discovered; and thereupon sharp firing began on both sides, the Irish dragoons bearing the brunt of the encounter; and though the Scotch horse, in small detached bodies, made some fire, yet they were overpowered, driven out of the towns, and obliged to retreat to Twyford Bridge; and at length many of the King's party deserted, and the rest were constrained to quit the pass and make the best of their retreat, there being about thirty killed and several wounded in this skirmish.

Upon this ill success, and the King having no considerable forces left, the day before his going away he sent a letter to his general, the Earl of Feversham, to this effect:—" That things being come to that extremity, he had been forced to send away the Queen and his son, the Prince of Wales, lest they should fall into his enemy's hands, he was resolved to secure himself the best way he could; and if he could have relied on all his troops he was resolved to have at least one blow for it; but that his lordship knew, and both his lordship and several of the general officers of the army had told him, that it was not safe to venture at the head of his troops, or to think to fight the Prince of Orange with them; and, therefore, it only remained for him to thank those officers and soldiers that had been truly loyal to him, not expecting they should further expose themselves in resisting a foreign enemy and a poisoned nation." In pursuance of this letter, the Earl of Feversham sent another to his Highness the Prince of Orange, to let him understand that " he had received a letter from the King, with the unfortunate news of his resolution to go out of England, and he was actually gone, with orders to make no opposition against any one, which he thought convenient to let his Highness know as soon as it was possible to hinder the effusion of blood, having already given orders to that purpose to all the troops under his command, which would be the last order they should receive from him."

The King's departure being publicly known, the multitude got together in divers places, as is usual in such disturbances, and dissolutions of government, spoiling and demolishing the newly-erected mass-houses and chapels; pulling down, burning and destroying all before them, they plucked down the new convent for monks at St. John's, which had been two years in building, at vast expense, and burnt the greatest part of the timber and materials in Smithfield, having before seized upon the goods, as they were removing, and burnt them in Holborn; they likewise defaced the chapels in Lime-street and Lincoln's-Inn Fields with that of the Spanish ambassador's at Wild-house, where some common thieves mixed with the more harmless boys, they got great store of plunder in plate, money, and rich goods; they likewise committed violences at the lodgings of the resident of the Duke of Florence, and much defaced the dwelling-houses of several eminent Papists, who were fled for fear of being secured; and though the magistrates laboured to quiet these tumults and disorders, yet they found their authority too weak till the mobile had in some measure vented their rage, they being grown so numerous that neither the watches nor trained bands thought it safe to oppose their fury.

Therefore, for redress of these mischiefs, the Lords, spiritual and temporal, then in town, repaired to Guildhall, and sending for Colonell Skelton, then Lieutenant of the Tower, demanded the keys, which being by him readily resigned, they committed the charge of that important place to the Lord Lucas, a person of known honour and integrity to his coun-

try; nor were they less active in suppressing those lawless rioters; that in a short time they were all dispersed and quelled, and some of the principal committed to prison, and then taking into consideration the great and dangerous conjuncture of the time, in regard of the King's having withdrawn himself, they drew up a declaration to this effect:—
"That they did reasonably hope that the King having issued out his proclamation and writs for calling a free Parliament, they might have rested securely under the expectation of that meeting, but that the King having withdrawn himself, as they apprehended, in order to his departure out of the kingdom, by the pernicious counsels of persons ill affected to the nation, they cannot, without being wanted to their duty, be silent under the calamities wherein the Popish councils, which had so long prevailed, had miserably involved them; and therefore unanimously resolved to apply themselves to his Highness the Prince of Orange, who, with so great kindness to these kingdoms, so vast expense, and so much hazard to his own person, had undertaken, by endeavouring to procure a free Parliament, to rescue them, with as little effusion of Christian blood as possible, from the imminent dangers of Popery and slavery; declaring further that they would, with their utmost endeavours, assist his Highness in the obtaining of such a Parliament with all speed; wherein their laws, liberties and properties might be secured, the Church of England in particular, with a due liberty to Protestant dissenters; and, in general, the Protestant religion and interest over the whole world might be supported and encouraged, to the glory of God, the happiness of the established government, and the advantages of all Princes and States in Christendom, that may be therein concerned."

This was signed by the Archbishops of York and Canterbury, twenty-two temporal lords, and five bishops; and the Earl of Pembroke, Lord Weymouth, Lord Bishop of Ely, and the Lord Culpepper, were ordered to attend his Highness with the said declaration at Henley-upon-Thames. The same day the Lord Mayor, aldermen and common council assembled in the same place, and drew up an humble address to be presented to his Highness in their names, on the behalf of the City, of like effect with the declaration, four aldermen being appointed to wait upon the Prince therewith; and the Lieutenancy of London meeting that day, also, drew up an address to his Highness, on behalf of themselves and the rest of the militia, to the like purpose, which were accordingly presented to the Prince, and very favourably received, imploring his Highness's protection, and beseeching him to repair to the city, were he would be received with universal satisfaction.

The next day, the tumults being somewhat allayed, search was made in divers places for such as were fled from justice; and among others, to the great rejoicing of the people, the Lord Chancellor Jeffries was taken in an obscure house at Wapping, disguised like a sailor, and endeavouring to make his escape in a vessel that lay there for Hamburg; who being brought before the Lord Mayor, with a numerous and enraged guard of attendants, his lordship was suddenly seized with such a frightful indisposition that he was incapable of examining the matter, so that the Chancellor was carried to the Tower by his own consent, to preserve himself from the fury of the rabble.

Dec. 14, his Highness by easy marches came to Windsor, where he was received with all kinds of respect and submission by the mayor and aldermen, in their formalities, and congratulated in an elegant speech, the Prince of Denmark's lodgings being provided for his reception. Whilst his Highness was preparing for London, he had noticed that the King designing to pass the seas in disguise, having betaken himself, accompanied only by two or three persons, in a small vessel to sea, was forced by foul weather upon the coast of Kent, near Feversham, and as soon as he came to the town was seized upon by the multitude, there being a report at that time that several persons were making their escape out of the land, and being ignorant who he was, they carried him to a house in the town, rifling him of some jewels, a considerable quantity of gold, and his crucifix, which he very much valued; but at last the King being known by a gentleman who came to see the prisoners they had taken, and fell on his knees to pay him duty, the common people were strangely surprised, a great number instantly retiring, and others begged his pardon, offering to restore what they had taken from him; but the King refused to take his gold again, giving it them freely; however, his person was detained till the news of his being there could be carried to London.

 The Lords who first assembled in the city, being then at Whitehall, and having notice of it, sent the Lords Feversham, Aylesbury, Yarmouth and Middleton to the King, with their earnest desires that he would be pleased to return to his royal palace at London; to which, though at first he showed some unwillingness, yet being pressed thereto, he at length condescended; the servants of his household, who went along with the lords, having brought him money and clothes, those he had being old, and rent in the searching him before he was known; but his

Highness the Prince of Orange being fully determined to come to London with all speed, it was upon consultation thought very inconvenient, in regard it might create daily disputes and quarrels between the soldiers of both parties, and in divers other respects for the King and himself to be there at one and the same time ; therefore, upon notice of the King's returning, Monsieur Zulestein was sent to meet him on the way, and to entreat him to return to Rochester, which the King would certainly have done had not Monsieur Zulestein missed him by taking another road ; so that the King arrived at Whitehall on Sunday, Dec. 16, in the evening, attended by three troops of life-guards, and a troop of grenadiers, a set of boys following him through the city and making some huzzas, while the rest of the people silently looked on. From thence the King sent the Earl of Feversham to the Prince, then at Windsor, to invite his Highness to come to St. James' and take that palace as his residence, with what number of troops he thought convenient. The Prince, deliberating with the Lords about this message, was advised by no means to accept of this invitation, and there being a necessity his Highness should be in town the next day, the following paper, signed by the Prince, was ordered to be carried to the King next day, by the Lords therein mentioned :—

" We desire you, the Lord Marquis of Halifax, the Earl of Shrewsbury, and the Lord Delamere, to tell the King that it is thought convenient for the greater safety of his person, that he do remove to Ham, where he shall be attended by guards, who will be ready to preserve him from any disturbance. Given at Windsor, Dec. 17, 1688."

And further to prevent the possibility of any disturbance, it was resolved that his Highness' guards should be possessed of all the posts and avenues about Whitehall before the paper was delivered, and it was computed that these guards might have reached Whitehall by eight o'clock at night, but they were so hindered by the foulness of the ways that it was past ten before they arrived, and there being difficulty made of withdrawing the King's guards, so much time was spent that the Lords could not proceed in their message till past twelve, so that the King was in bed; but to preserve decency and respect, and not break hastily in upon him, they sent the Lord Middleton, his principal Secretary of State, the following letter:—

"My Lord,

"There is a message to be delivered to his Majesty from the Prince, which is of so great importance that we who are charged with it desire we may be immediately admitted, and therefore desire to know where we may find your lordship, that you may introduce, my lord, your lordship's most humble servant," &c.

The Lord Middleton upon the receipt thereof came and introduced them to the King, and their lordships having made an apology for coming at a time that might disturb him, the Prince's message was delivered to the King, who, reading it, said that he would readily comply. The Lords, as they were directed, humbly desired that if it might be with his Majesty's conveniency, he would be pleased to remove so early, so to be at Ham by noon, thereby to prevent his meeting the Prince in his way to London. To this the King readily agreed, and asked if he might not appoint what servants should attend him. The Lords replied it was wholly left to his Majesty. The Lords then took their leave, but were instantly sent for back by the King, who told them he had forgot to acquaint them with his resolution before the message came, to send the Lord Godolphin the next morning to the Prince, to propose his going back to Rochester, he finding by the message Monsieur Zulestein was charged with that the Prince had no mind he should be at London, and therefore he now desired that he might rather return to Rochester. The Lords replied that they would immediately send an account to the Prince, and doubted not of an answer to his satisfaction, and accordingly, despatching a messenger to the Prince, who was then at Sion House, the Sieur Bentwick, by eight next morning, sent a letter by the Prince's order, agreeing to the King's proposal, and the guards and barges being prepared to attend him, and his coaches and sumpters to follow, he reached Gravesend on the 18th, in the evening, and passed overland in his coach, attended by the Earl of Arran and several others, and made his residence in Sir Richard Head's house.

In the afternoon of the same day, his Highness, with a very splendid equipage and a numerous attendance, arrived at St. James's, and received the congratulations of all the nobility and persons of chiefest quality in the town—the people crowding to see their deliverer, and expressing their satisfaction at so happy a resolution by ringing of bells, bonfires, and all the public demonstrations of joy imaginable.

A remarkable accident happened between the King's first going to Rochester and his return to London, a general alarm being given one night—

about midnight—at almost one and the same time, in the most considerable cities and towns in England, upon pretence that the Irish were killing, burning and destroying all before them, which seemed to be carried on industriously by persons sent on purpose to spread that false report, or else it can hardly be imagined how it should have been done at so many distant places at once, which threw the people into a great surprise and consternation, till the day appeared and convinced them of the fallacy; but the real occasion hereof was never yet generally understood.

Upon the arrival of his Highness, the Common Council of London assembled, and unanimously agreed that the sheriffs and all the aldermen of the city, with their deputies, and two common councilmen for each ward, should wait on and congratulate his Highness upon his happy arrival in the City of London, and accordingly, on the 20th of December, the Lord Mayor being indisposed by sickness, Sir George Treby, the Recorder, in a most elegant speech, thus addressed his Highness :—

" May it please Your Highness,

" The Lord Mayor being disabled by sickness, your Highness is attended by the aldermen and commons of the capital city of this kingdom, deputed to congratulate your Highness upon this great and glorious occasion, in which, labouring for words, we cannot but come short in expression. Reviewing our late danger, we remember our Church and State overrun by Popery and arbitrary power, and brought to a point of destruction by the conduct of men that were our true invaders—that broke the sacred fences of our laws and, which was worse, the very constitution of our Legislature, so that there was no remedy left us. The only person under heaven that could apply this remedy was your Highness. You are of a nation whose alliance at all times has been agreeable and prosperous to us; you are of a family of most illustrious benefactors to mankind; to have the title of Sovereign Prince, Stadtholder, and to have worn the imperial crown, are among the lesser dignities; they have long enjoyed a dignity singular and transcendent—that is, 'To be champions of Almighty God, sent forth in several ages to vindicate His cause against the greatest oppressions.' To this divine commission our nobles, our gentry, and amongst them our brave English soldiers, render themselves and their arms upon your appearing.

"Great Sir! when we look back the last month, and contemplate the swiftness and fulness of our deliverance, astonished, we think it miraculous. Your Highness, led by the hand of heaven, and called by the voice of the people, has preserved our dearest interest—the Protestant religion, which is primitive Christianity; restored our laws, which are our ancient title to our lives, liberties, and estates, and without which the world were a wilderness. But what retribution can we make to your Highness? Our thoughts are full charged with gratitude. Your Highness has a lasting monument in the hearts, in the prayers, in the praises of all good men among us, and late posterity will celebrate your ever glorious name till time shall be no more."

At the same time the high sheriff, nobility and gentry of the County of Cambridge, presented another address to his Highness, wherein they implored his protection and aid to rescue the nation from Popery and slavery, and assured him they would contribute their utmost endeavours for perfecting so glorious a work, returning his Highness their unfeigned thanks for the progress he had made therein with so much cost, labour, and hazard, both by sea and land.

But in the midst of these transactions, the King, having continued some days at Rochester, on the 22nd December, between two and three in the morning, going a back way, with great secrecy and caution, hastened to the sea-side, taking only with him Mr. Ralph Sheldon and Mr. Delabody, with whom he embarked in a vessel that lay for his transportation to France, to follow his Queen, as had been agreed betwixt them, leaving the following paper of reasons behind him for withdrawing himself from Rochester, said to be written by his own hand, and ordered by him to be published:—

"The world cannot wonder at my withdrawing myself now this second time. I might have expected somewhat better usage after what I wrote to the Prince of Orange by my Lord Feversham, and the instructions I gave him; but instead of an answer such as I might have hoped for, what was I to expect after the usage I received by making the said Earl prisoner, against the practice and law of nations! the sending his own guards at eleven at night to take possession of the posts at Whitehall, without advertising me in the least manner of it; the sending to me at one o'clock, after midnight, when I was in bed, a kind of an order, by three lords, to be gone out of mine own palace before twelve that same morning? After all this, how could I hope to be safe, so long as I was in the power of one who had not only done this to me, and invaded my kingdoms without any just occasion given him for it, but that did by his first declaration lay the greatest aspersion upon me that malice could invent, in that clause of it which concerns my son? I appeal to all that know me, nay, even to himself, that in their consciences neither he nor they can believe me in the least capable of so unnatural a villainy, nor of so little common sense to be imposed on in a thing of such a nature as that. What had I then to expect from one who, by all arts, hath taken such pains to make me appear as black as hell to my own people, as well as to all the world besides? What effect that hath had at home all mankind hath seen, by so general a defection in my army, as well as in the nation amongst all sorts of people.

"I was both free, and desire to continue so; and though I have ventured my life very frankly on several occasions for the good and honour of my country, and am as free to do it again (and which I hope I yet shall do, as old as I am, to redeem it from the slavery it is like to fall under), yet I think it not convenient to expose myself to be secured, as not to be at liberty to effect, and for that reason to withdraw, but so as to be within call whensoever the nation's eye shall be opened, so as to see how they have been abused and imposed upon by the specious pretences of religion and property. I hope it will please God to touch their hearts, out of His infinite mercy, and to make them sensible of the ill condition they are in, and bring them to such a temper that a legal Parliament may be called, and that, amongst other things which may be necessary to be done, they will agree to liberty of conscience for all Protestant dissenters, and that those of my own persuasion may be so far considered, and have such a share of it, as they may live peaceably and quietly, as Englishmen and Christians ought to do, and not to be obliged to transplant themselves, which would be very grievous, especially to such as love their own country; and I appeal to all men, who are considering men, and have had experience, whether anything can make this nation so great and flourishing as liberty of conscience? Some of our neighbours dread it. I could add much more to confirm all I have said, but now is not the proper time.

"Rochester, December 22, 1688."

Upon these reasons we make these few cursory remarks: that as to the detaining of the Earl of Feversham, who was sent without a pass in a time of war, it may be very well justified, he likewise having disbanded the army, and left them at large to lie upon the country. The message for his removal from Whitehall was managed, as we have heard, with all the respect and decency imaginable, and absolutely necessary upon several accounts, as well as for the preservation of his own person, whose late actions, especially his extraordinary severity in the west, had raised him many inveterate enemies, who now might have taken the opportunity of offering violence to him. That his Highness had sufficient reason for this glorious expedition, the King had made the nation too sensible of; and as for the business of the child, it is well known that his zeal for the Catholic cause made him shut his eyes to all other considerations whatsoever; and, besides, it was managed with such a number of suspicious circumstances, that we are told that one of his comrades in Ireland should say that "the Prince of Orange had one plausible pretence for his invasion, namely, that of the Prince of Wales; since, if it was a real birth the Court managed the matter so as if they had industriously contrived the nation should give no credit to it." As to his hopes of conquering us, we have as great hopes and better reasons to believe the contrary, since the people will scarce ever be fond of giving up their religion, laws, liberties, and estates to the will of an arbitrary prince, or even submit to a French government. As to a Parliament, we may think that he did not design to call any, since, some time before his departure, he ordered all the writs that were not sent out to be burnt, and a caveat to be entered against the making use of such as were already sent into the countries. As to liberty of conscience, which he seems so much to value, his proceedings in Ireland, and against the universities, together with his recalling the Protestant ministers from preaching to the English merchants in Popish countries, with many other instances that might be given, are sufficient demonstrations of the reality of his intentions therein.

Soon after we had an account that the King was arrived in France and gone to the court, where his Queen came some time before, having, as soon as she landed, sent, it is said, the following letter to the King:—

"An unfortunate Queen, all bathed in tears, has deemed it no trouble to expose herself to the greatest perils of the sea, on purpose to seek an asylum and protection in the dominions of the greatest and most glorious monarch in the world. Her bad fortune has procured her a happiness, which far distant nations have sought with eagerness; nor does the necessity lessen the value, while she makes choice of the same sanctuary before any other that she might have found in any other place. She is persuaded that His Majesty will look upon it as a demonstration of the singular esteem she has of his great and royal qualities, that she entrusts him with the Prince of Wales, who is all she has most dear and precious in the world. He is too young to partake with her in the acknowledgments due for his protection; that acknowledgment is entirely in the heart of his mother, who, in the midst of all her sorrows, enjoys this consolation, to live sheltered under the laurels of a prince who surpasses all that ever was of most exalted and mighty upon earth."

These fulsome flatteries, which were so admired by that King, doubtless moved him to entertain her with great tenderness, and made way for the reception of the King, her husband, who soon after arrived there, and had St. Germains allowed for their residence, with such an allowance as the King could spare from his other mighty expenses for their subsistence; though it is a question whether King James consulted his own interest in flying to the French King, for certainly, after all he had done at home, to see him harbour himself with the enemy of the English name, the contriver and adviser of all the mischiefs for several years perpetrated in the kingdom—what could more convict him of the oppressions of his reign, or more inveterately alienate the people's affections from him? Upon the King's second withdrawing, Portsmouth, that held out with some obstinacy, under the Duke of Berwick and Sir Edward Scott, deputy-governor, submitted, and received a garrison sent thither by the Prince's order.

And now to fill up this breach and rupture in the Government, the Lords spiritual and temporal immediately met in the House of Peers at Westminster, where they drew up an humble address, which they presented to his Highness, requesting him, in this conjecture, to take upon him the administration of public affairs, both civil and military, and the disposal of the public revenue for the preservation of the Protestant religion, rights, laws, liberties, properties, and the peace of the nation, and to take into his particular care the present condition of Ireland, and to use speedy and effectual means to prevent the danger threatening that kingdom.

At the same time, these honourable lords further humbly requested " That his Highness would please to cause letters to be written, subscribed by himself and the Lords spiritual and temporal, being Protestants, to the several counties, universities, cities, boroughs, &c., directed to the chief magistrates of each, within ten days after the receipt thereof, to choose such a number of persons to represent them as are of right to be sent to Parliament." Both which addresses were presented to the Prince at St. James's who answered that he had considered their advice, and that he would endeavour to secure the peace of the nation till the meeting of the Convention, Jan. 22nd next, and that he would forthwith issue out letters to that purpose; and that he would apply the public revenues to their proper use, and likewise endeavour to put Ireland into such a condition as that the Protestant religion and the English interest might be maintained in that kingdom; further assuring them that as he came hither for the preservation of the Protestant religion and the laws and liberties of the kingdom, so he should always be ready to expose himself in any hazard for the defence of the same.

His Highness likewise sent for all such as had been members of Parliament in the reign of Charles II., together with the aldermen and common council of the City of London, to meet him at St. James's,

L

to advise the best manner how to pursue the ends of his declaration in calling a free Parliament for the preservation of the Protestant religion, the restoring of the rights and liberties of the kingdom, and settling the same, that they might not be in danger of being again subverted. Upon which they met accordingly, and after his Highness had thus graciously expressed himself to them, they instantly concluded to go to the House of Commons, where being sate, they chose Henry Powle, Esq., their chairman, and then drew up an address to the Prince returning his Highness their hearty thanks, and expressing their extraordinary acknowledgment for the care he had taken of their religion, laws, and liberties, humbly entreating him to take upon him the administration of the government, &c., which being presented to his Highness at St. James's he returned the same answer as he had done to the lords.

The news of his Highness' success and prosperous proceedings arriving in Holland, all the persons of quality that were at the Hague appeared at Court to compliment her Royal Highness the Princess of Orange thereupon, and soon after their Electoral Highnesses of Bradenburgh arrived there, and were entertained very splendidly upon that occasion; and the States General sent three deputies to England to congratulate his Highness, who, landing at the Tower, were received with the discharge of the cannon, and conducted to the lodgings appointed for them, with a very splendid equipage.

December 30, his Highness issued out a declararation, to authorize sheriffs, justices of the peace, and all other officers except Papists to continue and act in their respective places till further orders; and a second declaration, for the better quartering of soldiers; that none should be quartered upon private houses, without the free and voluntary consent of the owner; and awhile after, the following association for the preservation of his Highness's person, which had been promoted and signed through most counties of England, with great cheerfulness and alacrity, was signed also by several noblemen and others at St. James's:—

"We whose names are hereunto subscribed, who have joined with the Prince of Orange for the defence of the Protestant religion, and for maintaining the ancient government and the laws and liberties of England, Scotland and Ireland, do engage to Almighty God, to his Highness the Prince of Orange and to one another, to stick firm to this cause, and to one another in defence of it, and never to depart from it till our religion, our laws and liberties are so far secured to us in a free Parliament, that we shall be no more in danger of falling under Popery and slavery. And whereas we are engaged in this common cause under the protection of the Prince of Orange, by which means his person may be exposed to dangers, and to the desperate and cursed attempts of the Papists, and other bloody men; we do therefore solemnly engage, both to God and to one another, that if any such attempts are made upon him, we will pursue not only those that made them, but all their adherents, and all that we find in arms against us, with the utmost severity of a just vengeance, to their ruin and final destruction; and that the execution of any such attempt (which God of His mercy forbid) shall not divert us from prosecuting this cause, which we do now undertake; but that it shall engage us to carry it on with all the vigour that so barbarous a practice shall deserve."

After this, his Highness published a declaration to command all Papists to depart within three days out of London and Westminster, and ten miles about, under penalty of suffering the utmost severity of the law; and about the same time the country people seized a great number of persons in Kent and other places, endeavouring to make their escape beyond sea, who were committed to several prisons till further orders. And to show the readiness and zeal of the people to support his Highness, he had no sooner signified to the City of London that the necessary expenses he had been at had near exhausted the public revenues, but that they instantly ordered a committee to attend him, to know what sum might be necessary, and one hundred thousand pounds being named, the generous citizens immediately came to Guildhall, and made subscriptions for three hundred thousand pounds, which was paid in to admiration within a very few days.

Affairs being now in a promising way of settlement in England, let us take a brief view of Scotland, to which his Highness, before his arrival, had likewise sent a declaration to the same effect with that sent to England, some expressions only being varied according to the different circumstances of both nations, his Highness declaring, "That by the influence of these evil counsellors, who designed to render themselves the absolute masters of the lives, honours, and estates of the subjects, without being restrained by any rule or law, a most exorbitant power had been exercised in imposing bands and oaths upon whole shires; in permitting free quarters to soldiers; in imprisoning gentlemen without any reason, forcing them to accuse and witness against themselves; in imposing arbitrary fines; frighting and harrassing many parts of the country with inter-communing; making some incur the forfeiture of life and fortune for the most general and harmless converse, even with their nearest relatives outlawed; empowering officers and soldiers to act upon the subjects living in quiet and full peace, the greatest barbarities; in destroying them by hanging, shooting and drowning them, without any form of law, or respect to age or sex, not giving some of them time to pray to God for mercy; and this for no other reason but because they would not answer or satisfy them in such questions as they proposed to them, without any warrant of law, and against the common interest of mankind, which frees all men from being obliged to discover their secret thoughts; besides a great many violences and oppressions, to which that poor nation hath been exposed, without any hope of having any end put to them, or to have relief from them. And that the arbitrary and illegal proceedings of these evil counsellors might be justified, such a declaration hath been procured by them, as strikes at the root of the government, and overturns the most sacred rights of it; in making all Parliaments unnecessary, and taking away all defences of religion, liberty and property by an assumed and asserted absolute power, to which obedience is required without reserve, which every good Christian is persuaded is due to God Almighty alone, all whose commandments are always just and good," &c.

Upon his Highness's arrival and happy progress in England the terror thereof wrought so effectually upon those Popish and arbitrary Ministers of State in Scotland, who were sensible of their own guilt, that they thought of nothing but to make their escape from justice, which some had the luck to do; others were seized; and the multitude, rising in divers places, demolished the mass houses, and burnt the Popish trinkets, yea, proceeded to several violences and disorders, which occasioned the death and wounding of many persons, even in Edinburgh itself; of which the Scotch noblemen and gentlemen in London having notice, they resolved to attend his Highness the Prince of Orange, and lay before him the willingness of the people of Scotland to submit to his protection, and his Highness having notice of their intentions caused such of them as were in town to be advertised to meet him at St. James's, January 7th, to whom he made the following speech :—

My Lords and Gentlemen,

"The only reason that induced me to undergo so great an undertaking was, that I saw the laws and liberties of these kingdoms overturned, and the Protestant religion in imminent danger, and seeing you are so many noblemen and gentlemen, I have called you together, that I may have your advice what is to be done for the securing of the Protestant religion, and restoring your laws and liberties, according to my declaration."

After which the Lords and gentlemen went to the Council Chamber at Whitehall, and, choosing the Duke of Hamilton their president, they drew up an address, which they presented to the Prince to this effect : " That they rendered his Highness their humble thanks for his pious and generous undertaking, &c., desiring him to take upon him the administration of affairs, civil and military, in Scotland, till the general meeting of Estates, which they humbly prayed his Highness to call to be held at Edinburgh, March 14th, following." This address was subscribed by thirty lords and eighty gentlemen. His Highness assured them that he would do all they required, and the news thereof coming to Edinburgh, was received with the utmost demonstrations of joy and satisfaction.

The elections for the convention at Westminster had in some places been generally made without those strivings and heats that are usual upon such occasions, and seemed to be a good prognostic that their debates would be calm, and tend to a speedy settlement; and accordingly, the 22nd of January being come, the Lords spiritual and temporal, and Commons assembled at Westminster. The Lord Marquis of Halifax officiated as Speaker in the House of Lords, and the Commons chose Henry Powle, Esq., to be their Speaker. After which a leeter from his Highness the Prince of Orange was read in both houses, on the occasion of their meeting, wherein his Highness declared that " he had endeavoured to the utmost of his power to perform what was desired of him, in order to the public peace and safety, and that he did not know anything which had been omitted that might tend to the preservation of them, since the administration of affairs was put into his hands; and that it now lay upon them to lay the foundation of a firm security for their religion, laws, and liberties; that he did not doubt but that by such a full and free representation of the nation as was then met, the ends of his declaration would be attained; and since it had pleased God hitherto to bless his good intentions with such great success, he trusted in Him that he would complete His own work by sending a spirit of peace and union to influence their councils, that no interruption might be given to a happy and lasting settlement. He then represented to them the dangerous condition of the Protestants in Ireland, and the present state of things abroad, which required their early assistance against a powerful enemy, who had declared war against them, and which he did not doubt, but without any unseasonable divisions among themselves, they would take effectual care about."

This letter being read and approved of, the Lords and Commons presented an address to his Highness. "That being highly sensible of the great deliverance of this kingdom from Popery and arbitrary power, and that their preservation, next under God, was owing to his Highness, they returned him their humble thanks as the glorious instrument of so great a blessing, and did farther acknowledge the great care he had taken in administering the public affairs to that time, humbly desiring that his Highness would continue the administration thereof till further application should be made by them, which should be expedited with all convenient speed." This address being presented January 23rd, 1688, his Highness returned them this answer:

"My Lords and Gentlemen

"I am glad that what I have done has pleased you; and since you desire me to continue the administration of affairs, I am willing to accept it. I must recommend to you the consideration of affairs abroad, which maketh it fit for you to expedite your business, not only for making a settlement at home upon a good foundation, but for the safety of all Europe."

After this the Lords and Commons ordered a day of public thanksgiving to be kept throughout the kingdom, to render praise to Almighty God for having made his Highness the Prince of Orange the glorious instrument of the great deliverance of this kingdom from Popery and arbitrary power.

As to the condition of Ireland, the Earl of Tyrconnel, a violent Papist, being made Lord Lieutenant of that kingdom by King James, as a fit instrument to carry on his designs, gave the Irish great hopes of subduing the English, by his first cashiering the Protestant officers and soldiers that were in arms, and then by turning out the officers and ministers of Justice; and though complaints were made against his proceedings in the Court of England, yet they were not regarded, but he rather encouraged in his enterprises, which occasioned such dread of future mischiefs that divers left the kingdom, some going for Holland, others for Scotland and England. Things continued in this dangerous posture till the news of the intended enterprise of the Prince of Orange arrived there, upon which Tyrconnel was very active to secure the Roman Catholic interest in Ireland, imprisoning and disarming the Protestants, and sending over three thousand of the choicest Irish soldiers to assist King James; but upon notice of his flight into France, he called his Popish Council together, and told them that now was the time for their standing up for their country, to secure it against all their enemies; and as for his part, if his master himself should command him to deliver up the sword he should think it his duty to refuse it in this juncture; and thereupon spreading the news all over the country, he caused the Irish everywhere to arm themselves with such weapons as they could get. This tumultuous rabble herding together, plundered the Protestants' houses, drove away their cattle, fired their stacks of corn and hay, murdered some, and barbarously used others; insomuch, that the Protestants being extremely affrighted many of them fled for their lives leaving their estates behind them; and though several of the Protestant nobility and gentry made head in the north, yet they found themselves unable to resist the fury of their numerous adversaries; however, they defeated several parties of Irish, fortified Londonderry, Sligo, the Isle of Enniskillen, and other places they thought tenable; for now Tyrconnel gave orders for stopping the ports, to prevent any more from going away, and made many large and plausible proposals to induce them to join with him, though they had very little effect upon them.

The conventions at Westminster were still upon serious debates about the present condition of the kingdom, and in the meantime it was thought necessary to have the presence of her Highness the Princess of Orange in England; whereupon a squadron of English and Dutch men-of-war were ordered to wait upon her till her equipage could be got ready, and the wind served to bring over her Highness; and after the Lords and Commons had duly weighed the circumstances of the King's departure, they at length came to the following resolution:

"*Resolved*, That King James II. having endeavoured to subvert the constitution of this kingdom, by breaking the original contract between King and people; and by the advice of Jesuits and other wicked persons, having violated the fundamental laws, and having withdrawn himself out of this kingdom, hath abdicated the Government, and the throne is thereby vacant."

In pursuance of which resolution the following declaration was drawn up in order to such an establishment as that the religion, laws, and liberties of the kingdom might not again be in danger, and for vindicating the ancient rights and liberties of the people, in these words:

"Whereas the late King James II., by the assistance of divers evil counsellors, judges and ministers, employed by him, did endeavour to extirpate the Protestant religion, and the laws and liberties of this kingdom, by assuming and exercising a power of dispensing with and suspending of laws, and the execution of laws, without consent of Parliament: By committing and prosecuting divers worthy prelates, for humbly petitioning to be excused from concurring to the said assumed power: By issuing and causing to be executed a commission under the Great Seal, for erecting a court called 'The Court of Commissioners for Ecclesiastical Causes: By levying money for, and to the use of, the Crown, by pretence of prerogative, for another time and in another manner than the same was granted by Parliament: By raising and keeping a standing army within this kingdom in time of peace, without consent of Parliament, and quartering soldiers, contrary to law: By causing several good subjects, being Protestants, to be disarmed at the same time when Papists were both armed and employed, contrary to law: By violating the freedom of election of members to serve in Parliament: By prosecutions in the Court of King's Bench for matters and causes cognizable only in Parliament; and by divers other arbitrary illegal courses.

"And whereas of late years, partial, corrupt and unqualified persons have been returned, and served on juries in trial, and particularly divers jurors in trials for high treason, who were not freeholders;

and excessive bail hath been required of persons committed in criminal cases, to elude the benefit of the laws made for the liberty of the subject; and excessive fines have been imposed; and illegal and cruel punishments inflicted, and several grants and promises made of fines and forfeitures, before any conviction or judgment against the persons upon the same were to be levied; all which are utterly and directly contrary to the known laws and statutes, and freedom of this realm. And whereas the said late King James II., having abdicated the government, and the throne being thereby vacant.

"His Highness the Prince of Orange (whom it hath pleased Almighty God to make the glorious instrument of delivering this kingdom from Popery and arbitrary power) did by the advice of the Lords spiritual and temporal, and divers principal persons of the Commons, cause letters to be written to the Lords spiritual and temporal being Protestants, and other letters to the several counties, cities, universities, boroughs and cinque ports, for the choosing of such persons to represent them as were of right to be sent to Parliament, to meet and sit at Westminster, January 22, 1688, in order to such an enactment as that their religion, laws and liberties might not again be in danger of being subverted; upon which letters, elections have been accordingly made.

"And thereupon the said Lords spiritual and temporal, and Commons, pursuant to their respective letters and election, being now assembled in a full and free representation of this nation, taking into their most serious consideration the best means for attaining the ends aforesaid, do, in the first place (as their ancestors in like case have usually done), for the vindicating and asserting their ancient rights and liberties, declare that the pretended power of suspending of laws, or the execution of laws by regal authority, without consent of Parliament, is illegal; that the pretended power of suspending of laws, or the execution of laws by regal authority, as it hath been assumed and exercised of late, is illegal; that the commissions for erecting the late Court of Commissioners for Ecclesiastical Causes, and all other commissions and courts of like nature, are illegal and pernicious; that levying money for, or to the use of, the Crown by pretence of prerogative, without grant of Parliament, for longer time or in other manner than the same is or shall be granted, is illegal; that it is the right of the subjects to petition the King, and all commitments and prosecutions for such commitments are illegal; that the raising or keeping a standing army within the kingdom in time of peace, unless it be with consent of Parliament, is against law; that the subjects which are Protestants may have arms for their defence suitable to their conditions, and as allowed by law; that election of members of Parliament ought to be free; that the freedom of speech, and debates or proceedings in Parliament, ought not to be impeached or questioned in any court or place out of Parliament; that excessive bail ought not to be required, nor excessive fines imposed, nor cruel and unusual punishments inflicted; that jurors ought to be duly impannelled and returned, and jurors which pass upon men in trials for high treason ought to be freeholders; that all grants and promises of fines and forfeitures of particular persons before conviction, are illegal and void; and that for redress of all grievances, and for the amending, strengthening and preserving of the laws, Parliaments ought to be held frequently.

"And they do claim, demand, and insist upon all and singular the premises as their undoubted rights and liberties; and that no declaration, judgments, doings or proceedings to the prejudice of the people in any of the said premises, ought in any wise to be drawn hereafter into consequence or example; to which demand of their right they are particularly encouraged by the declaration of his Highness the Prince of Orange, as being the only means for obtaining a full redress and remedy therein.

"Having, therefore, an entire confidence that his said Highness the Prince of Orange will perfect the deliverance so far advanced by him, and will still preserve them from the violation of their rights; which they have here asserted, and from all other attempts upon their religion, rights, and liberties, the said Lords spiritual and temporal, and Commons, assembled at Westminster, do resolve that William and Mary, Prince and Princess of Orange, be and be declarred King and Queen of England, France, and Ireland, and the dominions thereunto belonging, to hold the crown and royal dignity of the said kingdom and dominions to them, the said Prince and Princess, during their lives, and the life of the survivor of them; and that the sole and full exercise of the regal power be only in and executed by the said Prince of Orange, in the names of the said Prince and Princess, during their joint lives; and after their decease, the said crown and royal dignity of the said kingdoms and dominions to be to the heirs of the body of the said Princess; and for default of such issue, to the Princess Ann of Denmark, and the heirs of her body; and for default of such issue to the heirs of the body of the said Prince of

Orange; and the Lords spiritual and temporal, and Commons, do pray the said Prince and Princess to accept the same accordingly; and that the oaths hereinafter mentioned be taken by all persons, of whom the oaths of allegiance and supremacy might be required by law, instead of them; and that the said oaths of allegiance and supremacy be abrogated.

"I, A. B., do sincerely promise and swear, that I will be faithful and bear true allegiance to their Majesties King William and Queen Mary; so help me God."

"I, A. B., do swear, that I do, from my heart, abhor, detest and adjure, as impious and heretical, this damnable doctrine and position, that Princes, excommunicated or deprived by the Pope, or any authority of the see of Rome, may be deposed or murdered by their subjects, or any other whatsoever.

"And I do declare that no foreign prince, persons, prelate, state or potentate, hath or ought to have, any jurisdiction, power, superiority, pre-eminence or authority, ecclesiastical or spiritual, within this realm; so help me God."

This declaration being presented to their Highnesses the Prince and Princess of Orange, in the banqueting-house at Whitehall, on Wednesday, February 13, 1688, and their consent thereunto received, they were both, the same day, proclaimed King and Queen of England, France, and Ireland, &c., at Whitehall-gate, Temple Bar, and the Royal Exchange, many of the Lords and Commons attending, and the people proclaiming their joys by repeated shouts and acclamations. The tenor of the proclamation was as followeth:

"Whereas it hath pleased Almighty God, in His great mercy to this kingdom, to vouchsafe us a miraculous deliverance from Popery and arbitrary power, and that our preservation is due, next under God, to the resolution and conduct of his Highness the Prince of Orange, whom God hath chosen to be the glorious instrument of such an inestimable happiness to us and our posterity; and being highly sensible and fully persuaded of the great and eminent virtues of her Highness the Princess of Orange, whose zeal for the Protestant religion will, no doubt, bring a blessing along with her upon this nation: and whereas the Lords and Commons now assembled at Westminster have made a declaration, and presented the same to the said Prince and Princess of Orange, and therein desired them to accept the crown, who have accepted the same accordingly; we, therefore, the Lords spiritual and temporal, and Commons, together with the Lord Mayor and citizens of London, and others of the commons of this realm, do, with full consent, publish and proclaim, according to the said declaration, William and Mary, Prince and Princess of Orange, to be King and Queen of England, France, and Ireland, with all the dominions and territories thereunto belonging, who are accordingly so to be owned, deemed and taken, by all the people of the aforesaid realms and dominions, who are, from henceforward, bound to acknowledge and pay unto them all faith and true allegiance, beseeching God, by whom Kings reign, to bless King William and Queen Mary with long and happy years to reign over us. God save King William and Queen Mary.

"JOHN BROWN,

"Clericus Parliamentorum."

It is reported that His Majesty should thus generously express himself upon this occasion: "That though the regulations seemed somewhat harsh, they were easy to him that desired only to be a great King; but with respect to one that aimed to be a tyrant, they were not strict enough."

Having thus brought their Majesties to the throne, let us make a few remarks upon this wonderful and unparalleled revolution, and so conclude the history of the House of Orange.

Had a Prince of less secrecy, prudence, courage and interest, undertaken this mighty affair, it might probably have miscarried; but as his cause was better, so his reputation, conduct and patience infinitely exceeded that of King James. He would not stir till he saw the French forces sit down before Philipsburgh, and that he was sure France and Germany were irrecoverably engaged, and that he should have no other opposition than what the Irish and English Roman Catholics could make against him, for no English Protestant would fight his country into vassalage and slavery to Popish priests and Italian women; when a Parliament, sooner or later, must have determined everything in controversy, except they were resolved, once for all, to have given up their religion, laws, liberties and estates to the will of their arbitrary kings, and submitted for ever to the French Government; and, indeed, a nation of less sense than the English might have been imposed upon; of less bravery and valour, might have been frighted; of a more servile temper, might have neglected their liberties till it had been too late to recover them again; and none but a parcel of Jesuits, unacquainted with their temper and constitution, would ever have hoped to have carried two such things as Popery and arbitrary power, both at once, upon a people so jealous as the English are, and who hate idolatry and tyranny above any nation in the world. As for King James II., had he undertaken anything but these two, his vast revenue, his reputed personal valour, and the fame he had gained, both at home and abroad, by the defeat of Monmouth's invasion, would have gone near to have effected it; and after all, if he had, in the beginning of October, freely granted all the proposals made him by the nobility, and suffered a Parliament to have met, and given up his evil ministers to justice, and permitted the birth of the pretended Prince of Wales to have been freely debated and determined in Parliament, it would, in all probability, have prevented this expedition of the Prince of Orange; but whilst he thought to preserve the pretended succession, the dispensing and suspending power, and the ecclesiastical commission, to promote his future design, when he had once baffled the Prince of Orange, the nation saw through the project and he lost all.

As for the English in general, their interest centres in the maintaining the rights and franchises of their kingdom, which renders them this day the freest nation in Europe; a character, so far from supposing them to be like other nations, a people headstrong and inconsistent, that it shows them to be the most considerate and understanding people in the world. In short, though the example of a neighbouring Prince had served for a platform for other crowned heads to enlarge their power beyond the limits prescribed by the constitution of the kingdom, we see that at the very moment that the King began to act like his neighbour, they presently put a stop to his design, without the least respect to his dignity; they saw how sovereign authority reigned in France, as independent of the laws as in Turkey; they beheld the face of the kingdom of Sweden and Denmark changed, by introducing hereditary succession, whereas they were elective before; they viewed the face of the kingdom of Hungary, heretofore the seat of liberty, disfigured by the same innovation; and Poland, that boasts to have preserved the ancient laws entire, has, notwithstanding, suffered injurious alterations. In short, which way soever we cast our eyes, we shall find attempts of the same nature prosper, only in England they have failed, whence we may conclude that, maugre all which has been said of the English nation, they are the wisest and most prudent people that we know of under the sun.

THE HISTORY OF

KING WILLIAM AND QUEEN MARY.

King William and Queen Mary being proclaimed in all the counties and chief cities of England with the general joy of the people, addresses were daily presented them from several parts, to testify their extreme satisfaction and content in their being advanced to the throne; and the Convention being by an Act signed by the King turned into a Parliament, in the same manner as the Convention was, upon the restoration of Charles II., 1660, they proceeded to enact several laws for settling the government upon its true and ancient basis; and several vacant offices and employments were supplied by their Majesties, and Dr. Gilbert Burnet was made Bishop of Salisbury, in the room of Dr. Seth Ward, deceased.

I have been very brief upon the affairs in England till the happy revolution in 1688, because I have lately published a book of the same value with this entitled—

"The History of the Two Late Kings, Charles II. and James II., being an impartial account of the most remarkable transactions, and observable passages during their reigns, and the secret French and Popish intrigues managed in those times."

Neither shall I enlarge upon the affairs of Ireland, intending soon to publish the history of that kingdom from the first conquest thereof by King Henry II. to its total reduction by the arms of their present Majesties.

And now both Houses of Parliament presented an humble address to His Majesty about the speedy relief of Ireland; in pursuance whereof the King sent over a proclamation of pardon to all the Irish Papists that would lay down their arms, and live peaceably under the government, with the full enjoyment of their estates, and the private exercise of their religion, which if they refused, they were declared rebels and traitors to the Crown of England, and their estates to be forfeited and distributed among those who should aid and assist in reducing them to obedience; but Tyrconnel endeavoured to hinder the effect thereof, by promising them speedy succours from France, and that King James would come in person with a numerous army to their assistance, and sent several detachments of his tattered regiments to seize divers considerable Protestants in their houses, who upon notice escaped into the north, and strengthened their party. The priests stirred up these rascally vermin, that were armed with pitchforks, bills, staves and other weapons, to commit all manner of outrages, to the damage of some Papists as well as Protestants, and it was reported that at a consultation in the Council, wherein some Popish bishops assisted, it was moved that the only way to clear the country of heretics was by a general massacre, but Tyrconnell opposed it. In March, the late King James took post from Paris to Brest, and soon after landed in Ireland, with a numerous train of officers, but very few soldiers.

The Estates of Scotland met the same month at Edinburgh, in pursuance of His Majesty's circular letters, and King William sent them the following letter:

" My Lords and Gentlemen,

" We are very sensible of the kindness and concern which your nation has evinced towards us and our undertaking for the preservation of your religion and liberty, which are in such imminent danger. Neither can we in the least doubt your confidence in us after having seen how far so many of your nobility and gentry have owned our declaration, countenancing and concurring with us in our endeavours, and desiring us that we would take upon us the administration of affairs, civil and military, and to call a meeting of the estates for securing the Protestant religion, and the ancient laws and liberties of that kingdom, which accordingly we have done. Now it lies on you to enter upon such consultations as are most proper to settle you on sure and lasting foundations, which we hope you will set about with all convenient speed, with regard to the public good, and to the general interest and inclinations of the people; that after so much trouble and great suffering they may live happily and in peace, and that you may lay aside all animosities and factions that may impede so good a work. We are glad to find that so many of the nobility and gentry, when here in London, were so much inclined to a union of both kingdoms, and that they did look upon it as the best means for procuring the happiness of both nations, and settling of a lasting peace among them, which would be advantageous to both, they living in the same island, having the same language and the same common interest of religion and liberty, especially at this juncture, when the enemies of both are so restless in endeavouring to make and increase jealousies and divisions, which they will be ready to improve to their own advantage and the ruin of Britain. We, being of the same opinion as to the usefulness of this union, and having nothing so much before our eyes as the glory of God, establishing the reformed religion, and the peace and happiness of the nations, are resolved to use our utmost endeavours in advancing everything that may conduce to effecting the same. So we bid you heartily farewell. From our Court at Hampton, March 7, 1689."

This letter being read, commissioners were named to draw an answer full of acknowledgment and respect. The late King James had likewise sent a letter to the Estates, but before they proceeded to read it, they passed an Act, that notwithstanding anything that might be contained in the letter, for dissolving or impeding their procedure, yet they were a free and lawful meeting of the States, and would continue undissolved till they had settled the government; which done, the letter was read, but the Convention took so little notice of the late King's exhortations to declare for him, that the messenger was first secured, and then, not being thought worthy detaining, dismissed with a pass instead of an answer.

After this commissioners were chosen for drawing up the settlement of the government, out of which the bishops were left, as having disgusted the generality of the States, by their prayers at the beginning of the seasons, that God would have compassion on King James, and restore him, and other passages, which discovered their disaffection to their Majesties, and the government then about to be erected. The Duke of Gordon, who had the command of Edinburgh Castle, after he had for some time amused the Convention by his delays, so soon as he heard the late King was arrived in Ireland, set up his standard to signify his resolution to hold out that place, and fired all the cannon, without bullets, to the great terror of those that lay under the mercy of his great shot.

April 12, both Houses of Parliament in England presented an humble address to the King, wherein they declare that being highly sensible of their late great deliverance from Popery and arbitrary power, whereof it had pleased God to make His Majesty the glorious instrument, and desiring to the utmost of their abilities to express their gratitude for so great and generous an undertaking, no less necessary for the support of the Protestant interests in Europe than for recovering and maintaining the civil rights and liberties of these nations, so notoriously invaded and undermined by Popish counsels and counsellors, and being likewise fully convinced of the restless spirits, and the continued endeavours of their Majesties' and the nation's enemies, for the extirpation of the Protestant religion, and the subversion of our laws and liberties, unanimously declare that they would stand by and assist His Majesty with their lives and fortunes in supporting his alliances abroad, in reducing Ireland, and in defence of the Protestant religion and of the kingdom.

In answer hereto, the King assured them of his great esteem and affection for Parliaments, especially for this, which would be much increased by the kindness they showed to him, and their zeal for the public good, and that he would never abuse the confidence they put in him, nor give any Parliament cause to distrust him, because he would never expect anything from them but what it was their interest to grant; that he came hither for the good of the kingdom, and since, by their desire, he was in that station, he would still pursue the same ends that brought him; that God had been pleased to make him instrumental to redeem them from the ills they feared, and it was still his desire as well as his duty to endeavour to preserve their religion, laws, and liberties, which were the only inducements that brought him into England, and to those he did ascribe the blessings that had attended his undertaking. He then reminded them of assisting his allies, especially the Dutch, and to consider the deplorable condition of Ireland, which by the zeal and violence of the Popish party, and the assistance and encouragement of the French, required a considerable force to reduce it, &c., and that a fleet may be likewise provided, which in conjunction with the States, might make us entire masters of the seas; and as they freely offered to hazard all that is dear to them, so he should as freely expose his life for the support of the Protestant religion, and for the safety and honour of the nation.

In Scotland, the Viscount Dundee, having made escape from Edinburgh, went to the north, where he stirred up the Highlanders to join with him, and declare for King James; upon which the Convention ordered a number of horse, foot, and dragoons to march against them, and in the meantime the Lord Ross, who was sent with a letter to King William in England, returned, and brought an answer thereunto; after which the Estates drew up an instrument of Government for settling the crown upon King William and Queen Mary; wherein they recapitulate their grievances and proposed remedies for the same; and then declare "That King James VII., being a professed Papist, did assume the royal power and acted as a King without ever taking the oath required by law, and hath by advice of evil and wicked counsellors, invaded the fundamental constitution of the kingdom, and altered it from a legal limited monarchy to an arbitrary despotic power, and did exercise the same to the subversion of the Protestant religion, and the violation of the laws and liberties of the kingdom, inverting all the ends of government, whereby he hath forfeited the right to the crown, and the throne is become vacant; and they do pray the King and Queen of England to accept the crown and royal dignity of the kingdom of Scotland," etc.

And an oath of allegiance was drawn up, to be taken by all persons to them, together with a coronation oath; and April 11, being the day of the coronation of their Majesties at Westminster, they were proclaimed at Edinburgh, with universal joy and acclamations. Commissioners were also dispatched for London—that is, the Earl of Argyle, Sir James Montgomery, of Skelmerly, and Sir John Dalrymple, of Stair, younger, from the meeting of the Estates, with an offer of the crown of that kingdom to their Majesties, and May 11, 1689, they accordingly at three o'clock met at the council chamber, and from thence were conducted by Sir Charles Cottel, master of the ceremonies, attended by most of the nobility and gentry of the kingdom, who resided in and about this place, to the Banqueting-House, where the King and Queen came, attended by many persons of quality, the sword being carried before them by the Lord Cardross; and their Majesties being placed on the throne, under a rich canopy, the first presented an address from the Estates to His Majesty; then the instrument of government; thirdly, a paper containing the grievances which they desired might be redressed; and, lastly, an address to His Majesty for turning the meeting of the said Estates into a Parliament, all which being signed by His Grace the Duke of Hamilton as president of the meeting, and read to their Majesties, the King returned to the commissioners the following answer:

"When I engaged in this undertaking, I had particular regard and consideration for Scotland, and thereof I did emit a declaration in relation to that as well as to this kingdom, which I intend to make good and effectual to them. I take it very kindly that Scotland hath expressed so much confidence in and affection to me; they shall find me willing to assist them in everything that concerns the welfare and interest of that kingdom, by making what laws shall be necessary for the security of their religion, property, and liberty, and to ease them of what may be justly grievous to them."

After which the coronation oath was tendered to their Majesties, which the Earl of Argyle spoke word by word distinctly, and the King and Queen repeated it after him, holding their right hands up, after the manner of taking oaths in Scotland.

The meeting of the Estates of Scotland did authorize their commissioners to represent to His Majesty that clause in the oath, in relation to the rooting out of heretics, did not import the destroying of heretics; and that by the law of Scotland no man was to be persecuted for his private opinion; and even obstinate and convicted heretics were only to be denounced rebels, or out-lawed, whereby their moveable estates are confiscated. His Majesty, at the repeating that clause in the oath, did declare, that he did not mean by these words, that he was under any obligation to become a persecutor. To which the commissioners made answer, that neither the meaning of the oath or the law of Scotland did import it. Then the King replied, that he took the oath in that sense and called for witnesses, the said commissioners and others present; and then both their Majesties signed the said coronation oath. After which, the commissioners and several of the Scotch nobility kissed their Majesties' hands.

The Parliament in England proceeded to enact many laws for the ease of the people and security of the kingdom; one for taking away the revenue arising from the hearth-money, by His Majesty's own desire, who willingly resigned up his right therein, because it was found grievous to the people, though it occasioned a great diminution to the revenue of the crown; another Act was passed for exempting their Majesties' Protestant subjects dissenting from the Church of England, from the penalties of certain laws; another for abrogating the oaths of supremacy and allegiance, and appointing other oaths; another for prohibiting all trade and commerce with France, with divers more; and about the same time the House of Commons presented His Majesty the following address:

"We, your Majesty's most loyal and dutiful subjects, the Commons in Parliament assembled, most humbly lay before your Majesty our earnest desires that your Majesty would be pleased to take into your most serious consideration the destructive methods taken of late years by the French King, against the trade, quiet and interest of your kingdom, and particularly the present invasion of your kingdom of Ireland, and supporting your Majesty's rebellious subjects; and we not doubting in the least, but through your Majesty's wisdom the alliance already made, as well as those that may be hereafter concluded on this *occasion by your Majesty may be effectual to reduce the French King to such a condition that it may not be in his power hereafter to violate the peace of Christendom, nor prejudice the trade and prosperity of this your Majesty's kingdom. *To this end we most humbly beseech your Majesty to rest assured upon this our hearty and solemn promise and engagement, that when your Majesty shall think fit to enter into a war with the French King we will give your Majesty such assistance in a Parliamentary way as may enable your Majesty (under the protection and blessing that Almighty God has ever afforded you) to support and go through with the same."

To this request and resolution of the House of Commons, which was so graceful to the nation in general, his Majesty was pleased to return this answer:

"Gentlemen,

"I receive this address as a mark of the confidence you have in me, which I take very kindly, and shall endeavour, by all my actions, to confirm you in it. I assure you that my own ambition shall never be an argument to incline me to engage in a war that may expose the nation either to danger or expense; but in the present case I look upon the war so much already, in effect, by France against England, that it is not so much an act of choice as an inevitable necessity in our own defence. I shall only tell you that I have ventured my life, and all that is dear to me, to rescue the nation from what it suffered; so I am ready still to do the same, in order to the preserving it from all its enemies; and as I doubt not of such an assistance from you as shall be suitable to your advice to me to declare war against a powerful enemy, so you may rely upon me that no part of what you shall give for the carrying it on with success shall by me be diverted to any other use."

Soon after a declaration of war was published against France, and the reasons thereof, namely, "The unjust methods of the French King these late years to gratify his ambition, by invading the territories of the empire now in amity with us, and in manifest violation of the treaties confirmed by the guarantee of the crown of England, His Majesty, therefore, can do no less than join with his allies in opposing that King's designs, as the disturber of the peace and the common enemy of the Christian world; likewise the many injuries done to His Majesty and his subjects are a sufficient justification for their taking arms, since they have called upon His Majesty so to do; and though no notice has been taken nor reparation demanded of late years, for reasons well known to the world, yet His Majesty will not pass them over without a public and just resentment of such outrages; also the encroachments and invasions of the French on our trade and fishing of Newfoundland, and their hostilities upon the Caribbee Islands, New York, and Hudson Bay, seizing the forts, burning the houses, robbing the English of their goods, imprisoning some, inhumanly killing others, and driving the rest to sea in a small vessel, without food or necessaries, and this even at a time when that King was negotiating a treaty in England, of neutrality and good correspondence in America; also his countenancing the seizure of English ships by French privateers; his disputing the right of the flag in the narrow seas which, in all ages, has been asserted by His Majesty's predecessors, and which he is resolved to maintain for the honour of the crown and of the English nation; and that which most nearly touches His Majesty is his un-Christian persecution of many English Protestants in France, contrary to the law of nations and express treaties, forcing them to abjure their religion, strange and unusual cruelties, imprisoning some English masters and seamen, and condemning others to the gallies, upon pretence of having on board either the persons or goods of some of his own miserable Protestant subjects; lastly, as he has, for some years past, endeavoured by insinuation and promises of assistance to overthrow the government of England, so now by open and violent methods, and the actual invasion of Ireland, and supporting the rebels there, he is promoting the utter extirpation of the Protestants there. His Majesty being therefore necessitated to take up arms, and relying on the help of Almighty God in his just undertaking, hath thought fit to declare war against the French King, and will, in conjunction with his allies, vigorously prosecute the same by sea and land, since he hath so unrighteously begun it; being assured of the hearty concurrence and assistance of his subjects; in supporting of so good a cause, forbidding all correspondence or communication with that King or his subjects; and that all the French nation in His Majesty's dominions, who shall demean themselves dutifully, and not correspond with his enemies, shall upon the King's royal word, be safe in their persons and estates, and free from all molestation and trouble of any kind."

About the same time the King of Spain proclaimed war against France, and the Emperor of Germany sent a letter to His Majesty, wherein, after he had returned thanks to the King for taking care that no violence should be offered to the Roman Catholics, he promises the same thing in respect to the Protestants. His Majesty gave advice to the Switzers of his advancement to the throne; so that now King William and Queen Mary were acknowledged for lawful Sovereigns of Great Britain by all the Protestant and the greatest part of the Roman Catholic Princes and States, for (besides the Emperor and the King of Spain) the Duke of Bavaria, the three Ecclesiastical Electors, the Duke of Newberg, the Elector Palatine, and the Bishops of Liege and Munster, all Roman Catholics, declared themselves enemies to France, and by this we may observe that the French politicians were greatly deceived in their measures, for upon notice of the Prince of Orange's expedition into England, it is reported some of them thus discoursed King Lewis: "Sir," said they, "there is a civil war kindling in England, which will last this two or three years, and disable that Island and the United Provinces from acting. In this time your Majesty will have conquered all, or the greatest part of Germany. If King James has the worst, we will persuade all the Roman Catholic Princes to unite and restore him. All this while your Majesty will be the head of the league, will preserve your conquests, and King

James cannot refuse you Ireland, or any other portion of his kingdom, for the expenses of the war. This done, your Majesty can fall upon Holland which shall be weak, and unprovided of men and money, and shall be able, in a little time, to oppress the remainder of the Protestants, and so become Emperor of all Europe." But, unfortunately for them, King James too soon forsook his country, and then they cried, "Religion is ruined unless all endeavours are used for his restoration;" upon which some would fain know what religion the French King is of, who persecutes Papists as well as Protestants, and thinks that he must be either a Pagan or Mahometan, or else of a christianity of his own contriving, to carry on his perjuries and usurpations upon his neighbours.

May 1st, a squadron of English men-of-war, under Admiral Herbert, sailing toward the coast of Ireland, to prevent the French from landing forces and provisions there, understanding they were got to sea under favour of the night, they got sight of them lying in the Bay of Bantry, in the west of Ireland, and resolved to attack them with nine ships in the harbour, they being about forty-four sail in all, whereupon next morning the fight began. We continued battering, upon a stretch, till five in the afternoon, when the French Admiral tacked from us and stood further into the Bay. In this action Captain Aylmer and ninety-four seamen were killed, and about two hundred and fifty wounded; but the enemy were reported to have two hundred slain, and many more wounded, and having landed some few men, for fear of a second engagement, retreated; after which our squadron returned to Portsmouth whither his Majesty came soon after and declared his royal intention of conferring the title of earl upon the admiral, and accordingly he was afterwards created Earl of Torrington, Baron of Torbay, &c., and the Captains Shovell and Ashbay were knighted, and ten shillings a man given to those seamen that had been engaged against the French.

King James found himself, at this time, greatly mistaken in Scotland, which he called his ancient kingdom, where he thought himself absolute master, by making so many creatures and friends, whereas that kingdom in general now owned King William; and the rebels, whose numbers were inconsiderable, were discovered and secured. The Lord Dundee alone escaped, who roamed about the north parts with some few followers, and General Mackay at his heels. Letters, about this time, were intercepted from the late King and his secretary, Melfort, to the Lord Balcarris and others, wherein were some expressions that highly incensed the Scots against them. "You will ask me, without question," says Melfort to Claverhouse, "how we intend to pay our army; but never fear that, so long as there are rebels' estates, we will begin with the great ones and end with the little ones." In another to Balcarris, says he, "The estates of the rebels will recompense us. Experience hath taught our illustrious master that there are a good number of people that must be made Gibeonites, because they are good for nothing else. You know that there are several lords that we marked out, when we were both together, that deserve no better. These will serve for examples to others." After the reading of these letters, the President of the Convention, addressing himself to the members of the Assembly, "You hear, gentlemen," said he, "our sentence pronounced, and that it behoves us either to defend ourselves or die;" upon which the Lords Balcarris and Lochore, and Lieutenant-Colonel Balfour were committed to prison, and being thus forewarned, they resolved to keep the army afoot which they thought of disbanding. As to the hopes of the enemies of that kingdom, that the abolishing of episcopacy may occasion another revolution, there is no reason to believe it, since the late carriage of the Scotch bishops has utterly alienated the affections of the greater part of the people from them; so that if they were Protestants at the bottom of their souls, yet they appeared to be men of no policy, nor conduct, for they sent an address to King James, wherein they highly congratulated the birth of the pretended Prince of Wales; they read that King's declaration for liberty of conscience, in favour of the Papist, and the abolition of penal laws; and how could they imagine when they knew it was a long time before, that they could gain that single point of the superiority of bishops over private ministers, that the Scots would never endure Popery and arbitrary power to domineer over them? Experience shows us that they only want a leader before this time, so that when the Prince of Orange's design was once discoursed of, it caused an universal joy over Edinburgh and the whole kingdom, only the prelates wrote to King James that they looked upon this enterprise as a "detestable invasion;" and after the same manner they behaved themselves to the end, some absenting from the convention, others attending only to thwart the proceedings, and show their disaffection by their public prayers; so that some wise men have affirmed had the bishops of Scotland showed the same constancy with those of England, their zeal and virtue had gained the hearts of the Scots, and given them an opportunity to continue episcopacy, but their ill conduct during the last two reigns, in their obstinate supporting the Roman Catholic party, that had already invaded all the liberties of the people, annulled their privileges, and changed a government, limited by law, into arbitrary power, rendered them the abomination of the people, who were convinced that their dignities were the only things they regarded which made them deviate from the rules of the Gospel, looking no farther than their present enjoyments, little minding the betraying the interests of religion and the kingdom, out of treacherous compliance with the will and pleasure of a Popish court, to whom they made themselves slaves.

June 15, the Estates of Scotland met after their late adjournment, and the Duke of Hamilton acquainted them that His Majesty had been pleased to send him a commission to represent his royal person, and that he had orders to give his consent to an Act for the turning the meeting of the Estates into a Parliament, which was done accordingly, and soon after they made an Act for recognizing and asserting their Majesties' royal authority and right to the crown, and another for all persons to take an oath of faith and allegiance to them; and about the same time the English forces under General Mackay and others being entered that kingdom, the Duke of Gordon, who till this time had possession of the castle, finding no hopes of relief, surrendered it upon articles to Sir John Lanier; and so that important place, which so long had been a terror to the city of Edinburgh, was put into safe hands, the Duke casting himself upon the King's mercy without making any article for himself, and it was reported he said, "That he had so much respect for all the Princes of King James VI. line as not to make conditions with them for his own particular interest." After this a reward of eighteen thousand marks was, by proclamation, promised to those that should apprehend Dundee, dead or alive, and indeed he survived not long after; for July 26, Major-General Mackay, marching from St. John's Town with four thousand foot and four troops of horse and dragoons, and coming within two miles of the Blair of Athol, had notice that Dundee advanced toward him with six thousand foot and one hundred horse. The fight began between four and five o'clock in the afternoon, and lasted till night, with great courage and resolution on both sides; but at length, Mackay's forces being overpowered with number, he retired toward Stirling, with a body of fifteen hundred men in good order: many were killed on both sides, but the enemies' loss was greater by the death of Viscount Dundee, who, charging furiously at the head of the Highlanders to encourage them, was slain with a shot, though he had armour; after which a division happened between the Lord Dunfermline and Colonel Cannon, who should succeed in command of the rebels, at which time Major-General Mackay, hearing that five hundred of their foot and two troops of horse were sent to St. John's Town to surprise the stores of provisions there, resolved to be revenged for his late loss; and marching out of Stirling with a party of horse and dragoons, met the rebels, and gave them a total rout, killing and taking prisoners the greatest part of them, and Captain Hacket, their commander. Soon after another defeat was given to Colonel Cannon's men, consisting of about four thousand with the addition of the country, by the Earl of Angus's regiment, under Lieutenant-Colonel Cleland, who, after three hours' sharp dispute, forced the rebels to fly back, with a loss of above three hundred and not above thirty of the King's men, among whom was the Lieutenant-Colonel. This defeat put an effectual stop to the incursions of the Highlanders, who lost all their courage with the death of their commander, being never able to make any considerable head afterward; and though the Earl of Dunfermline pretended to manage them, yet several of the chief nobility and gentlemen came in and craved the benefit of the proclamation of indemnity which the King had published some time before, to all those who, before the third of September, should lay down their arms and swear fidelity to King William and Queen Mary; and Colonel Cannon, who only maintained the interest of the late King, retreated with his few followers to the Isle of Mull, doubtful whether to continue longer there or return to Ireland. Lieutenant-General Mackay having put a garrison into the castle of Blair, returned to Edinburgh, where several Earls that were in prison had their liberty, giving sufficient security for their peaceful behaviour; so that several troops of the King's forces in that kingdom were embarked for Ireland. And about the same time the Parliament there passed several Acts which were touched with the royal sceptre, by the Lord High Commissioner, and among others, an Act for abolishing prelacy, purporting, "That whereas the Estates of the kingdom, by their claim of right, April 11th last, had declared that prelacy and supremacy in any office of the church above Presbytery had been a grievous burden to the nation ever since the Reformation; that therefore the King and Queen's Majesty did abolish episcopacy, &c., and would establish that church government which was most agreeable to the people."

And now the Parliament of England having given the King plentiful supplies for the reduction of Ireland, the army marched from all parts towards Chester and Highlake, to embark under the Duke of Schomberg, consisting of near thirty thousand men, with great store of all sorts of ammunition and provisions, and considerable sums of money, and His Majesty appointed a camp on Hounslow Heath for the remainder of the forces, August 14th, which continued only two or three days, and in the meantime a declaration of war was published against France in Scotland; and now several Protestants in the north of Ireland having got possession of the Isle of Enniskillen and the City of Londonderry, they resolved to defend them against King James and his army of Irish Papists, who were marching from Dublin against them; and hearing that Lieutenant-General Macarty was abroad with a strong detachment, plundering and ravaging the country, Lieutenant-Colonel Barry fell upon them with such vigour, that it is judged three thousand of the Irish were slain and drowned in the Lough, near Newton-Butler, into which they desperately threw themselves to escape the sword. King James, arriving at Londonderry, imagined the terror of his arms would oblige the English to surrender the town upon his first appearance, and though Colonel Lundy and others despaired of holding it against an army of forty thousand men, with a train of artillery and divers mortars, yet the enraged people resolved to defend it against the utmost efforts of the enemy, and having declared Mr. George Walker, a minister, and Major Baker, their Governors, they chose colonels and other officers, and regimented their men, consisting in the whole of seven thousand and twenty soldiers, and three hundred and forty-one officers, and rejecting all the terms of surrender offered them, they fired upon the enemy, and much astonished King James, who was within reach of their cannon, and expected they would have opened their gates to him, who thereupon resolved to reduce them by force, and within a day or two broke ground, and ran their trenches within a furlong of the walls, where placing a demiculvern, they battered the town but with little success, unless some small damage to the market-house, the cannon from the town in the meantime killing many Irish; and, to prevent their further approach, the garrison made a sally, killing two hundred of the enemy, with Mamow, the French General, and other officers of note. Several other gallant sallies were made out of the town, in one of which above two hundred were killed and five hundred wounded, with the loss of three of the defenders, and twenty wounded. June 4th, the besieged made an attack upon the work near the windmill, and though the Irish came upon them with loud huzzas, and though the foot had faggots, and after these failed, took up dead bodies to defend themselves, and the horse were mostly in armour, yet they were beaten off, four thousand of them killed, and but a few of the garrison. In some of these attacks Lieutenant Douglas and Captain Cunningham were taken prisoners, and, after quarter given, barbarously killed. In the night the enemy played their bombs of two hundred and seventy-three pounds weight, which ploughed up the streets and killed several sick people; and in the day time their cannon played incessantly against the walls, insomuch that the garrison, by sickness, more than shot of the enemy, was reduced to six thousand one hundred and eighty-five men, and began to be distressed; but June 15th, a fleet of thirty sail under Major-General Kirk, with men, provisions, and ammunition for their relief, came into the Lough, and though several ships attempted to sail up the river, yet the fire of the enemy from the batteries on shore, and also a boom made of timber, chain and cable, across the narrowest part of the river, prevented their design; however, they contrived to give Major-General Kirk an account of their extremity, and he sent an answer assuring them that they should suddenly be supplied with all necessaries, which he had aboard in abundance. The enemy being sensible of their exigencies, pressed on the siege with more vigour, under their new French Marshal, General Rosen, who, by threats and promises, used his utmost efforts to reduce the town. June 30th, Major Baker died, to the great regret of the besieged, and soon after the garrison was reduced to four thousand eight hundred and ninety-two men; yet they made a vigorous sally to fetch in some cattle, but did not succeed, losing a great number of their men. This made the famine increase in the city, so that horse-flesh was sold for twenty pence per pound, the quarter of a dog for five shillings and sixpence, a dog's head two shillings and sixpence, a cat four shillings and sixpence, and other things proportionately, as rats, mice, tallow, grease, &c. But now, when all hopes failed them, July 13th the *Mountjoy* and *Phœnix*, convoyed by the *Dartmouth* frigate and other men-of-war, came up to the town with little loss, when they reckoned but upon two days' life, having only nine lean horses left, and one pint of meal to each man, four thousand two hundred only being left, whereof a fourth part were rendered unserviceable. The enemy perceiving that these ships had furnished the besieged with provisions, July 31st, they raised the siege in some disorder, blowing up several castles, with all the houses down the river, and setting the country for ten miles in a flame in their retreat.

August 13, 1689, the Duke of Schomberg landed at Carrickfergus with all the forces under his command, and the Protestants joining with him in great numbers, he soon reduced that town, and sent two regiments to Belfast; and the General having made proclamation, "That if the enemy continued to burn as they had begun, if any of them fell into his hands, they must expect no quarter." They thereupon quitted Dundalk without any damage. After this, about five thousand Irish attempted to take Sligo, which was in the hands of the English; but the Enniskillen men, with about one thousand horse, foot and dragoons, charged them with such celerity and courage that seven hundred of them were cut off, and four hundred taken prisoners; and besides arms and ammunition, eighteen thousand head of cattle were taken from them, which they had plundered the country people of. In November the English army decamped from the plains of Dundalk to Lisneegarvee and Lisburn, the enemy, though superior in number, having of late attempted little; only one morning early, they had hopes of surprising our advanced parties at Newry, killing the out sentinels, and getting into the town, but were soon beaten out again by a party of Colonel Ingoldby's regiment; and several other parties beat the enemy in divers places, and gained great booties of cattle. Colonel Woolsey defeated the Irish at Cavan, though the Duke of Berwick was sent to reinforce them, so that though the garrison consisted of four thousand men, yet three hundred of the enemy were killed, and among them many officers; two hundred taken prisoners, and Cavan taken and burnt, which the English were constrained to do, to get the soldiers out of the town to resist the Irish, who made a strong sally out of the fort.

In England Her Royal Highness the Princess of Denmark was delivered of a Prince in August, who was christened by the Lord Bishop of London, and named William, His Majesty being godfather, and Her Majesty and the Queen of Denmark godmothers. October 19, the Parliament met at Westminster, and granted His Majesty two millions sterling towards the expense of the next year's war. In Scotland Colonel Cannon continued still in the Isle of Mull, with an inconsiderable party of islanders and others. Some few rebels appeared about this time under the Lord of Lochelly, burning and plundering wherever they came; about eight hundred marched out of Inverlochy, thinking to have surprised the fort of Inverness, but were defeated of their design. The Earl of Pembroke, upon his return from being Ambassador in Holland to England, was made a Privy Councillor. Some persons were seized about this time for endeavouring to raise disturbance against the Government.

December 16, 1689, an Act was passed declaring the rights and liberties of the subject, and settling the succession of the crown: "That whereas the Lords spiritual and temporal, and Commons assembled at Westminster, lawfully, fully and freely, representing all the estates of the people of this realm, did, on February 13, 1688, present to their Majesties, then called and known by the names and style of William and Mary, Prince and Princess of Orange, being present in their proper persons, a certain declaration in writing, made by the Lords and Commons (of which you have already an account). Upon which their said Majesties did accept the crown and royal dignity of these kingdoms, according to the resolution and desire of the said Lords and Commons contained in the said declaration, and thereupon their Majesties were pleased that the Lords and Commons, being the two Houses of Parliament, should continue to sit, and with their royal concurrence to make effectual provision for the settlement of the religion, laws and liberties of this kingdom, so that the same for the future might not be in danger again of being subverted. Now, in pursuance of the premises, the Lords spiritual and temporal, and Commons in Parliament assembled, for the ratifying, confirming and establishing the said declaration, and the articles, clauses, matters and things therein contained, by the force of a law made in due form by authority of Parliament, do pray that it may be declared and enacted, that all and singular the rights and liberties asserted and claimed in the said declaration, are the true, ancient and indubitable rights and liberties of the people of this kingdom, and so shall be esteemed, allowed, adjudged, deemed and taken to be, and that all and every the particulars aforesaid shall be firmly and strictly holden and observed, as they are expressed in the said declaration, and all officers and ministers whatsoever shall serve their Majesties and their successors according to the same in all times to come ; and do further declare that King James II. having abdicated the government, and their Majesties having accepted the crown and royal dignity as aforesaid, did become, were, and of right ought to be, by the laws of this realm, our sovereign liege Lord and Lady, King and Queen of England, France and

Ireland, &c. And for preventing all questions and divisions, by reason of any pretended titles to the crown, and to preserve a certainty in the succession, the Lords and Commons beseech their Majesties that it may be enacted, established and declared, that the crown and royal dignity shall be and continue in their Majesties during their lives, and the life of the survivor of them; and after their decease to the heirs of Her Majesty; and in default of issue, to the Princess Ann of Denmark and her heirs; and for default of such issue, to the heirs of the body of His Majesty; and that the Parliament in the name of the people will submit themselves and their heirs, and posterities for ever, and stand by, maintain and defend this limitation and succession of the crown, to the utmost of their powers, with their lives and estates, against all that shall attempt anything to the contrary. And whereas it hath been found by experience, that it is inconsistent with the safety and welfare of this Protestant kingdom to be governed by a Popish Prince, or by any King or Queen marrying a Papist, they do further pray that it may be enacted, and all persons that are or shall be reconciled to, or hold communion with the see of Rome, or shall profess the Popish religion, or shall marry a Papist, shall be excluded, and be for ever incapable to possess, inherit or enjoy the crown and dignity of this kingdom, of Ireland, &c. And that in all such cases, the people are absolved from their allegiance, and the crown shall descend to the next heir being a Protestant, as should have inherited and enjoyed the same, as if the persons so reconciled, or marrying, were naturally dead: and that every King or Queen that shall succeed hereafter shall, on the first day of the meeting of their Parliament, sitting on the throne of the House of Peers, in the presence of the Lords and Commons, or at their coronation which shall first happen, audibly repeat the declaration in the statute of the 30th of King Charles II., entitled 'An Act for the more effectual preserving of the King's person and Government,' etc. But if such King and Queen shall be under the age of twelve years, then to perform the same the first Parliament after that age; all which are by their Majesties, by and with the consent of the Lords spiritual and temporal, and Commons declared, enacted and established to stand, remain and be the law of this realm for ever."

About this time the Queen of Spain was convoyed by a squadron of English men-of-war from Holland to the Groin, in Spain. February 6, the Parliament was dissolved, and another summoned to appear at Westminster, March 20th, following, which accordingly met and confirmed all the acts of the preceding Parliament, passing many others, both for raising money, for carrying on the present war, and for the benefit of the people. In Scotland some attempts were made by the rebels, for in May, 1690, the Colonels Buchan and Cannon, being with two thousand men (which they expected to be four thousand in a few days) at their rendezvous at Strathspey, Sir Thomas Livingstone, upon notice thereof, marched towards them with his forces, surprising them in the night in the camp, killed four hundred and took one hundred prisoners, most gentlemen and officers, Buchan and Cannon hardly escaping, upon which the Castle of Lethindy, in which the enemy had a garrison under Colonel Buchan's nephew, surrendered at discretion, in which was found store of arms and ammunition, with four hundred bolls of meal and the standard design to have been set up by the late King James; and yet in this whole action it was very remarkable that the English lost not one man, and had only four or five wounded.

In Ireland affairs proceeded very successfully, for May 11th, the strong garrison of Charlemont surrendered upon articles, the Governor Teage O'Regan, and the Irish, about eight hundred strong, having almost consumed all their provisions, marched out, leaving a good quantity of ammunition, seventeen brass cannon, and two mortars. The King now resolved, if possible, to make a sudden reduction of Ireland, that it might no longer be a diversion from his attacking the French vigorously in Flanders; and in pursuit of this magnanimous design, His Majesty concluded to go thither in person, by his presence and conduct to facilitate the same, and accordingly, June 4, 1690, with a splendid equipage departed from Whitehall, and coming to Chester, embarked on the fleet attending him, and June 14 landed at Carrickfergus, being received by Duke Schomberg, and the army and all the Protestants with general joy and loud acclamations; and from thence His Majesty marched with his forces in two bodies, and encamped at Dundalk, intending to go for Dublin, or else oblige the enemy to a battle, which the late King James was aware of, and therefore with his army which consisted of about thirty-six thousand Irish and French, besides fifteen thousand in garrisons, he marched from Dublin towards Drogheda, but seemed to distrust his success, for to provide for the worst, he sent an order to Waterford to prepare ships for carrying him off. June 31, King William resolving to force the enemy to fight or to retreat, marched by break of day from his camp at Ardee toward Drogheda, and found the Irish army encamped along the River

Boyne, above the town; and according to his usual custom, with undaunted resolution, he passed the river, notwithstanding the utmost opposition of the enemy, and fell upon them with such fury, that in a few hours their whole army were utterly routed and dispersed, about three thousand being killed and divers prisoners of note being taken, most of the enemy's baggage, as chariots, tents, arms, cannon, ammunition and provisions, and some money falling into the hands of our soldiers.

The late King James, who had stood at a distance to see the fight, perceiving the defeat of his forces, fled with all speed toward Dublin, with a very few attendants, and having staid there one night, filling the place with fear and confusion, upon an alarm that King William was on his way thither, accompanied with the Duke of Berwick, the Marquis of Powis, and some others, he left the city, and hastened to Waterford, where a ship lay ready for him, having neither slept nor eat till he had got out at sea, and stood away for France. Upon this the Protestants at Dublin, who were imprisoned had their liberty, and a few days after the King arrived there, to the unspeakable joy of the people. The loss of the English in obtaining this great victory was not considerable, only Duke Schomberg and Doctor Walker were both slain. After this, Waterford, Wexford, and several other places were reduced, and upon a proclamation of pardon, many of the Irish laid down their arms, and returned to their former places of abode.

This glorious success was somewhat clouded nearer home, for the French King, to favour his design in Ireland, had now sent forth the greatest fleet that ever sailed on the ocean out of France, and stood toward our coast, as if they designed to fight our navy under the Earl of Torrington, who June 24, sailed from St. Helen's toward them. They were seen the night before off Freshwater Gate, in the Isle of Wight; but the wind taking them short, the Admiral came to anchor off Dunnose, five leagues off the French, so that a battle was soon expected, which the enemy did not seem to decline. The English seamen were also full of courage, and desirous to engage; but the French being much stronger both for number and bigness of ships, consisting of eighty-two men-of-war, besides fire-ships, and tenders, it was not thought fit to fight in the open sea, so that the Earl of Torrington avoided it, till he came to Bevesire, off Beachy, which was favourable for his purpose, and there he received the Queen's orders not to delay engaging, if the wind and weather would permit, which was the reason that we went to seek the enemy, who expected us in order of battle, and about nine in the morning the engagement began. The Dutch that had the vanguard fought bravely, and both sides fired desperately three hours, till the French, not liking their entertainment, bore away with all speed; but about one o'clock there happened a calm, which not only prevented the Hollanders' pursuit, but put them into a little disorder. The French not being able to get away, were constrained to begin the fight again, which lasted till five in the evening with extraordinary fury. As for the English, some fought well; but the Admiral's unexpected standing away prevented them from seconding the Dutch, so that the rest stood lookers-on, while the main body of the French fell into the rear of the Dutch, who having fought from morning till night, and defended themselves so long against a prodigious number of the enemy that assailed them on every side, they were so much battered, that hardly three were capable of making any defence, which constrained them to make their way through the French fleet to the coast of England. The Hollanders lost two Admirals and a Captain; and some of their ships, that could not be got off, were burnt. The English lost two sea and two marine Captains. Admiral Everston declared that all the Dutch officers and seamen had done their duties; and had ours engaged heartily, no doubt the French had gone home in a worse condition than the Spaniards did in 1588. After the fight, the French fleet sailed westward, and sent their boats ashore at Teignmouth, a small village of fishermen's cots, which they set on fire, with two or three small vessels in the harbour, and stealing a few sheep, after having lain some time on our coast to little purpose, they returned to Brest.

At the time the French lay off the coast of Kent one Godfrey Cross, an innkeeper in that country, was seen to go on board one of their boats, which carried him to the fleet, whereupon, at his return, he was seized, and treasonable letters being found about him he was committed prisoner, and soon after tried for high treason at the King's Bench bar, Westminster, and being convicted was hanged and quartered for the same, and care was taken by her Majesty, in whom the regency resided during the King's absence, to put the militia of the counties into such a posture as to defeat any evil designs of the enemies to the Government; and the militia of London, consisting of about ten thousand men, made a gallant appearance before Her Majesty at Hyde Park, and declared their resolution to defend their Majesties and the Government against all its opponents, and the whole Militia of England, computed to be about one hundred and fifty thousand, horse and foot, showed the same forwardness. Upon complaint against the Earl of Torrington for the miscarriage of the fleet, he was committed by the Council to the Tower. After the French had quitted our coasts and were gone into harbour, the militia were discharged, and all diligence was used to repair and equip the fleet for sea.

About this time we had news of the great success of the English against the French in the West Indies, having beaten them out of St. Christopher's and many other considerable places, and taken great booties of cattle, corn and other stores and provisions, and that we had reduced the fort in the Island of Statie, and two of our privateers falling in with twelve French merchantmen bound for St. Malo's, under the convoy of a frigate of twelve guns, took four of them, forcing the rest on shore about Cherbourg, where they were all shipwrecked, except the frigate, and most of the men drowned.

The rebels in Scotland, promising themselves great advantages from the French being on our coasts, and being deceived by false reports, fifteen hundred of them got together in the county of Murray, under Buchan and Cannon, threatening the people to burn and destroy their houses and goods if they did not join with them; but Sir Thomas Livingstone advancing by speedy marches, came upon them so surprisingly, that they made little resistance, but fled with all imaginable confusion, and being pursued, four hundred of them were killed, and the rest totally routed and taken prisoners, with a great quantity of claret and other provisions, and a great number of officers were brought to Edinburgh and committed to the Tolbooth. Soon after, the remaining rebels who escaped, designed to have surprised the garrison of Inverness, but were happily prevented and defeated by the Earl of Drumlanrig and Major-General Mackay.

In Ireland, the King having secured Dublin in safe hands, caused his army to march towards Limerick, where Tyrconnel and Lauzun had drawn together the late King's broken forces; and having made their approaches, against all opposition, His Majesty ordered the trenches to be opened, and planted several batteries of cannon, which made great breaches in the walls, and a general assault was expected; but on August 28th, at night, the rain fell so excessively, that the rivers overflowed, and the garrison being extremely strong, the King, to spare his men, and to avoid the many inconveniences of the approaching season, was pleased to order the raising the siege, and to defer the reducing the city till a more favourable opportunity; after which his Majesty returned for England, and was received with all imaginable expressions of joy throughout the kingdom.

About this time a fleet was prepared by His Majesty's order, consisting of thirty-two English and twenty-eight Dutch men-of-war, on board of which were embarked eight regiments of foot, besides the marine regiments, commanded by the Earl of Marlborough as General, and Trelawney as Major-General, who, on the 21st of September, arrived at Cork, in Ireland, which was obliged to surrender upon articles, and soon after Kinsale ran the same fate. A horrible design of the Irish was now discovered to have set the city of Dublin on fire, but it was happily discovered and prevented.

In October the Parliament met at Winchester, and congratulated His Majesty on his safe return, and likewise returned their humble acknowledgments to Her Majesty for her goodness, wisdom and courage, manifested in the greatest dangers, even when a powerful enemy was upon the coasts. The Earl of Torrington was tried on board the *Kent*, in the river Medway, by a jury of sea captains, and, after a long hearing of the witnesses and his defence, upon a long debate, he was acquitted. The Parliament continued to sit, and passed many Acts, both supplying His Majesty for the war and settling the kingdom, to whom the King gave an account, that the posture of affairs abroad required his presence at the Hague; and, accordingly, on the 6th of January, His Majesty left Whitehall, attended by the great officers of his household, and divers others of the nobility and gentry, and soon after arrived in Holland, though with some difficulty, by reason of the ice. At the Hague, His Majesty was received with great joy, which they expressed by erecting several triumphal arches, redounding to the glory of his gallant achievements since His Majesty had left that country.

And now a conspiracy was discovered, managed by several persons, for introducing our former bondage and slavery, and the Lord Preston, John Ashton and Edmund Eliot were seized as they were designing to go for France, with letters and papers of pernicious consequence, and on the 17th of Jaunary the Lord Preston was tried for high treason at the Old Bailey, and two days after Mr. Ashton, who were both found guilty; and Mr. Ashton was executed for the same, but the Lord Preston was reprieved, together with one Crone, formerly sentenced upon the same account, and the trial of Eliot was deferred; after which a proclamation was issued out, for apprehending Dr. Turner, late Bishop of Ely, William Pen, and James Graham, Esquires.

The Duke of Savoy, whose family had for above a hundred years past been trampled on by France, and would this day have been entirely enslaved by that King, took this favourable occasion to set himself at liberty, while all Europe almost lent him a helping hand, and thereupon some months since he declared openly against that crown, and released and gave liberty to all his Protestant subjects, and entertained them into his service, entering likewise into the confederacy with the Princes and States of Christendom, now in arms to reduce that grand usurper to reason, and incapacitate him from being any longer dangerous to his neighbours. And in the latter end of 1690, his Highness sent an envoy to congratulate their Majesties' accession to the throne, and to express his passionate desire to unite himself to His Majesty's friendship, by an indissoluble union.

Upon the King's arrival at the Hague, several Princes daily came thither, as well to have the honour to wait upon His Majesty, as to confer about the state of affairs. March 5, the King, accompanied by the Duke of Zell, and several of his own nobility, departed for Loo, and by the way had news that the French had invested the city of Mons the day before; upon which His Majesty ordered the Dutch troops to march immediately into Flanders, to the general rendezvous, and soon after followed in person, being received in the camp with extraordinary joy, that they should fight under the banner of so undaunted a Prince. The French King arrived before the town five days after the siege had begun, having amassed all his forces together upon this enterprise, leaving only sufficient to defend their garrisons, so that by their continual firing and attacks, and the folly of the burghers, who would not admit above six thousand men into the town, whereas they ought to have had at least four thousand horse, and ten thousand foot, this important place was taken in eight days' time, the Governor not being able to make such vigorous sallies as he might have done, because he was willing to spare his men; but the burghers being by this means stronger than the garrison, obliged the Prince of Berghes to a surrender before the confederates could possibly have leisure to relieve the town. After which the French King returned to Versailles, and King William came back to England, viewing some part of the fleet in his return, and arrived safe at Whitehall, where His Majesty nominated several new bishops to succeed to those that had forfeited their bishoprics by refusing to swear allegiance to their Majesties. He likewise took a view of the troops that were to go to Flanders; and having provided for security of the kingdom, and happily settled all affairs in Scotland and Ireland, His Majesty declared his resolution of returning into Flanders, and arrived May 2nd, 1691, in the army encamped within two miles of Brussels, being about seventy thousand strong, and the French, under the Duke of Luxemburg, no less numerous. And in July, Baltimore and Athlone, in Ireland, were taken by General Ginkle, and the Prince Wirtemberg. Monsieur St. Ruth, the French King's general, being killed in the great battle at Aughrim, soon after, with the loss of seven thousand of the Irish, and the taking of Galway, which followed, with most of the other forts, and castles, and towns, except Limerick, which was also invested the latter end of August, upon which Lieutenant-General Sarsfield, who was retired to the mountains with four thousand horse and dragoons, resolved to return to that city, but was met by the

General Ginkle and a party of the English, who so vigorously charged them, that they instantly fled, and were pursued to the very gates of the town, above six hundred Irish being slain, and seventy officers taken prisoners. The besieged, seeing themselves shut up within the walls of one single town, which was now almost battered down about their ears, hopeless of succour, and reduced to the last extremities, October 13th, surrendered up Limerick, upon articles, whereby all Ireland was wholly reduced to their Majesties' obedience.

In Flanders, September 19, there happened an engagement between the French and confederate armies in the absence of the King of England, who, finding he could not oblige the enemy to a battle, departed to Brussels, and from thence to Loo, in order to his return to England, leaving the command of the army to Prince Waldeck, who, decamping from Loo to retire to Cambron, the enemy having note thereof, detached about thirty squadrons who marched all night, and by favour of a thick mist, unexpectedly fell upon fifteen squadrons of the confederates' rear guard. The conflict was very sharp, and though inferior in numbers, the allies made a vigorous defence till several other regiments came up to their relief, which caused the enemy to retreat. The French lost near seven hundred men with many officers, and the confederates about the same number, after which both armies went into winter quarters.

The English and Holland fleets, under the command of Admiral Russell, had in vain sought to engage the French this summer at sea, and having lain some time on the coast of Ireland, to prevent the French from sending forces thither, came now into harbour after a very tempestuous season, and the Holland fleet separated, and safely arrived in their several ports, and the French fleet returned to Brest. His Majesty being returned to England, October 19, and the Parliament sitting, the King declared himself to them, who thereupon unanimously resolved to raise such supplies as should enable him to continue the war with France, and in March following His Majesty arrived again in Holland, and from thence went to Loo, where several Princes met him, to concert the affairs of the next campaign. He having an army of thirty thousand English in Flanders this summer, March 26, 1692, the Elector of Bavaria, who was made Governor of the Spanish Netherlands during life, arrived at Brussels, being received there with much joy and solemnity.

His Majesty having designed to make a descent upon France this summer, the news so alarmed the French King that he resolved to land some forces in England, and King James at the head of them, some Jacobites and discontented people here having given him assurance of joining with him upon his landing; to which end the French supplied ships, troops and Louis d'ors, so that nothing was wanting but to cross the sea, and a squadron of sixteen ships and two bombing vessels were fitted at Toulon, under Count d'Estree, to convey the transport ships thither, under the protection of the French fleet, commanded by Vice-Admiral Tourville, in the Channel, to prevent the joining of the Dutch and English fleets, and to fight all that should oppose their passage: but Providence ordered the winds and rocks to fight d'Estree, he losing two of his largest ships near Ceuta, on the coast of Africa, and the rest, miserably shattered, went to Portugal to refit, so that instead of being at Brest the beginning of April, he did not arrive there till the beginning of July, and came a minute too late, as he said, to join Tourville. The Queen of England, upon notice of the embarking of so many men, gave out all necessary orders for securing the coasts, and several horses were seized, whose owners designed to have joined the enemy upon their descent, which was intended to have been about Portsmouth and the Isle of Wight. King James with his Irish forces was come to Cherbourg, upon the coast of Normandy, and Monsieur Tourville had great confidence in the courage of his French mariners, upon James's assurance that the English would not fight, but be spectators only.

The English and Dutch fleets being happily joined, without any obstruction from the enemy, Admiral Russell set sail from St. Helens, and on the 19th of May got sight of the French fleet near Cape Harfleur. Admiral Tourville, having the wind, hastened up to the English, but the wind slackening, the French vanguard of fifteen great men-of-war could not come up to the English till eleven next morning. Five of the fifteen did their duty, but the other ten kept out of cannon shot. The Dutch were not able to come up, the wind being in their teeth. The fight lasted between them that could engage about three hours, and then the French made all the sail they could to get away, and the Dutch had much ado to turn their ships to follow them, by reason of the calm, during which two main bodies of the fleet laboured to the utmost to come up with the enemy, and being happily got up with them engaged resolutely for four hours, and then Tourville, as his vanguard had done before, retreated with all speed, and by favour of a mist got out of sight. In the afternoon the English blue squadron, which could not come up for the calm, fell upon the French blue squadron, where the most obstinate fight was maintained, till the night and mists gave opportunity to the enemy to hasten toward their own coasts. The next day being clear, Admiral Russell discovered them two leagues off, but could not come up by reason of a sudden mist. About eleven at night the French weighed anchor by moonlight, and the confederates pursued them, who, to save themselves, ventured among the rocks of Jersey and Guernsey. On the 21st of May the Admiral discovering several men-of-war upon a bank, near Cape Harfleur, detached Vice-Admiral Delaval, with eight or nine vessels and three fire-ships, to set fire to them, which, next day, was happily effected. The *Royal Sun*, that magnificent ship, commanded by Admiral Tourville, which was the wonder of the world, both for the exquisiteness of her carving and the beauty of her shape, being twenty years in the building by the most skilful shipwrights in Europe, carrying one hundred and ten guns; the *Admiral*, of one hundred and two, and the *Strong*, of eighty guns, with two less frigates and three transport ships, were all sacrificed to the flames, and the next day twelve more were burnt in a bay behind the Isle of Alderney, and this without the loss of one English or Dutch ship; the rest of the French fleet fled to Brest, St. Malo's, and other ports to secure themselves. King James was upon a hill, and through a perspective glass saw the fight; and, upon the first firing of the English, he declared that it was only a signal to come over to the French; but he soon found himself deceived, and that it was Admiral Russell he had to do withal, and that the intrigues of his Jacobites had not succeeded. Thus it pleased Heaven to crown their Majesties' navy with a glorious victory, and to preserve us from the chains prepared for us by the two dear allies; for notwithstanding the specious declaration published by King James, upon his assurance of being restored, yet we have all the reason in the world to believe his pardon would not have secured the nation from Popish vengeance, but that we should have all felt the utmost effects of his rage and fury, as well as the honourable and worthy persons following, whom he excluded from all hope of mercy—that is, the Duke of Ormond, the Marquis of Winchester; the Earls of Sunderland, Bath, Dandy and Nottingham; the Lords Newport, Delamere, Wiltshire, Colchester, Cornbury, Dumblane, and Churchill; the Bishops of St. Asaph and London; Dr. Tillotson and Dr. Burnet; Knights, Sir Ro. Howard, Sir J. Worden, Sir S. Grimstone, Sir S. Fox, Sir George Treby, Sir Basil Dixwell, and Sir John Oxendon; Esquires, F. Russel, R. Levison, J. Trenchard, C. Duncombe; Citizens of London, Edwards, Napleton and Hunt; fishermen, with all others that offered indignities to him at Feversham, with Ashton and Crosse's judges and jurymen; also all spies, and those that have betrayed his councils in his absence.

May 15, 1692, the French army, having made many marches and countermarches, invested the strong fortress of Namur, being encouraged thereto by the treacherous Baron de Bersey, who, being born a subject of Spain, and having received some disgust from that court, was corrupted by the French, and, making his escape out of the town, informed the enemy of the condition thereof, of which he had got full information by his intimacy with the governor, the Prince of Brabançon, so as to inform them of the best places for the attack, which was strong and yet weak, so that the town surrendered in five days; and awhile after, William's fort and castle were likewise delivered up. It is very well known that the King of England took all the pains imaginable to get his army of several nations together before the siege; and that the Duke of Luxemburg, who lay with a strong detachment to cover the besiegers, used all manner of caution to avoid a battle, by encamping in places where he could not be assaulted, being sufficiently acquainted with the temper of King William, to whom it was natural to despise danger, and who pushed on the relief of the place to the utmost; for as soon as he came to Mehaine, he instantly caused bridges to be built in the night to cross the river next morning, and to attack Duke Luxemburg in the morasses, which he had certainly done if an extraordinary rain had not fallen, and if all the Generals had not unanimously dissuaded him from it, because of the impossibility of forming a line of battle in a place so full of water. After the surrender of Namur, the King being informed that the Duke of Luxemburg was upon his march from Enguien, resolved to advance with all speed to the same place, but the French got there before him, and posted themselves between that place and Steinkerken, among hedges and woods. However, King William resolved to attack him there, which much surprised Luxemburg, who, upon view of the advantageous situation of his camp, had said that "none but an Alexander or a Cæsar durst attack him in that place;" but it was William the Great who performed that part, and, marching silently all night, fell upon the French with such fury next morning that in a few hours above seven thousand of the enemy were slain, with a great number of nobility and officers, and afterwards retreated at leisure, the French not having the courage to fol low them, so that the attack and retreat were equally glorious, the King having exposed himself amidst the cannon and musket shots where the fight was hottest, riding continually from one end to the other to give necessary orders, so that it was next to a miracle that his sacred person was preserved among so many imminent dangers. Thus His Majesty gloriously ended this campaign by a signal victory over the French at sea, and by having several times braved his enemies by land, harrassing them by his continual marches and attacking them in their entrenchments, seeking only an opportunity of putting an end to the war by a general battle, and so to procure to Europe a solid and durable peace.

On the contrary, the French King dares never to appear at the head of his troops, but endeavours to make himself renowed by treachery and violation of oaths; these are his fortress; and assassinations and poisonings are crimes which in that court are not prohibited. Witness the valet de chambre who poisoned the Duke of Lorraine; the French cook who, at the instigation of the French ambassador, poisoned Mr. Harbord at Belgrade, for being vigorous in procuring a peace betwixt the Emperor and the Turks; and lastly, Sieur de Granval, who was with some others hired by the Marquis of Barbesieux, secretary to the French King, to murder King William, being also encouraged thereto by King James and his Queen, who told him, "If you and the rest do me this service, you shall never want." But this horrid villainy being happily discovered, Granval was about this time deservedly executed for the same. In October, His Majesty returned again to England, and the Parliament being met he made a gracious speech to them, after which they unanimously voted a supply of near five millions, for carrying on a vigorous war against France.

[NOTE.—Burton's History of the House of Orange closes here, but to complete the History of King William and Queen Mary, the following has been taken from Lord Macaulay's history during that period.]

The state of Ireland will now engage our attention for a moment. On the 5th October, 1692, the Irish Parliament met at Dublin in Chichester House. It was very differently composed from the Assembly which had borne the same title in 1689, and there can be no doubt that in many respects it was very unsatisfactory in its constitution. The Session opened with a solemn recognition of the paramount authority of the mother country, and the Commons ordered their clerk to read to them the English Act which required them to take the oath of supremacy, and to subscribe the declaration against Transubstantiation. Addresses of a loyal description were voted, and certain members who had proved unfaithful to the Protestant interests were expelled. Large supplies were eagerly voted, but considerable discontent was subsequently occasioned by the conduct of Lord Lieutenant Surrey, who, without any sufficient foundation, attributed to the Irish House of Commons a desire of unduly trenching upon the prerogatives of the Imperial Parliament and the provisions of what was known as " Poyning's Act." Both Houses addressed the King on the state of Ireland; they mentioned no delinquent by name, but they expressed an opinion that there had been gross maladministration, that the public had been plundered, and that undue partiality had been shown to the Roman Catholics. William promised that the matter should be inquired into. Sydney was soon after recalled, and the government of Ireland was for a time entrusted to the Lords Justices, among whom Sir Henry Capel held a foremost place.

In the life of King William, the year 1693 is memorable as the date of the great battle of Landen, which is the name of a small stream convenient to the village of Romsdorff. On the right of this stream lay the village of Neerwinden. Here it was that William had his army entrenched. Both villages were, after the fashion of the Low Countries, surrounded by moats and fences, and within these enclosures the little plots of ground occupied by different families were separated by mud walls five feet in height and a foot in thickness. William had them repaired with so much rapidity that Saint Simon, a competent authority who surveyed the ground after the battle, declared that he could not believe that defences so extensive and so formidable could have been created with so much rapidity. Luxemburg, the valorous and experienced opponent of King William, was determined to try whether even this position could be maintained against the superior numbers and impetuous valour of his soldiers. Soon after sunrise the roar of the cannon began to be heard, and while the French army was getting itself placed, William's artillery did much service. The fight began in real earnest about eight in the morning, and for several hours continued with terrific fury. Again and again Luxemburg brought up his troops within pistol shot of the breastwork, but again and again they recoiled from the heavy fire which was poured on their front and on their flanks. The day had nearly gone in favour of the allied forces, when a hurried council of war was held, the result of which was that Luxemburg determined to make an effort to carry the village of Neerwinden, and the invincible household troops, the conquerors of Steinkirk, must lead the way. A third time the town was taken by them, and a third time William tried to retake it. At the head of some English regiments he charged the Guards of Louis with such fury that, for the first time in the memory of the oldest warrior, that far-famed band gave way. This terrific attack, if standing alone, would shed imperishable lustre on the Prince of Orange. By this time, however, the centre and left of the allied army had been so much thinned for the purpose of supporting King William at Neerwinden that other points could no longer be defended, and a little after four p.m. the whole line gave way. It was only on such occasions as this that the whole greatness of William's character appeared. Amidst the rout and uproar, while arms and standards were flung away, while multitudes of fugitives were choking up the bridges and fords of the river, or perishing in its waters, the King, having directed Talmash to superintend the retreat, put himself at the head of a few regiments, and by desperate efforts arrested the progress of the enemy. Doing this he exposed his life to imminent danger, but he only smiled when told that the star on his breast was a good mark for the enemy. Many fell on his right hand and on his left. Two led horses, which in the field always closely followed his person, were struck dead by cannon shots. One musket ball passed through the curls of his wig, another through his coat, a third bruised his side and tore his blue ribands to tatters. Many years later, Chelsea Hospital pensioners used to relate how King William charged at the head of Galway's horse; how he dismounted four times to put heart into the infantry; how he rallied one corps which seemed to be shrinking, by saying, "That's not the way to fight, gentlemen. You must stand close up to them; thus, gentlemen, thus." Four days after the battle an eye-witness wrote: "You might have seen him with his sword in his hand throwing himself upon the enemy. It is certain that, one time among the rest, he was seen at the head of two English regiments, and that he fought *seven* with these two in sight of the whole army, driving them before him above a quarter of an hour. Thanks be to God that preserved him." The French were victorious, but they had purchased victory dear. More than ten thousand of the best troops of Louis had fallen. Neerwinden was a spectacle at which the oldest soldiers stood aghast. The streets were piled breast high with corpses. During many months the ground was strewn with skulls and bones of men and horses, and with fragments of hats and shoes, saddles and holsters. The next summer the soil, fertilized by twenty thousand corpses, broke forth into millions of poppies. The traveller who, on the road from Saint Trou Tirelemont, saw that vast sheet of rich scarlet spreading from Landen to Neerwinden, could hardly help fancying that the figurative prediction of the Hebrew prophet was literally accomplished—that the earth was disclosing her blood and refusing to cover her slain. The French army was too much exhausted to pursue, and a short delay was sufficient to enable King William to recruit his forces. His character appears to great advantage in this hour of extreme peril. As soon as he was safe he wrote to assure his wife of the fact. During the fight he had lost sight of his friend Portland, who was then in feeble health, and had therefore run more than the ordinary risks of war. A short note that he sent to him a few hours afterwards is still extant: "Though I hope to see you this evening, I cannot help writing to tell you how rejoiced I am that you got off so well. God grant that your health may be quite restored. These are great trials which He has been pleased to send me in quick succession. I must try to submit to His pleasure without murmuring, and to deserve His anger less." What a noble example of confiding trust in the providence of God! His forces rallied rapidly, and in the short space of three weeks he had a greater force than on the morning of the bloody day of Landen. Much discontent followed, and the Jacobites were not slow to avail themselves of it. A common expression among them was: "Box it about; it will come to my father." This was really a Romish password, meaning that if sufficient disorder were created, the kingdom would ultimately revert to James.

The space at our disposal will not permit us to refer even briefly to the state of political parties in England during this ever-memorable epoch. Between 1690 and 1693 several very serious defeats had been sustained by the arms of England, but the importance of these was greatly exaggerated by the political animosities by which William was assailed. At length, in 1694, the tide had begun to turn. The French arms had made no progress, and altogether matters were looking hopeful both at home and abroad. The year '94 was not destined to pass without becoming for ever memorable in the domestic history of King William. The terrible plague of small-pox broke out, and towards the end of the year the infection spread to the palace and reached the young and blooming Queen. She received the intimation of her danger with true greatness of soul. She gave orders that every lady of her bedchamber, every maid of honour, nay, every menial servant who had not had the small-pox, should instantly leave Kensington House. She locked herself up during a short time in her closet, burned some papers, arranged others, and then calmly awaited her fate. The disease alternated for a few days, but at length all doubt was over, and it was only too plain that the Queen was sinking under small-pox of the most virulent type. All this time William remained night and day near her bedside. The sight of his misery, the Dutch Envoy wrote, was enough to melt the hardest heart. Nothing seemed to be left of the man whose serene fortitude had been the wonder of old soldiers on the disastrous day at Landen, and of old soldiers on that fearful night among the sheets of ice and banks of sand on the coast of Gorey. Even the household servants saw tears running unchecked down that face, of which the stern composure had seldom been disturbed by either triumph or defeat. Several of the prelates were in attendance. The King drew Burnet aside, and gave way to an agony of grief. "There is no hope," he cried; "I was the happiest man on the earth, and I am the most miserable. She had no fault. None. You knew her well; but yet you could not know her. Nobody but myself could know her goodness." Archbishop Tenison undertook to tell her that she was dying. She soon caught his meaning, and with a gentle womanly courage, which so often puts our bravery to shame, submitted herself to the will of

God. She called for a small cabinet in which her most important papers were locked up, gave orders that as soon as she was no more it should be delivered to the King, and then dismissed worldly cares from her mind. She received the Holy Communion, and repeated her part of the office with unimpaired memory and intelligence, though in a feeble voice. After she had received the Sacrament she sank rapidly, and uttered only a few broken words. Twice she tried to take a last farewell of him she had loved so truly and entirely; but she was unable no speak. The public sorrow was great and general; for Mary's blameless life, her large charities, and her winning manners had conquered the hearts of her people. When the Commons next met, they sat for a time in profound silence. At length an address of condolence was moved, and the House broke up without proceeding to any other business. The Dutch Envoy informed the States General that many of the members had handkerchiefs at their eyes. The most respectable of the Jacobite party respected the sorrows of the King. There were, however, exceptions; for at Bristol the adherents of Sir John Knight rang the bell as if for a victory. It has often been repeated, and is not at all improbable, that a nonjuring divine, in the midst of the general lamentation, preached on the text, "Go, see this cursed woman and bury her, for she is a King's daughter." This is exactly what we would expect from priests who favoured the Popish tendencies of the banished King. But we cast a veil over their conduct. The funeral was long remembered as the saddest and most august that Westminster had ever seen. Both Houses followed the hearse, the Lords robed in scarlet and ermine; the Commons in long black mantles. No preceding Sovereign had ever been attended to the grave by a Parliament, for till then Parliament had always expired with the Sovereign. The whole magistracy of the City swelled the procession, and the banners of England, France, Scotland and Ireland were carried by the great nobles before the corpse. On the gorgeous coffin of *purple and gold* were laid the crown and sceptre of the realm. No day could have been more suitable. From a dark and troubled sky there dropped a few ghastly flakes of snow on the black plumes of the funeral carriage. The body was deposited under a splendid canopy while the Primate preached the funeral sermon. Through the whole service the distant booming of the cannon was heard from the Tower.

What was the spirit evinced by her Popish father? It was this: James strictly prohibited all mourning at St. Germains, and prevailed upon Louis to issue a similar edict at Versailles, and the great nobles of France who were related to the House of Nassau, and had always, when death visited that house, punctiliously observed the decent ceremonial of sorrow, were now forbidden to wear black. The sharp-witted courtiers whispered to each other that there was something pitiful in this revenge taken by the living on the dead—by a parent on a child. *But James was a pious Romanist.*

During the month which followed the death of Mary, the King was incapable of exertion. Even to the addresses of the two Houses of Parliament, he replied only by a few inarticulate sounds. During some weeks the important confidential correspondence between the King and Hemsius was suspended. At length William forced himself to resume it, but his first letter was that of a heart-broken man. "I tell you in confidence," he wrote, "that I feel myself to be no longer fit for military command, yet I will try to do my duty, and I hope that God will strengthen me."

During the two years and a half which followed the execution of Granval, no serious design had been formed against William's life. James never pretended to feel any scruple about removing his enemies by those means which he had justly thought base and wicked when employed against himself. If any such scruple had arisen in his mind there was no want under his roof of casuists willing and competent to quiet his conscience with the specious sophisms of Popery which had before then corrupted far nobler natures. To question the lawfulness of assassination in cases where assassination might promote the interests of the Church, was to question the authority of the most illustrious Jesuits, of Bellarmine and Suarez; of Molina and Mariana; nay, it was to rebel against the Chair of St. Peter. One Pope had walked in procession at the head of his Cardinals; had proclaimed a jubilee; had ordered the guns of St. Angelo to be fired in honour of the perfidious butchery in which Coligni had perished. Another Pope had in solemn allocution hymned the murder of Henry the Third of France, in rapturous language blasphemously borrowed from the ode of the Prophet Habbakuk, and had extolled the murderer above Phinehas and Judith. Thus by an infallible Pope, whose system is *semper eadem*, William was regarded at St. Germain, pretty much as he is still regarded by the bulk of Irish Papists everywhere, as a monster, compared with whom Coligni and Henry III. were saints. For some time James refused to sanction any attempts against the life of King William, and his reasons are well worthy of attention from Protestants of the present day, particularly as they breathed, in an eminent degree, the spirit of Popery. He did not affect to think that assassination was a sin which ought to be held in horror by a Christian, or a villainy unworthy of a gentleman; he merely said the difficulties were great, and that he would not push his friends on extreme danger when it would not be in his power to second them effectually. Protestants should bear in mind that Popery has not changed since then. In the spring of 1695 the scheme of assassination was submitted to James, but in order to keep himself free in case it should fail, he delayed making any formal reply, and on the principle that "silence gives consent," the conspirators proceeded to make arrangements of their own; but before these had been finally completed, William set out for Flanders, and the plot against his life was necessarily suspended until his return.

We must now pass over the events connected with the fall of Namur. In all the countries which were united against France the event was received with much satisfaction, but in England the joy was almost unbounded. And not without reason. For several generations previous, our ancestors had achieved nothing considerable by land against foreign enemies; we had indeed occasionally furnished to our allies small bands of auxiliaries who had well maintained the honour of the nation, but until the days of King William there had been on the continent no campaign in which British troops had borne a principal part. At length our ancestors had again, after an interval of near two centuries and a half, begun to dispute with the warriors of France the palm of military prowess. The struggle had been a hard one. The genius of Luxemburg and the consummate discipline of the household troops of

Louis had prevailed in two great battles; but the result of these battles had been long doubtful; the victory had been dearly purchased, and the victor had gained little more than the honour of remaining master of the field of slaughter. Steinkirk and Landen had formed the volunteers who had followed Cutts through the pallisades of Namur. The judgment of all the great warriors whom all the nations of Western Europe had sent to the confluence of the Sambre and the Meuse was, that the English subaltern was inferior to no subaltern, and the English private soldier to no private soldier in Christendom. The fall of Namur was the great military event of the year 1695. Ths maritime superiority of England and Holland was now fully established. During the whole year Russell was the undisputed master of the Mediterranean, passed and repassed between Spain and Italy, bombarded Palamas, spread terror along the whole shore of Provence, and kept the French fleet imprisoned in the harbour of Toulon. Meanwhile Berkeley was undisputed master of the channel, sailed to and fro in sight of the French coast, threw shells into St. Malo, Calais and Dunkirk, and burned Granville to the ground. The navy of Louis which five years before had been the most formidable in Europe, which had ravaged the British seas unopposed from "the Downs" to the Land's End, which had anchored in Torbay and had laid Teignmouth in ashes, now gave no sign of existence except by pillaging merchantmen which were unprovided with convoy. Such was the state of matters in the month of October, 1695, when William, leaving his army in winter quarters, returned to England, where he was received with great enthusiasm. He made a progress through the country, and at every stage received marks of the good-will of his subjects. About this time there was a general election, and amongst those returned to the new Parliament was Admiral Russell. He had won the battle of La Hague; had commanded two years in the Mediterranean, and had there shut up the French fleet in the harbour of Toulon, and had stopped and turned back the French armies in Catalonia. He had taken many vessels, and among them two ships of the line, and he had not, during his long absence in a remote sea, lost a single vessel either by war or by weather. He had made the red cross of St. George an object of terror to all the princes and commonwealths of Italy. The result of the general election proved that William had chosen a fortunate moment for dissolving, and of the members returned by far the larger part were favourable to the Government. It was very fortunate that such was the case, because at that particular juncture it was absolutely necessary that the House of Commons should aid the King in remedying several domestic evils which had assumed gigantic proportions. The silver coin, which was then the standard coin of the realm, was in a state at which the boldest and most enlightened politician stood aghast. The hammered coins and the milled coins were current together. They were received without distinction in both public and private payments. There were those who foolishly imagined that the new money would soon displace the old; yet any man of understanding might have known that when the State treats perfect coin and light coin as of equal value, the perfect coin will not drive the light coin out of circulation, but will itself be driven out. A clipped crown, on English ground, went as far in the payment of a debt or a tax as a milled crown. The politicians of that day marvelled exceedingly that

everybody should be so perverse as to use light
money in preference to good money. In other words,
they marvelled that nobody chose to pay twelve
ounces of silver when ten would serve the same purpose. Several schemes were proposed. On the
22nd November the House met. The King opened
with a speech very skilfully framed; he congratulated his hearers on the success of the campaign on
the Continent. That success he attributed to the
bravery of the English army. He spoke of the evils
that had risen from the deplorable state of the coin,
and of the necessity of applying a speedy remedy,
and he intimated very clearly that he thought the
expense of this should be borne by the State, but
that he would refer the whole matter to the great
Council. The speech was well received both by the
House and by the public. Ultimately the House
resolved itself into a Committee of the Whole on the
state of the nation. When the Speaker had left the
chair, Howe, who had already made himself con-
spicuous, harangued as vehemently against the war
as he had in former years harangued for it. He
found little support. The great majority of his
hearers were fully determined to put everything to
hazard rather than submit to France. "We did
not," said the Protestant orators, " degrade ourselves
by suing for peace when our flag was chased out of
our own Channel; when Tourville's fleet lay at
anchor in Torbay; when the Irish Papists were in
arms against us; when every post from the Netherlands brought news of some disaster; when we had
to contend against the genius of Louis in the cabinet
and Luxemburg in the field; and are we to turn
suppliants now, when no hostile squadron dares to
show itself even in the Mediterranean; when our
armies are victorious on the Continent; when God

has removed the great statesman and great soldier whose abilities long frustrated our efforts, and when the weakness of the French Administration indicates in a manner not to be mistaken, the ascendency of a female favourite?" Finally, it was resolved that the money of the kingdom should be recoined according to the old standard of weight and fineness, and that the loss on the clipped pieces should be borne by the public; that a time should be fixed after which no clipped money should pass at all.

It has been already mentioned that the plan fostered against the life of King William by the banished King was suspended in consequence of William having gone to the Continent, but it was now thought that the time had arrived for resuming it. One part of the infamous scheme was under the Duke of Berwick, and the other part under Sir George Barclay, a Scotch gentleman. Barclay was told to steal across the Channel and to repair to London, where it was said he would be followed by a number of officers and soldiers. That they might have no difficulty in finding him, he was to walk on Mondays and Thursdays in the piazza of Covent Garden, after nightfall, with a white handkerchief hanging from his coat pocket. He was furnished with a large sum of money and a commission, which was not only signed, but written from beginning to end by James himself. This commission authorized the bearer to do, from time to time, such acts of hostility against the Prince of Orange as should most conduce to the service of King James. Such language as this requires no explanation. Barclay arrived in England in January, 1696. His chief agent was a monk, who, under several names, heard confessions and said masses at the risk of his neck. Shortly afterwards some twenty or more trusty followers arrived from St. Germains, and, with Barclay and some others, at once set about their murderous undertaking. Various plans were proposed, but it was ultimately decided to adopt one originally suggested by a person named Fisher. William was in the habit of going every Saturday from Kensington to hunt in Richmond Park. There was no bridge over the Thames between London and Kingston. The King, therefore, went in a coach, escorted by some of his body-guards, through Turnham Green to the river, which he crossed in a boat, and was met on the other side by a new set of guards. It was deemed best to attack him on one of these occasions when he was returning. Time and place were fixed. The place was to be a narrow and winding lane, leading from the landing-place, and the time the afternoon of Saturday, 15th February. On that day the forty conspirators were to assemble in small parties at public-houses convenient to the locality. When the signal was given that the coach containing the King was approaching, they were to take horse and repair to their posts. As the cavalcade came up the lane, Charnock was to attack the guards in the rear, Rookwood on one flank, Porter on the other. Meanwhile Barclay, with eight trusty men, was to stop the coach and do the deed. All this time Berwick was actively engaged in persuading the Jacobite aristocracy to rise in arms; he was in constant communication with Barclay, and was therefore perfectly well aware of the dreadful crime about to be committed. Both James and Louis awaited the result with feverish anxiety. Louis sent down orders to Calais that his fleet should be in such readiness as might enable him to take advantage of the great crisis which he anticipated. But God, who had already preserved the King in a most remarkable manner, had willed that his enemies should not triumph. Even those very enemies were made to work their own destruction. The first whose heart failed him was Fisher. Even before the time and place of the crime had been fixed, he obtained an audience of Portland, and told him that a design was forming against the King's life. Some days later Fisher brought more precise information, but his character was not such as entitled him to much credit; Portland, therefore, thought little further about the matter. But on the evening of the 14th of February he received a visit from a person whose testimony he could not treat lightly. This was a Roman Catholic gentleman, of known courage and honour, named Pendergrass. He had on the day preceding come up from Hampshire in consequence of a summons from one of the conspirators, named Porter. This man had been almost a father to Pendergrass, but the latter was a conscientious man, and felt that he could not commit murder. What was he to do? Perhaps it might be possible to save William without harming Porter. At all events he would try, and so proceeded to Portland's residence and told him as he valued the King's life not to let him hunt on the following day. Portland went to the King, and with great difficulty dissuaded him from going out on the following day. Saturday, the 15th, came. The forty murderers were ready, when they received intelligence that the King did not mean to hunt that day. The delay was vexatious, but Saturday, the 22nd, would do as well. In the meantime a second informer appeared, and even William began to feel that there was real danger. Pendergrass was sent for to the royal closet. William with courtesy and animation, which he never showed without making a deep impression, urged Pendergrass to speak out. "You are," said William, "a man of true probity and honour. I am deeply obliged to you; but you must feel that the same considerations which have induced you to tell so much ought to induce you to tell something more. The cautions which you have as yet given can only make me suspect everybody that comes near me. They are sufficient to embitter my life, but not sufficient to preserve it. You must let me know the names of these men." At last Pendergrass said he would give the information required if he could be assured that it would be used only for the prevention of crime, and not for the destruction of the criminals. "I give you my word of honour," said William, "that your evidence shall not be used against any person without your own free consent." It was long past midnight when Pendergrass wrote down the names of the chief conspirators. Again the wished-for Saturday came, but again the conspirators were doomed to disappointment. The King had changed his mind, and would not hunt. In the course of the afternoon it became known that the guards had been doubled at the palace. Before the dawn of Sunday, Charnock was in custody; a little later, Rockwood and Bernadi. Seventeen traitors were seized before noon. On Monday morning all the train bands of the City were under arms. The King went in State to the House of Lords, sent for the Commons, and from the throne told the Parliament that but for the protection of a gracious Providence he should at that moment have been a corpse, and the kingdom would have been invaded by a French army. The danger of invasion, he added, was still great, but he had already given such orders as would, he hoped, suffice for the protection of the realm. Sir Rowland Gwyn, an honest country gentleman, made a motion of which he did not at all foresee the important consequences. He proposed that the members should enter into an Association for the defence of their Sovereign and their country. An instrument was immediately drawn up, by which the representatives of the people, each for himself, solemnly recognized William as the rightful and lawful King, and bound themselves to stand by him and by each other against James and against James's adherents. Lastly, they vowed that if His Majesty's life should be shortened by violence, they would avenge him signally on his murderers, and would with one heart strenuously support the order of succession settled by the Bill of Rights. It was ordered that the House should be called over next morning. The attendance was consequently great. "The Association," engrossed on parchment was on the table, and the members went up, county by county, to sign their names—so that this, like similar Associations of a later date, was organized for defensive purposes.

Three of the principal conspirators—Charnock, King and Keys—were tried and executed, and afterwards others of less note. In the May of that year (1696), William proceeded to Flanders and took command of the allied forces. The King spent some time with the armies, but the pressure on the currency question and other matters necessitated his return in the autumn of that year. On the 20th of October the House of Commons met. William addressed them in a speech remarkable even among all the remarkable speeches in which his own high thoughts and purposes were expressed. In the dignified and judicious language of Somers, the Keeper of the Great Seal, "There was," the King said, "great reason for congratulation. Overtures tend-

Q

ing to peace had been made. What might be the result of these overtures was uncertain; but this was certain, that there could be no safe or honourable peace for a nation which was not prepared to wage vigorous war. I am sure we shall all agree in opinion that the only way of treating with France is with our swords in our hands." The Commons returned to their Chambers, and Speaker Foley read the speech from the Chair. A debate followed which resounded throughout all Christendom, and it forms one of the proudest days in the history of the English Parliament. One hundred years after, Burke, the eloquent Irish orator, held up the proceedings of that day as an example to the statesmen whose hearts had failed them in the conflict with the gigantic power of the French Republic. Before the House rose on that occasion, the Chancellor of the Exchequer proposed and carried three memorable resolutions: *First*—That the Commons should support the King against all foreign and domestic enemies *Second*—That the standard of money should not be altered in fineness, weight or denomination. *Third* —That the House make good all deficiencies of all Parliamentary funds established since the King's accession. As an evidence of the temper of the times, it may be mentioned that within a fortnight two millions and a half were granted for the military expenditure of the approaching year, and nearly as much for naval purposes. Provision was made without any dispute for 40,000 seamen; and on a division of two hundred and twenty-three to sixty-seven, the King was granted a land force of 87,000. The matter which next occupied the attention of the country was the Bill of Attainder which had been brought into the Commons against Sir John Fenwick. After much acrimonious discussion the Bill passed both Houses, and on the 28th January, 1697, the unfortunate man was executed. Our space will not permit us to enter into the events connected with the peace of Ryswick; suffice that it produced the greatest possible amount of satisfaction. The rejoicings in London and elsewhere were carried out on a scale of unusual magnitude. The Parliament met on the 2nd December, 1697, and with the return of peace came the important question of what was to become of the standing army. Was any part of those eighty-seven thousand excellent troops to be retained in the service of the State? A fierce conflict arose on the point. The words which the King used when he opened the Parliament brought the matter to a speedy issue. He said he felt obliged to tell them that for the present England was not safe without a land force. A Bill for disbanding the army was ultimately passed, and there can be no doubt but the King regarded it with anything but favour; however, his strong understanding mastered his own feelings in the matter, and he gave his consent to the Bill. The public mind was much excited, and the Jacobites came in crowds, hoping to see King William mortified. The hope was disappointed. He came down to the House and told them that he was prepared to assent to the Bill, although he considered that it left the country too much exposed. We must pass with rapidity over the intervening sessions of Parliament until we reach the early part of 1701. About this time James II. had had several paralytic attacks. On the 13th September he had a second fit in his chapel, and it soon became clear that this was the final stroke. Louis, the French King, entered the bedchamber of the dying monarch, and promised to acknowledge his son as King of England, Scotland, and Ireland; and after the unhappy man's demise, the mockery of the proclamation of the poor lad was gone through. This raised a popular flame in England, and when King William returned from the Hague, where he had been detained for a few weeks, the enthusiasm of the people knew no bounds. Deputations from cities, counties, universities, besieged him daily. Shortly afterwards an election took place, which caused more than the usual share of excitement consequent on such events. We have now reached the year 1702, and we find alarming reports constantly in circulation respecting the state of King William's health, It would appear that he had consulted all the most eminent physicians in Europe, and fearing that they might flatter him if they knew who he was, he had invariably written under feigned names. To Fagon, the celebrated French physician, he wrote, describing himself as a parish priest. The blunt reply of the great physician was for the patient to prepare himself for death. Afterwards he consulted him openly, but the great King's days were numbered. He had no longer a firm seat on his horse, although he still rode and hunted. Still the King's care was for the future. With Heinsius he maintained a constant and affectionate correspondence. Heinsius was suffering from indisposition, which was a trifle when compared with the maladies under which William was sinking. There was nothing selfish in King William's character. On the 20th February he wrote to Heinsius, and he never once mentioned his own sufferings. "I am," he said, "infinitely concerned to learn that your health is not quite re-established. May God be pleased to grant you a speedy recovery. I am unalterably your friend,—WILLIAM." On the day he wrote that letter he was riding through Hampton Court Park a favourite horse named Sorrel. He urged the horse into a gallop just at the spot where a mole had been at work; the animal stumbled, and the King was thrown off, breaking his collar-bone. The bone was set and the King returned to Kensington in his coach. In consequence of the jolting, it was necessary to reduce the fracture again, and a constitution so much impaired as William's was unable to bear this. On the 28th February, the House of Commons listened with uncovered heads to the last message that bore King William's sign manual. He told them an unhappy accident had compelled him to forego the pleasure of addressing them personally. He was anxious to see a union consummated between England and Scotland, as he considered it would be for the interest of both. It was resolved to take the matter into consideration on the 7th March, but in the meantime alarming symptoms showed themselves. On the 4th of March he was attacked by fever; on the 5th he was sinking fast. Two important bills were awaiting his signature. A Commission was prepared, and the Adjuration and Malt Bills became law on Saturday, the 6th. The following day was Sunday. Albemarle had arrived from the Hague, and reported that everything was in the best of order. William received the intelligence with the calmness of a man whose work was done. "I am," said he, "fast drawing to my end." His intellect was not for a moment clouded, and his fortitude becomes the more remarkable when we remember that he had no particular wish to die. He had recently said, "You know I never feared death; however, there have been times when I should have wished it, but now that this great new prospect is opening before me, I do wish to stay here a little longer." Yet no weakness, no repining, no dissatisfaction at the will of his Heavenly Father marred the close of that noble career. Burnet and Tenison remained with him for many hours; to them he solemnly professed his firm and unshaken faith in the truth of the Christian religion, and received the Holy Communion from their hands with great seriousness. Crowding around this last awful scene were the steadfast friends of his early youth and more mature manhood—men who had served him faithfully when others betrayed him. He strained his feeble voice to thank Averquerque for the affectionate and loyal service of thirty years. By this time he could scarcely respire. "Can this," said he to the physicians, "last long?" He was told the end was approaching. He took a cordial and then asked for Bentinck. These were his last articulate words. Bentinck instantly came to his bedside, bent down and placed his ear close to the King's mouth. The lips of the dying man moved but nothing could be heard. The King took the hand of his earliest friend and pressed it tenderly to his heart. It was now between seven and eight in the morning. He closed his eyes and gasped for breath. The Bishops knelt down and read the Commendatory prayer, and while it was being offered up, the soul of the great Champion of Protestant liberty returned peacefully to its Creator. When his remains were laid out, it was found that he wore next to his skin a small piece of black silk ribbon, containing a gold ring and a lock of his beloved wife's hair.

At the time of his demise William was in the fifty-second year of his age, having reigned thirteen years. He was a man prematurely old. Left an orphan at a very tender age, he had learned in a hard school to be self-reliant and reserved. He possessed a courage that was calm amid every kind of danger, and never did he rejoice so much as in the day of battle. In his reign it became established that Parliament is alone responsible for the administration of Government. By this great constitutional principle, the Sovereign has always the power of freeing himself from popular odium by dismissing his Ministers; and if that should prove insufficient by also dissolving Parliament and summoning the election of a new one, when the future course of government is left to the determination of the constituencies. King William's submission to the will of God is not the least praiseworthy of the qualities which distinguished this great man. It should be imitated by all. In the roll of fame there is no more illustrious hero than William the Third, Prince of Orange.

A SKETCH

OF

THE ORANGE INSTITUTION.

IN the Introduction to this work, we intimated that the seeds of what subsequently became the Orange Institution were sown in the days of King William. But to the proper understanding of this subject, it is well to bear in mind that "the Press," which has since then grown into a mighty power, was in the days of the Orange Prince in its swaddling clothes. The Protestants of Great Britain were confronted with all the formidable organizations of Rome, and at a very early stage in the contest with that Power our forefathers felt how necessary combination was, it might almost be said, to their very existence. If they had neglected the very obvious duty of banding together for the prosecution of a common purpose, it would have been equivalent to allowing themselves to be defeated by piecemeal; but this they were not prepared to do, and accordingly we see what an unprecedented degree of success attended the motion of Sir Rowland Gwyn. He proposed " that the members of the House should enter into an Association for the defence of their Sovereign and their Country." Montague improved upon this hint, " and an instrument was immediately drawn up by which the representatives of the people, each for himself, solemnly recognized William as rightful and lawful King, and bound themselves to stand by him and by each other against James and James's adherents." "After making," says Lord Macaulay, "the largest allowance for fraud, it seems certain that THE ASSOCIATION included the great majority of the adult male inhabitants of England who were able to sign their names. The tide of popular feeling was so strong that a man who was known not to have signed ran considerable risk of being publicly affronted. In many places nobody appeared without wearing in his hat a riband on which was embroidered the words, 'GENERAL ASSOCIATION FOR KING WILLIAM.'" We do not refer to this for the purpose of showing that Orangeism has a consecutive history from the days of King William; what we wish to make clear is this—namely, that the principles of the Orange Society, as it now exists, are identical with the principles which were recognized and contended for by the early champions of the cause of civil freedom and religious toleration. This point being, as it must be, conceded, we have all that we can possibly require. With the abatement of the acts of disloyalty which called the ASSOCIATION into existence, we, to a great extent, lose sight of its operations in the succeeding reigns. There can be no doubt whatever but "the Association" rendered good service to the cause which was mainly instrumental in calling it into existence. It consolidated a feeling of loyalty and attachment to the Protestant dynasty, and crushed for all time to come the possibility of a Romish Sovereign on the British Throne. With this brief reference, it will be sufficient for our present purpose to say that several Associations were formed in the days of King

William, having as their ground-work principles analogous to those that are at present recognized as essential in the Orange institution as it now exists, not alone in Ireland and Canada, but in all the British Colonies. Since Rome with unhallowed hands touched "The Emerald Isle," peace and happiness may be said to have taken their departure from that unhappy country. The Irish National Church at one time rejoiced in an independence that sadly annoyed the arrogant pretensions of the Bishop of Rome, and this despotic Priest determined at all hazards to reduce her to submission. It was not accomplished without a severe struggle, but Rome has been amply repaid for the labour which she bestowed in corrupting the faith of St. Patrick. Ireland has been in the past, as she is admittedly in the present, a thorn in England's side. Why is this? Simply because she is made so by Romanism. For a long time after the crushing defeat which the cause of the Popish King sustained at the hands of his son-in-law, Irish Romanists were kept on their good behaviour by means of penal enactments; but even penal enactments were found powerless against the turbulent agitators who kept the country in a continual fever of discontent by their secret societies and by their lawless conduct. Even some Presbyterians were for a moment so far forgetful of their duty as to join hands in an unholy alliance; however, if they made a mistake on that occasion they have since amply redeemed it, and at the present day Her Gracious Majesty has no more loyal or devoted subjects than the Presbyterians of Ulster. Much doubt and some controversy has arisen as to the formation of the Orange Society, and up to the present, at all events, no real attempt has been made to give a reliable history of its institution.

We are quite aware that some enterprising individuals, with extravagant notions of their own capabilities and importance, have adventured such a work, but hitherto their efforts have not been attended with any marked degree of success. The Macaulay of Orangeism has not yet come to the front, and we must therefore content ourselves with giving, in the space at our disposal, a broad but nevertheless accurate outline of the Orange Institution since its inception in the latter years of the last century. In doing so we shall not inflict upon our readers unnecessary details nor ill-digested "authorities" of any kind. Such a work we could easily pitchfork together, but we prefer using our own intellects and giving results, rather than dry details, which have long since lost their interest even for the people in Ireland. In looking at the course pursued by the Irish Protestants at that day, cognizance must be taken of many circumstances which may escape the notice of even the most careful historian. That they suffered a great deal at the hands of their Roman Catholic fellow-countrymen is only too true; and even if they were occasionally guilty of reprisals we must bear in mind that there is a point beyond which the ordinary run of mankind do not look upon endurance as a virtue. We are not commending reprisals, nor are we justifying penal enactments; we are simply saying that, judged by the ordinary tests, the conduct of the Protestants of Ireland was, under great provocation, tolerant to the last degree; and the surprise is, not that the Orange Society was formed at a particular period, but why it had not been formed years before that date. Let us see what it was they had to contend against. Looked upon as *aliens*, and known to be *heretics*, the ordinary Irish Romanist hated them with a hatred as intense as it was unjustifiable. To the animosities of race were added the still more powerful antipathies of religion, and both were used by Romish Jesuits for their own particular purposes, and that with a degree of unscrupulousness that is unknown outside the Church of Rome. Disloyalty to the Crown was fostered; and hatred to the Protestants, as such, became a cardinal virtue. Crime ceased to be crime when the object was a Protestant, and so it came to pass that midnight outrages, murders, robberies and arsons became "as common as blackberries" in Ireland. This law and sanguinary spirit, we are sorry to add, grew and increased in intensity, until ultimately the very foundations of society were threatened. The lives and properties of Protestants were alike exposed to danger, and it was very difficult to predict what would be the final issue. In the prosecution of these disloyal and bloodthirsty schemes, those cut-throats banded themselves together under various names—that is to say, in different parts of Ireland they were called by different names—but the objects to be attained were identical. Amongst these confederacies the gang that obtained the most unenviable notoriety was "the Defenders." What they defended is a mystery even to the present day, because it is a well-established fact that the so-called "Defenders" were as cruel, as aggressive and as bloodthirsty a set of scoundrels as ever disgraced the name of Irishmen. Their villainies were as unbounded as their cruelties were heartless or devilish. This precious band was composed exclusively of Romanists; but working to a greater or less extent with, and participating in their plans were the "Peep-o'-Day Boys," and some other secret associations of less note. For a variety of reasons it was felt that an amalgamation of the "Defenders" and the "Peep-o'-Days" should take place. The chief reason of this lay, no doubt, in the fact that the "Peep-o'-Day Boys" were mainly Presbyterians, while the "Defenders" were, on the contrary, Roman Catholics. A primary object to be achieved was national independence, and the leaders in the movement knew perfectly well that after this had been obtained there would not be much difficulty in settling accounts with the Irish Protestants. In addition to all this, French influence began to be preceptibly felt, and this in turn served to moderate the fervour of the fanatics, who would have been quite willing to prosecute the war on a religious basis. But without stopping to discuss this aspect of the question, we proceed to notice a fact which, if taken by itself, appears somewhat singular—we refer to the immunity that the "Defenders" appear to have enjoyed from punishment of almost any kind. It may be asked, why was this? and in reply we are bound to say that no satisfactory answer can be given to the enquiry. That the Government of the day could have visited these murderers with the most condign punishment is a matter that hardly admits of dispute, and that it did not do so is equally certain. The notorious Father Sheehy and some others were executed, but until the formation of the Orange Society, the "Carders," "Hearts of Oak," "United Irishmen," "Thrashers," "White Boys," "Molly Maguire's Men," and all the rest of them, had things pretty much after their own minds; in fact, so early as 1772 the Government had commenced that system of conciliating Roman Catholics which since then has wrought so much mischief in Ireland. "In 1782 the Volunteers held their first meeting, but owing to several low persons, who turned out notorious traitors, assuming the rank of officers, they were by no means an efficient corps against the Romanists, who were now organized and united into National Guards and Defenders, under Wolfe Tone and Napper Tandy." Some competent hand must yet do justice to this chapter of Irish history, as it is of more than ordinary importance, particularly to the Protestants. About the year 1794-95 a perfect " Reign of Terror," with all its horrible accompaniments, was the order of the day throughout Ulster, but nowhere was its influence more severely or more disastrously felt than in the county of Armagh, and to this county above all others is due the credit of originating the Orange Institution. Our readers may infer for themselves the dreadful extent to which Defenders carried matters, when we tell them that they absolutely made an attack upon the life of the Lord High Chancellor, and that of his Grace the Lord High Primate and Mr. C. Beresford. If Protestants had any business to transact either at the fairs or markets, they were obliged to go together in crowds, and even then they were not safe from attack. This state of things continued, with but slight intermissions of peace, for the five or six years immediately preceding 1795. Hopes of French aid and the prospect of the speedy downfall of England kept the Popish population at fever heat, and they could not endure, with any degree of patience, the presence of the hated *Sassenach* and *heretic*, even for the short time that must, according to their notion of things, have elapsed before their final overthrow. In order to prepare for the massacre that was no doubt contemplated, the most frightful crimes were charged against the Protestants. Things went on from bad to worse until the month of September, 1795, when matters seemed to have reached a crisis. During the summer of that year, the outrages committed on the Protestants of Armagh were of a most aggravated character, but about the middle of September the atrocities became perfectly unbearable. What object the "Defenders" had in view in precipitating a conflict at that particular juncture need not now be inquired into; suffice that about the the 15th of September they assembled in large numbers in the vicinity of Loughgall, in the county of Armagh, to the great terror and consternation of the Protestant inhabitants. Contiguous to Loughgall is a small village called "The Diamond," and it was in the adjoining valley that the "Defenders" vowed vengeance on "the bloody heretics," as they were pleased to term the inoffensive Protestants of that neighbourhood. But here again Rome "reckoned without her host," and by her infatuated tyranny and bloodthirsty intolerance she evoked a spirit on that memorable occasion which from that day to this has pursued her with untiring hostility. The Protestants collected as rapidly as they could to oppose their ruffianly assailants, and succeeded to the extent, at all events, in keeping them in check for several days. Some "outpost" fighting, if we may be permitted the use of such a term, occurred, during the course of which the "Defenders" were almost invariably worsted. This intermittent warfare continued for the greater part of a week, and was ultimately concluded through the interference of a Protestant gentleman named Mr. Cope and the priest of the parish. The latter waited upon Mr. Cope, and assured him of the desire of his people to cease hostilities and to return peacefully to their homes. Mr. Cope expressed himself favourable to the proposition, but assured the priest, at the same time, that he had sent for military assistance, and that the lawless spirit of the Romanists would have to be crushed, if necessary, at the point of the bayonet. The parish priest gave his assurance that nothing of the kind should occur again, and relying upon this, both parties repaired to the house of Captain Atkinson, of Crow Hill, whose terms of treaty were arranged on what was deemed a satisfactory basis. While these stipulations were in course of progress, a large body of "Defenders" from the adjoining counties of Cavan, Monaghan, Louth and Tyrone, were on their way to join their friends at "The Diamond;" they arrived some hours after the treaty had been signed, and they were indignant at the idea of having to return without plunder. Now, it is alleged, and perhaps not altogether without reason, that the signing of the treaty was simply a "blind" for the purpose of taking the Protestants at a disadvantage. We rather incline to a contrary opinion, and we think that, so far as the Armagh "Defenders" were themselves concerned, the treaty was perfectly *bona fide*. Practically, however, the odium of its violation rests upon the Romanists, and no amount of special pleading will relieve them from the stigma so justly attached to their conduct. Apart from the institution of the Orange Society, the "Battle of the Diamond" is not an event of much importance. The "Defenders" began by attacking the house of an inoffensive Protestant named Winters, living at "The Diamond," and the Protestants, who had been induced, through the stipulations of the treaty, to seek their homes, were recalled in great haste. The result is a matter of history. The Protestants boldly faced their skulking and cowardly assailants, who, after having received a few well-directed discharges from Protestant muskets, precipitately fell back, and finally ran away, leaving some thirty or forty killed. Their flight was considerably accelerated by the appearance of the military. So many conflicting accounts have been published respecting these events that we make no apology for reproducing the account which was given by Lieutenant-Colonel William Blacker, when examined on the Select Committee on Orange Lodges, 4th August, 1835. Colonel Blacker's account is especially valuable for two reasons—First, because he was an actual participant in the contest; and secondly, because his version of the transaction has been endorssd as "*most authentic*" by the late William Archer, Grand Secretary to the Grand Orange Lodge of Ireland.

Question.—Are you a member of the Orange Society?

Answer.—I am.

Q. How long have you been so?

A. It wants about six weeks of forty years.

Q. You, of course, then are able to give the Committee some account of its origin?

A. I think I am.

Q. Can you do so from hearsay or from personal knowledge?

A. Both.

Q. From whom have you chiefly acquired your information?

A. My principal information was derived from a very respectable old gentleman in the County Armagh. Captain Atkinson, of Crow Hill, who took a principal part in the transaction that led to the origin of the Orangemen, and also from several others of a lower rank in society who were mixed up with these transactions.

Q. Do you consider the information you received from these persons to be authentic?

A. Perfectly so.

Q. Will you state the amount of it?

A. The amount of the information which I received at different times was, that a large body of persons called "Defenders" had made an irruption into a district of the County Armagh, near Loughgall, and the Protestants of that district assembled to oppose their progress. I believe their principal intention was to disarm the district: the Protestants assembled to oppose them, and there came to their assistance Protestants from other districts of the County, particularly from the neighbourhood in which I reside.

Q. What neighbourhood is that?

A. The neighbourhood of Portadown.

Q. Is this information derived from others?

A. Yes; it is derived from the authentic sources above mentioned.

Q. Can you state the date of it?

A. Monday was the 21st, the great day, and I think it began about the Wednesday before, in September, 1795. The parties skirmished, if I may use the expression, for a day or two without much harm being done. Mr. Atkinson on one side, and the priest of the parish on the other, did their best to reconcile matters, and though they had succeeded, as the "Defenders" had engaged on their part to go away, and the Protestants to return to their homes. At that time, as I understand a large body of "Defenders," not belonging to the County of Armagh, but assembled from Louth, Monaghan, and, I believe, Cavan and Tyrone, came down, and were much disappointed at finding a truce of this kind made, and were determined not to go home without something to repay them for the trouble of their march. In consequence, they made an attack upon the house of a man named Winters, at a place called "The Diamond;" it is a meeting of cross roads, where there are only three or four houses. Word was brought to the Protestants, who were on their return home, of what had taken place; they returned to the spot, attacked the "Defenders" and killed a number of them.

Q. Were you yourself at all mixed up with the transactions of the Diamond?

A. I was.

Q. To what extent?

A. I was a very young lad at the time; it so happened that my father was making some alterations in his house, which occasioned a quantity of lead to be removed from the roof. A carpenter's apprentice and myself took possession of a considerable quantity of this lead, ran it into bullets, and had it conveyed to the persons of my neighbourhood that were going to fight the battle of the Diamond.

Q. Were you at the spot when the battle was fought?

A. I was not in time to be under fire, but immediately as it was terminating.

Q. Can you speak from your knowledge as to the state of the Protestants prior to the battle?

A. I have always understood they were in a most persecuted state; that they were worried and beaten coming from fairs and markets upon various occasions.

Q. What did you see at the Diamond?

A. When I got up, I saw the "Defenders" running off in one direction, and the firing had nearly ceased—I may say had ceased, except a dropping shot or two—and I saw a number of dead bodies.

Q. Can you state about the number?

A. No; they were carrying them away upon cars in different directions, so that I could not make an exact calculation.

Q. Were there 30?

A. No; if there were thirty killed, that was the outside.

Q. Were there any Protestants killed?

A. None that I could hear of.

Q. How did that happen?

A. The Protestants were in a very commanding situation. Winters' house and "The Diamond" generally is at the foot of a very steep hill; the other party were in that hollow, and consequently men firing upon them from above could do great execution without being liable to be injured themselves.

Q. The "Defenders" were the assailants, were they?

A. Yes, they were.

Q. Was the *first* Orange Lodge formed then?

A. It was.

Q. Where?

A. I understand it was formed in the house of a man named Sloan, in the village of Loughgall.

Q. Have you seen any of the original warrants?

A. I have; I think I have one of them with me.

Q. Will you have the goodness to produce it?

(Produced and read as follows)

"Timakeel, July 7th, 1796.

" No. Eighty-nine.

"JAMES SLOAN.

"To be renewed in the name of Daniel Bulla, Portadown district."

Q. What was the principle upon which they were founded?

A. Wholly defensive.

Q. Has the Association ever varied from that principle since?

A. I do not consider it has in the slightest degree.

Q. Then you consider the Orange Society to be a strictly defensive Society, not in the slightest degree aggressive?

A. Certainly.

Q. Do you conceive that you have had opportunities of forming a fair estimate of the effects of the system?

A. I conceive that I have.

Q. Can you take upon yourself to say what these effects have been?

A. I consider, in the first place, that the establishment of Orange Lodges was the first thing that checked the march of republicanism and rebellion in the North of Ireland. When the United Irishmen were on foot, they afforded a rallying point for the loyalty of the country. I consider they have been productive of various advantages; besides, in a moral and religious point, I am sure that the discipline of these Lodges has gone far to prevent many young men from falling into vice of different kinds, such as intoxication. They had a character to support, and they felt it. I am sure it brought many to read God's Word and to attend God's worship, who but for that would have been ignorant and idle.

This testimony puts the foundation of the Orange Institution in a correct light before the public. Another trustworthy authority, speaking on this subject, says that "the rebels were two to one on the field." Quigley, their commander, was so confident of victory, that he ordered his father to prepare an entertainment for his forces on their return. The result, we may be sure, put a "damper" on the festivities. Protestants of all classes, seeing that a final stand must be made, joined in the fight, and partook of the honours of the victory, in commemoration of which the first Lodge was formed the evening of that day on the field of battle. The Orangemen were now vastly strengthened by the accession of all such as remained loyal, and desired to stand for their Sovereign and security of property. From this time they increased in numbers and good order, and during the rebellion of 1798 they rendered services that ought never to have been forgotten. The original warrants, as may be collected from the remarks of Col. Blacker, were simple slips of paper, with the number of the Lodge, the date of issue, and the signature "James Sloan." It was at the suggestion of this old veteran that the first Lodge was formed. There is an interesting anecdote told respecting the "Dian Lodge, No. 1." A few days after the struggle at "the Diamond," some men came from that place to Loughgall, to procure from Sloan the necessary authority for admitting members into Lodge. Sloan told them to go to the village to get writing materials. Meantime Wilson, on a similar errand from the Dian, arrived, and on being informed that there was neither pen nor ink, replied : " If that be all, I can provide against that, and 'tis best that the first Orange warrant should not be written by anything made by the hand of man." He then took a sprig from a tree of hyssop which grew in the garden, and handed it with the cover of a letter to Sloan, who signed the paper, and thus established the claim of the Dian men to a "number" which ought to belong to the place of victory. This Lodge is now in active operation near Caledon, County Tyrone. In its inception the internal workings were very simple, and the obligation short and to the point. During the course of years its ritual became elaborated, and from time to time additions were made, either because they were deemed useful or ornamental, or perhaps both.

To Ireland, and to Ireland alone, belongs the credit of the Orange Institution. The Society rapidly grew into importance, and the mere fact of its success was sufficient to create for it a host of enemies; notwithstanding, however, it made rapid progress, especially in the North of Ireland. Among the sturdy sons of Ulster it found a congenial soil, and even in several parts of the South and West of Ireland it made considerable progress. Previous to 1797 several County Grand Lodges were formed, but the awful forebodings of the times, darkened with the approaching storm of conflicting animosities, and which in '98 overwhelmed the country, warned the Protestants of the necessity of a closer union and a more perfect organization of their strength, which they hoped would be, and eventually was, the protecting shield of the faith and liberties in the sanguinary and turbulent times which ensued. To perfect the discipline of the Order, and organize its strength, the Grand Lodge was called into existence in the City of Dublin on the 4th of April, 1798. Thomas Verner, Esq., was appointed first Grand Master. As we have already intimated, we are not in favour of crowding together a lot of old documents to prove points that no one in his senses ever thinks of disputing. One almost turns sick at heart contemplating the atrocities perpetrated by the rebels in '98. The entire outbreak is unredeemed by a single feature of true manliness, while in many instances the page of history is blurred by the record of deeds of hellish cruelty, the perpetration of which would put even savages to shame. That Irish Orangemen, during the whole of this unhappy period, did good service in the cause of law and order, even their enemies are fain to admit. A few years later, all the sacrifices they had made and all the sufferings they had endured were forgotten, and torrents of abuse were heaped upon them; for example, the Rev. Mortimer O'Sullivan, D.D., one of the most eminent champions of Orangeism, in giving evidence before the Parliamentary Committee, stated that he had imbibed a strong feeling against Orangeism through reading the charges delivered by Mr. Justice Fletcher in 1814. It is well to bear in mind the change that was passing over English politicians some few years later. The memories of '98 were dying out. Roman Catholics were again asserting themselves with great boldness; professions of loyalty were not wanting from the more moderate of their leaders, and altogether it came to be a favourite maxim that Orangeism barred the way to a reign of all but universal peace. Agitation was now in full swing, and the Romanists of Ireland were in a state of mind that augured ill for the peace of the country. Intimately connected with this period are many names of historic note. Moore, " the poet of all circles and the idol of his own," it was feared, would be drawn into the net of the agitators, and so the Marchioness Dowager of Donegal, his early friend, wrote him on the subject. His reply, being the candid opinion of an intelligent Roman Catholic, is extremely valuable.

"If," says Moore in his reply, "there is anything in the world that I have been detesting and despising more than another for this long time past, it has been these very Dublin politicians whom you so fear I should associate with. I do not think a good cause was ever ruined by a more bigoted, brawling and disgusting set of demagogues; and though *it be the religion of my fathers*, I must say that much of this vulgar spirit is to be traced to the wretched faith which is again polluting Europe with Jesuitism and Inquisitions, and which, of all the humbugs that ever stultified mankind, is the most narrow and mischevous. So much for the danger of my joining Messrs. O'Connell, O'Donnell, &c." Hardly anything more severe than this has ever been written about Romanism by any educated Protestant. In 1821, Lord Talbot was Irish Viceroy; he attended the inauguration dinner of the newly-appointed Mayor of Dublin. On that occasion the charter toast was duly given and honoured. His successor, the Marquis of Wellesley, with a view to conciliate the disaffected Papists, refused to allow the toast to be drunk in his presence. Nor was this all. The Orangemen of Dublin were in the habit of decorating King William's statue, in College Green, and this display the worthy Viceroy determined should be put a stop to. His conduct gave great offence, and on a subsequent occasion, during a performance in the Theatre Royal, some empty bottles were thrown at the royal box. Two or three Dublin mechanics were tried for the offence, and very properly acquitted. It would be tedious and unprofitable to go into these matters in detail; let it suffice, that in the year 1836 King William IV. expressed a wish that the Society should be dissolved. "For nearly forty years—that is to say, from 1798 to 1836—the Grand Lodge continued to exercise its immense powers, through the press, on the platform, at the hustings, in the Senate and on the battle-field, in upholding the Crown of England. Ever obedient to the law, and to the chief magistrate of the law, the Sovereign of these realms, the Grand Lodge received with dutiful submission, but deep regret, the desire of the King that the Orange Institution should be dissolved. The vital importance of dissolution requiring the deepest consideration, a special meeting of the Grand Lodge was held in Dublin, when, on the 14th April, 1836, after three days' discussion, the resolution to dissolve the Grand Lodge of Ireland was passed, and it then ceased to exist." Persons reading this are liable to fall into the error of supposing that the Orange Institution itself was dissolved. This was not so. The dissolution of the Grand Lodge deprived the Society of a great deal of the lustre which it unquestionably enjoyed in consequence of the noble men that were then identified with it. We shall give their names:—

Grand Master.

His Royal Highness the Duke of Cumberland.

Prelate.

The Right Rev. the Lord Bishop of Salisbury.

Deputy Grand Masters.

The Right Hon. the Earl of Enniskillen.

Robert Hedges Eyre, Esq.

Colonel William Verner, M.P.

Right Hon. Lord Viscount Cole, M.P.

The Right Hon. Lord Longford.

Right Hon. Viscount Mandeville, M.P.

The Right Hon. the Earl of Roden.

The Right Hon. the Earl of Rathdown.

The Right Hon. Viscount Castlemaine.

The Right Hon. Lord Farnham.

The Most Noble the Marquis of Ely.

The Most Noble the Marquis of Thomond.

Right Hon. Viscount Powerscourt.

Right Hon. Randal E. Plunket.

The above list included some of the most influential noblemen in the country; and although the Grand Lodge was formally dissolved, they never ceased till the day of their death to countenance and support the Institution. In connection with the above, we subjoin a list of the first County Grand Masters, as well as a list of those who were County Grand Masters at the time of the dissolution.

COUNTY.	FIRST GRAND MASTER, 1798–9.	GRAND MASTER AT TIME OF DISSOLUTION, 1836.
Antrim	William Atkinson, M.D.	Commodore Watson.
Armagh	William Blacker.	William Blacker.
Carlow	Lieut.-Col. Rochfort.	Joseph Fishbourne.
Cavan	James H. Cottingham.	Richard P. Bell.
Cork County	William Longfield.	Robert Hedges Eyre.
" City	Dr. Harding.	Henry Brooke.
Donegal	Sir Edward Hayes, Bart.	Earl of Annesley.
Down		Nich. D. Cromelin.
Dublin County	Hon. Mayor Molesworth.	Earl of Rathdown.
" City	Thomas Verner.	John Judkin Butler.

THE ORANGE INSTITUTION.

COUNTY.	FIRST GRAND MASTER, 1798-9.	GRAND MASTER AT TIME OF DISSOLUTION, 1836.
Farmanagh	Thomas Verner.	Earl of Enniskillen.
Kildare	Samuel Montgomery.	None.
King's County	None.	Guy Atkinson.
Leitrim	William Perry.	William Perry.
Limerick	None.	Ralph Hill.
Londonderry	Thomas Verner.	Rev. John Graham.
Longford	Sir T. Featherstone.	William L. Galbraith.
Louth	None.	Earl of Roden.
Meath	None.	Hon. R. Plunket.
Monaghan	Alexander Ker, Barrister-at-Law.	A. H. Montgomery.
Queen's County.	None.	Chidley Coote.
Rosscommon	None.	Henry Fry.
Sligo	John Workman.	Ed. J. Cooper.
Tipperary	Simon Langley.	William P. Barker.
Tyrone	Thomas Verner.	None.
Trinity College	None.	Edward Spencer.
Waterford	Sir Richard Musgrave.	Thomas Harris.
Westmeath	William Webb, jr.	Col. G. S. Rochfort.
Wexford	Rt. Hon. George Ogle.	R. W. Phaire.
Wicklow	Rev. Richard Powell.	William Jones Westby.

Some years ago, the number of Lodges in the different counties of Ireland was estimated as follows:

Antrim	282	Londonderry City	19
Armagh	262	Longford	13
Cavan	104	Louth	6
Cork	44	Mayo	6
Carlow	4	Meath	6
Donegal	50	Monaghan	110
Down	269	Queen's County	14
Dublin	42	Sligo	17
Fermanagh	250	Tipperary	6
Kildare	3	Tyrone	238
King's County	5	Wexford	19
Leitrim	28	Wicklow	20
Londonderry County	124		

These numbers have, especially in the northern counties, greatly increased within the past few years. In the Dominion of Canada there cannot be less than 1,300 Lodges; and if to all these be added the Lodges in England, Scotland, New Zealand, Australia and the United States, the aggregate membership of the Order would figure up to nearly ONE MILLION of men.

We need not dwell at any great length on what followed. Orangemen were too conversant with the tricks and subterfuges of their enemies quietly to abandon a position which gave them so decided an advantage over their opponents, and notwithstanding the repeated assertions and declarations to the contrary, Orangemen persisted in believing that Romanism was unchanged, and that if opportunity served, the professors of that creed would be only too willing to disturb the settlement of 1688, and to bring the country again under the Egyptian bondage of Rome. A decade had hardly passed when it was made abundantly manifest that Emancipation and the innumerable concessions made to Rome, instead of producing loyalty, had only served to whet the appetite of that insatiable system. The agitators were again at work, and again the Government, in its hour of extremity, threw itself into the arms of the Orangemen of Ireland. It is not necessary to detail what followed.

"The Young Ireland party," as it was termed, after repudiating the advice of that wily politician, O'Connell, ended its inglorious career in the Ballingarry cabbage garden; but had their efforts amounted to anything really serious, the Orangemen of Ireland would have taught them such a lesson as they had not received since the memorable "Battle of the Boyne." As it turned out, however, half a dozen police constables were able to defeat the whole party, notwithstanding the heroics of "Vitriol John." The danger having subsided, the Orangemen of Ulster were treated rather like rebels than as loyal men. Witness, for example, "the Party Processions Act," and the prohibition issued by Lord Chancellor Brady against the Orange magistrates. The immediate cause of this prohibition was the unfortunate riots in Belfast, in 1857. In the July of that year very serious rioting took place, and in the following September a Special Commission was sent down to investigate the entire matter, and, as they were expected to do, the commissioners reported to the Lord Lieutenant that the riot was owing to the Orange celebrations. This was incorrect. It is alleged that the riot arose in this way: "A Roman Catholic, evidently with a malicious intention, attempted to induce a Protestant to show an orange lily in a part of Belfast inhabited principally by Roman Catholics. Not having succeeded with the Protestant, he procured a lily and wore it in a locality where he was not known. Immediately the object of effecting discord was obtained; offence was taken at the obnoxious display, and party feelings were aroused which resulted in riot and bloodshed." These riots were renewed in subsequent years, and there could be no doubt whatever but the Roman Catholics were the aggressors.

Naturally enough, the history of Orangeism centres a good deal in Ireland; but Canada may now be fairly considered as hardly of less importance; indeed, in many respects Canada has improved on the system which she received from the mother country. The same spirit of loyalty and attachment to the throne of Great Britain which characterizes the Orangemen of Ireland, characterizes their descendants in Canada, and our national history will be incomplete if it does not record the part they took in the defence of this country and for the suppression of rebellion. In the latter part of 1860, the Prince of Wales visited the United States, and what was then called Upper and Lower Canada. "His Royal Highness was attended by the late Duke of Newcastle, then Colonial Secretary, under whose guidance and direction he travelled. It was an unhappy circumstance that the Duke was called upon to accompany the Prince, for his Whig antecedents and Romanistic proclivities rendered him but an indifferent mentor for our young Telemachus. It is estimated that there were then in the two Provinces about 150,000 Orangemen—a number which has since then greatly increased. The great bulk of these belonged, of course, to Ontario. The Protestants, entertaining sentiments of sterling loyalty for their beloved Queen, were delighted to have an opportunity for manifesting their feelings. For this purpose preparations were made on a large and extensive scale for the Grand Master and the brethren to meet and give honour to the Prince, and in his person tender the fealty to the Queen. Lofty and magnificent arches were erected, and thousands of Orangemen, mostly congregated from remote districts, appeared, decorated in the insignia of the various orders in the Institution, marshalled by their respective officers, with waving flags and banners, accompanied by martial music. It had been previously intimated by the Duke that addresses would not be received from the Orangemen, but up to this time nothing was said as to the procession or wearing of colours. Processions in this country were not illegal; no impediment was anticipated; and the Orangemen hailed with joy an opportunity of giving expression to their true devotion to the Crown of Old England. A Committee having drawn up a programme for the intended reception of the Prince at Kingston, assigned a suitable position in it to the Orange procession, of which the county lodges being informed they, at much expense and toil, gladly obeyed the invitation, arriving in large masses from distant places, with all the paraphernalia of the Order; but as such a display would not accord with the Duke's anti-Orange feelings, he, having been informed of the intended demonstration, wrote a letter to Sir Edmund Head, who in turn wrote letters to the Mayors of Kingston and Toronto, in which he stated that the Duke had instructed him that the Prince of Wales would not pass under any Orange arch, nor should the Prince land at any place where the Orangemen appeared as a body with the flags or insignia of their Order. This intimation, most injudicious and dictatorial, which, in the words of the *Morning Herald,* placed the Duke's *ipse dixit* above the law of the land, calling upon the Orangemen to forego a *legal right* to assemble in the streets, and in the decorations of their Order present their humble duty to the son of their Queen, was what they would not, ought not, and did not accede to. Their obstinacy was firmer when told that one reason given by the Duke was that their Orange display "would be notoriously offensive to the members of another creed." This language coming from a man who at one time said he would not permit "any ovation in which the religious or political predilections of any party were made public"; and yet this same man permitted the Prince at Quebec to visit the Romish University, presided over by the Popish Archbishop, and he allowed the Prince to receive graciously the

s

whole Roman Catholic Bishops of Ontario and Quebec, gorgeously attired in their purple robes. Nor was this all: he also allowed the Prince to pay a visit to the Convent of the Ursuline Nuns and receive "a beautiful address," which was suitably replied to; and he permitted a Popish fraternity, called St. Patrick Society, to take part in a procession in Montreal, displaying the party colour (green), and decorated with the rebel emblem of "the Irish harp without a crown." These things determined the Orangemen of Kingston not to disown their colours. This course gave great offence to the Duke, who would not, in consequence, permit the Prince to land at the "Derry of Canada." Some have gone the length of saying that the Kingston brethren were not justified in the course they pursued. Let it be remembered that thousands of them had assembled there on the invitation of the Reception Committee, which had been appointed to make the necessary arrangements to meet the Prince. Many of them travelled long distances, and had never got the slightest hint that they would not be well received; in fact, the prohibition arrived but a few hours before the time the Prince was expected to land. Then they were informed, after toil, travel, anxiety and expense, that if they did not tear down their splendid arches, furl their Orange banners, disrobe them of their orange and purple scarfs, remove every insignia of their Order, the Prince would not land. Surely this was sufficient to provoke the very feeling which the Duke was so solicitous should not be called into play. The Orangemen stood forth, not alone on their loyalty, but on their *legality*, and recollecting the countenance shown elsewhere to Popery in its most objectionable forms, and feeling their hopes blasted, they determined not to yield an inch, and refused to relinquish their Orange demonstratiom in case the Prince should land. The Duke, however, was told that there was to be no procession or address presented, and that all they required was that the Prince would land and see the people, without officially recognizing the Orange Society. Yet the Duke was inflexible, and the Prince turned his back on Kingston because Orangeism would not submit to be put under the foot of Popery. The same unwise course was pursued throughout. In the City of Toronto an arch was erected on King Street, and decorated with a picture of King William on horseback; but even this very harmless display was too much for the Duke's stomach: he did not think it right that the heir to the crown of England should pass under the picture of one of the most illustrious kings that ever wore the royal diadem. These uncalled-for and perfectly unjustifiable indignities wounded the sensibilities of the loyal men of this country deeply, and no wonder, because they contained the sting of ingratitude. Men willing to risk their lives in defence of the throne and constitution had a right to expect better treatment. An address was at once prepared by the brethren, and sent over to the Queen, in which complaint was made that as the Orange Society in Canada was under no legal disability, their claim to recognition during the progress of the Prince of Wales should have been admitted. Her Majesty received the address graciously, and it is now admitted on all hands that the worthy Duke of Newcastle should have remained at home to guide his *own* son, and prevent him from squandering his patrimony as a low gambler and spendthrift.

The Duke must have known that he was pursuing a course of conduct for which an apology was possible. We cannot suppose that he was ignorant of the fact that the Duke of Cumberland had at one time made a remarkable speech from his place in the House of Lords on this very subject of Orangeism during the course of which he said that "he did not accept the office of Grand Master until he had the full concurrence of his late Majesty George IV., who not only said to him that he should be glad he did accept, but he knew it was in good hands." His Royal Highness further alleged, that "in the year 1798 or 1799 he saw the officers and men of the 4th Regiment (King William the Third's own regiment) wear orange and purple ribbons on their breasts at Swinley Camp, in the presence of George III.; and if not mistaken he believed the late King George IV. became a member of the Lodge in that regiment." In an edition of Rules and Regulations," published in Dublin in 1813, we read as follows:—"The enlarged Institution was copied from one which, since the Revolution, has existed in the 4th Regiment of Foot, raised by King William, into which Orange Lodge several Princes of the House of Hanover have not thought it beneath them to be initiated. We believe that the King was—we know the Prince of Wales and the Duke of York were made Orangemen. This Institution, nearly constituted as at present, dates therefore from the Revolution, and was kept up in small numbers until 1795." Thus it is manifest that if the present heir to the throne had even gone the length of patronizing the Institution, he would not have been acting without Royal precedent. However, we have no reason to suppose that His Royal Highness approved of the measures which the Duke adopted, but the exigencies of office and Court life were such as to leave His Royal Highness no option in the matter. The current history of the society is well known. In Great Britain it has been freed from the disabilities which for many years it laboured under, and many who formerly stood aloof are now joining the ranks. Within the past few years efforts have been made by the Orangemen of Eastern and Western Canada to secure Incorporation Bills, but their claims were disallowed in the Legislative Assembly. We give the names of the members who supported the Orange cause:—

Appleby,	Lauder,
Barr,	McDougall (Simcoe),
Bell,	McRae,
Bethune,	Meredith,
Boulter,	Merrick,
Broder,	Monk (Carleton),
Brown,	Mostyn,
Cameron,	Preston,
Creighton,	Richardson,
Flesher,	Robinson
Graham (Frontenac),	Rosevear,
Grange,	Tooley,
Haney,	Wigle,
Kean,	Wills.

On a recent occasion the Grand Master of Scotland announced the following as being the landmarks of Orangeism:

"1. An open Bible, and the right of all to read it.

"2. The doctrine that justification is by faith alone, of grace, and that man's salvation is to be ascribed to the finished work of Christ, and to the power and love of Christ, now glorified and living in heaven, not, in whole or in part, to any works of man himself; good works flowing from grace received, and necessarily flowing from it, but not in any degree contributing to procure grace, or to merit any of the blessings of salvation.

"3. The doctrine that, in consequence of the fall, all men are by nature sinful; and that no one can enter into the kingdom of heaven without being regenerated by the Holy Ghost, by whom also all true believers in Jesus Christ are sanctified, and so fitted for the fellowship of God, and kept, through faith, unto salvation.

"4. The only proper object of worship is God Himself, Father, Son and Holy Ghost; and prayer is to be made to God alone; and all prayer to the Virgin, to saints, angels, and the like, with all veneration of images and relics, is to be abhorred as idolatrous.

"5. The only priest of the Christian Church is the Lord Jesus Christ Himself, our Great High Priest, who has passed into the heavens; who, having made one and an all-sufficient sacrifice for our sins, the sacrifice of Himself, hath entered in, by His own blood, into the holy place not made with hands, there to appear in the presence of God for us, and ever liveth, a priest upon His throne making continual intercession for His people; and under Him, all His true people have equal and free access to God in prayer and all other exercises of worship.

"6. Confession of sins to be made to God alone, who alone can forgive sins; and auricular confession is to be rejected as having no authority in the Word of God, and, indeed, contrary to it.

"7. The pretended sacrifice of the mass is impiety, being plainly inconsistent with the all-sufficiency of the sacrifice of Christ, once offered for the sins of many.

"8. The doctrine of purgatory, so fruitful a source of gain to the Popish clergy, and a most powerful instrument for binding the souls of the people in slavish subjection to them, is to be detested as a virtual denial of the all-sufficiency of the sacrifice of Christ, and of the free and full forgiveness of sins for His sake.

"9. The Holy Scriptures of the Old and New Testaments are the only rule of faith, the traditions of the Roman Catholic Church and the decisions of the Pope being of no authority.

"10. Loyalty to the Sovereign and to the British Constitution is the duty of every one in this land—a duty plainly taught in the Holy Scriptures."

The same authority defined the duties of Orangemen in the following terms, which we heartily endorse. Such sentiments appropriately close this work:—

"Our duties, like our principles, are summed up in the two words, Protestantism and Loyalty. I have explained these words already—that Protestantism is pure Christianity; that Loyalty is not mere attachment to the person of the Sovereign, nor a particular Royal family, but it is such attachment subordinated to a regard for the constitution of the country. Let us seek, then, to be good Protestants—not mere haters of Popery, but true Christians, believers in Christ, rejoicing in Christ, walking by faith, walking in love, rejoicing in hope, adorning the gospel. May God make us so, and make us all more and more to abound in every grace, so that our lives may be lives of piety, and holiness, and active obedience to all God's commandments! May our Protestantism be that genuine and pure Religion which manifests itself in the family circle, and in all the intercourse of society, and in all the occasions and affairs of ordinary life! Let us be zealous against Popery; but let us also be in all things zealous Christians. Avoid *intemperance*, and honour the Sabbath day by attending your places of worship. And as to Loyalty, let our whole conduct show that we are faithful subjects of Queen Victoria; that we feel ourselves bound by that law which is above all laws, to pay respect to the laws of our land, living quiet and peaceful lives in all godliness and honesty; and that we in the highest degree esteem, and prize, and are thankful to God for, the civil and religious liberty secured to us by the British Constitution—that admirable Constitution which was established, let us hope, for all coming time, at the glorious Revolution of 1688."

THE REFORMATION;

AND

WHAT IT DID FOR SCOTLAND.

By the Late Rev. James Mackenzie, of Dunfermline.

Three hundred years have gone by since Scotland was a Popish country. A poor, wretched country it was in those days. Great part of the people were slaves, bought and sold like cattle, with the fields which they tilled. The land was full of violence. Bands of fierce robbers defied the law. Murder was common; and no wonder, for the murderer had only to lift with his red hand the latch of the nearest church, enter, and be safe. Such was the power of superstition!

The people were steeped in ignorance. Scarce one could read a word, or write his own name. A whole parish would have been filled with dread if, for a single day or night, the church bells had failed to ring to drive away evil spirits. The priests would give the people some trash to kiss, calling it a bit of Christ's cross, or a thorn of His crown, or, perhaps, a piece of the Virgin Mary's veil, or of the sail of Peter's boat. The poor, abused people paid for leave to kiss the relic, to draw virtue from it for the healing of their souls.

In all their troubles they cried to the saints. If fever raged they prayed to St. Roche. When lightning darted out of the thundercloud they prayed to St. Barbara. The farmer prayed to St. Anthony to take care of his cattle and swine. The soldier prayed to St. Sebastian to make the English arrows miss him in battle. People took long journeys to beg favours of particular saints. Insane persons were brought from all parts to be tied to St. Mungo's cross at Glasgow. When the madman, bound to the cross, had yelled and struggled a while his friends took him down, expecting that he would now return to his right mind. Persons dying of consumption dragged themselves to the East Nook of Fife to get health by kissing the " old cross of Crail."

The land swarmed with priests and monks, a debauched and vicious crew. There goes one, a stout, tall fellow, wrapped from head to heel in a long flowing black gown, with sleeves as wide as a sack's mouth. His cowl, thrown back, shows his head all shaven, except a ring of hair above his ears. There goes another with gown of grey, vast tippet, knotted rope round his middle, and wooden soles strapped to his bare and dirty feet. And there goes one of a third order, yellow gowned, white-mantled and broad hatted.

But to tell all the varieties of the monkish tribe would need a summer day. Their abodes were vast buildings like palaces, where they dwelt, fifty, a hundred, two or three hundred together, living in idleness on the fat of the land. Look at that stately person who rides along on his pacing mule, the silver bells of his bridle softly tinkling as he goes. People drop on their knees on the dirty streets, and remain kneeling till he is past. It is the proud lord of one of these monk palaces, with its broad lands, tributes, dues and offerings.

Let us visit yon cottage on the moor. It is the home of one who laboured a little patch of land for his family's bread. But some fatal disease has struck him down, and you see at a glance that he lies on a bed from which he will never rise. The sun is setting behind the hills, and time is setting with him. The death damp already gathers on his brow. A priest enters. He mutters some words in an unknown tongue, brings out a little box, and takes from it a morsel of bread, which he places in the mouth of the dying man, and then leaves him to go his dark road into eternity. Poor, ignorant, fearfully deceived soul, taught to worship a wafer and eat his god!

On the morrow the priest returns. The sufferer of yesterday is done with all his earthly toils. The children that play beside the cottage door are orphans now, and the widow presses her infant to her bosom as she weeps beside her dead husband. What brings the priest back to-day? The greedy priest has come to look after his dues. He must have his "corpse present." The best cow that belonged to the dead man now belongs to the priest, together with the covering of his bed, or the uppermost of his body-clothes. The widow brings out the coat which was wont to wrap her husband's manly form, and weeps anew as she hands it to the priest. The cow is driven away, the wondering orphans looking on. This was what the priests, in their filthy greed, used to do whenever a man died.

If we think of these things we may have some idea what Scotland was, and what look it bore, when it was a Popish country.

More than a hundred years before the Reformation there came to the north an Englishman who had fled for his life from the priests in his own country. This Englishman, John Resby by name, went about teaching the Scottish people the truth as it is in Jesus. Many heard, and some believed. But the priests seized this good soldier of Jesus, and burned him alive at Perth, the first of our martyrs. Far away in the city of Prague, in Bohemia, the people of God heard what had been done to the preacher of the Cross in dark, fierce Scotland. They found a man who was willing to come here and risk his life to tell perishing souls of a Saviour. The name of this noble, generous man was Paul Crawar. He was a doctor of medicine, and while he healed the diseases of the body he told his patients of Him who alone can heal the soul. The good which the blessed stranger did among our benighted fathers the last day will reveal. But the priests got hold of him also. They kindled his death-fire at St Andrews, and there they burned him to ashes. They forced a ball of brass into his mouth, lest he should speak to the people who gathered to see him die; and thus among cruel strangers, far from his fatherland, he endured his great dumb agony. Such was Scotland's welcome to the messengers of peace.

From the time of John Resby there never ceased to be a little hidden flock of Christ in Scotland. They met in great secrecy, to encourage one another in the faith and hope of the Gospel. The fear of discovery forced them to use many strange concealments. For example, one Murdoch Nesbit, an Ayrshire man, had a written copy of the New Testament. He dug a vault below his house, and there by the light of a burning splinter of bog-fir he was wont to read his precious book, a few trusty friends, who were in the secret, creeping into the murky den to hear.

As printing came into use copies of the English Bible were secretly brought into the country, and eagerly read by hundreds of little clubs like that which met in Murdoch Nesbit's hole. In this way the Word of God grew mightily and prevailed. The priests raged against it with all cruelty and blood. One most meek and gentle preacher of the truth, Patrick Hamilton, was the king's own kinsman born. Not the less for that was he burned at the stake. The fierce priests burned the bones of God's people to lime. But they could not stop: they only hastened God's work by that. The smoke of the burning martyrs infected all on whom it blew. When one blessed voice was silenced amid the roaring flames God sent another messenger to declare His truth. The ashes of Patrick Hamilton might be trampled by the feet of his murderers; but Wishart came and spoke as one who sees heaven open. Wishart, too, was burned. Fire, fire was the argument of the priests. But Knox was ready to lift up his mighty voice. He preached, and the hearts of his countrymen were moved as the trees of the wood are moved by the wind.

Slowly and long had God been preparing His own way. At last the power which had wrought in secret burst out like a flood. Scotland rose up to cast away its fetters, and put an end for ever to the tyranny of Rome. The Reformation had come, the hour of the good-will of Him who dwelt in the bush. The Popish Church was stripped of its enormous wealth, heaped up by ages of imposture and merchandise of the souls of men. The swarms of lazy, vicious monks, who ate up the nation's wealth, were scattered. The Word of God was made free. Over all the land the Gospel was preached, and thousands of thirsty souls drank the water of life. As fast as ever it could be got done, ministers were planted in all parishes, schools opened, and schoolmasters set to teach. This was the work of John Knox and the Reformers. It is three hundred years to-day since they first met in General Assembly to consult about the doing of it.

What, under God, made Scotland what Scotland is? What was it that came upon our country like spring after winter, like life from the dead? The Reformation. Then it was that morning rose on the hills and glens of Scotland and chased away the ancient night of ignorance and superstition. Without the Reformation ours would have been just such a poor, half-savage country as Spain is, or as the Popish parts of Ireland are to this day. Of all the precious blessings which our land enjoys, where is there one that had not its source in the Reformation? Our freedom? It was born at the Reformation, and its cradle was rocked in the storm that swept Popish tyranny away. Education? It is the rich inheritance which the Reformers bequeathed. Civilization? It came on the wheels of light which the Reformation lent it. The Word of God? The Reformation bought it, and laid it at every cottage door. All the best blessings of the life that now is, as well as the blessings of the life to come, entered Scotland by the same door, and became ours by the same glorious event—the Reformation.

This day, the 20th December, 1860, the three hundredth anniversary of the first meeting of the General Assembly after our country was freed from spiritual bondage, is a memorable day for Scotland.

Let us hope that while, in all the churches throughout the kingdom, ministers tell the story of our great deliverance, and give thanks to the Most High for His mercy to our land, the people will resolve, in His strength, to hand down to latest generations the blessings so dearly won.

www.ingramcontent.com/pod-product-compliance
Lightning Source LLC
Chambersburg PA
CBHW030815230426
43667CB00008B/1234